A
GLORIOUS
WAY
TO DIE

A GLORIOUS WAY TO DIE

The Kamikaze Mission of the Battleship Yamato, April 1945

RUSSELL SPURR

NEWMARKET PRESS
NEW YORK

FIRST EDITION

1   2   3   4   5   6   7   8   9   0   y   /   c

Library of Congress Cataloging in Publication Data

Spurr, Russell.
  A glorious way to die.

  Bibliography: p.
  1. Yamato (Battleship) 2. World War, 1939–
1945—Naval operations, Japanese. I. Title.
D777.5.Y33S68   940.54′5952   81-9663
ISBN 0-937858-00-5   AACR2

Manufactured in the United States of America

To my dear wife,
Rosemary,
whose patience, support, and assistance
proved invaluable

Contents

PART III
APRIL 6, 1945

PART IV
APRIL 6-7, 1945, NIGHT

PART V
APRIL 7, 1945, MORNING

PART VI
APRIL 7, 1945, AFTERNOON & EVENING

APPENDIXES

List of Maps

A SECTION OF ILLUSTRATIONS FOLLOW PAGE 118.

A
GLORIOUS
WAY
TO DIE

Now all is done,
And I can slumber for a million years . . .
　　　　　—Vice Admiral Takijiro Onishi,
　　　　　　　father of the Kamikaze naval air attack units.
　　　　　　　Farewell haiku written to his wife before his suicide

Old men forget: yet all shall be forgot,
But he'll remember with advantages
What feats he did that day.
　　　　　—Shakespeare, *Henry V*

Introduction

YAMATO WAS THE BIGGEST battleship ever built. She was the first of a class of superships covertly constructed by Japan before World War II. Equipped with 18.1-inch guns, sheathed in the heaviest armor ever milled, these mighty warships seemed virtually unsinkable and totally unbeatable. They were the secret weapon which would perpetuate Japanese naval dominance over the Pacific. But before these monsters could be thrown into the battle, they were rendered obsolete, and by none other than the Japanese themselves. Nine days before *Yamato* was commissioned they destroyed the battleship's traditional role as the backbone of naval warfare.

The Japanese carrier attack upon the unsuspecting U.S. Pacific Fleet at Pearl Harbor altered the way men fought at sea more decisively and more swiftly than any action in history. The impact of that ill-omened but brilliantly executed raid gave air power a supremacy in ocean conflict never quite achieved on land. Confirmation came all too soon at Midway. Carriers, not battlewagons, now clinched every important engagement on the wide wastes of the Pacific, whittling away the Japanese fleet until the emperor's desperate sailors fell back on suicide tactics to try to halt the vengeful American juggernaut.

In April 1945 it was *Yamato's* turn. With the U.S. already overrunning southern Okinawa, less than 400 miles from Japan, the time had come for a grand gesture. The impetuous faction controlling what was left of the Imperial Japanese Navy ordered its only operational battleship to sortie from the Inland Sea and sail southward to Okinawa with minimal escort and without air cover to engage the biggest fleet the world has ever seen. Some staff officers viewed this foredoomed operation as a suicidal "banzai" charge—the fitting, final exit for any samurai warrior—and their plans envisaged the supership blasting a trail of destruction through the American transports and their escorts before beaching close to the nearest Japanese positions. Surviving crewmen would then storm ashore to reinforce the defending garrison.

Of course this was fantasy. Most of those who took part already knew it. The navy's last serviceable ships and their devoted crews were being sacrificed to save the navy's face. Bombastic cables from headquarters spoke of honor and immortal glory. The army must not be seen fighting alone for Okinawa. The navy must do something, anything, no matter how futile. So why not use the pride of the fleet, the one great ship left? Better for *Yamato* to be sunk with all hands than to be ignobly surrendered . . .

I knew nothing of this story when I reached Japan in February 1946. Most of my war had been spent fighting the Japanese in Burma. I served in what was then the Royal Indian Navy. India was still under British rule. I was aboard the only Indian navy ship sent to Japan as part of the token Commonwealth occupation force. We were assigned to Kure, the vast navy base in southern Honshu. The mighty American fleet had gone to Yokosuka, not far from Tokyo.

It was my last naval station before I returned to England, a 23-year-old lieutenant due for demobilization. My fighting days were over. At least, that was how it looked at the time. I was not to know that in the years ahead I would be involved in endless conflict in southeast Asia, Indochina, Korea, and the Middle East as the peace we had fought for fell apart, producing a new and unsuspected crop of crises.

My combat duties had often carried me ashore on the amphibious coastal operations which punctuated the latter stages of the Burma campaign. There I saw many Japanese. Not more than two or three of them were alive; even in the retreat which finally turned to rout, the emperor's soldiers fought to the bitter end. What kind of men were these who preferred suicide to surrender? It was with mixed curiosity and apprehension that I arrived in Japan.

Kure was a wasteland. Shattered workshops, docks, and barracks stretched for miles along the bay. Beyond the railroad station lay the burned-out remnants of the town. A forest of 30-foot brick chimneys was all that remained of thousands of wooden houses. The fire raids had done their work. The destruction was every bit as bad as at nearby Hiroshima. Only two new buildings rose from the ashes: one a brothel, the other a dance hall where hungry would-be hostesses shuffled around in the mornings exploring the mysteries of the quickstep. A hand-wound phonograph ground out "Bye Bye Blackbird."

Men who would have done me to death only a few months before, or lost their lives trying, were no longer the formidable creatures we had learned to fear. They looked inexplicably mild and inoffensive in their shabby uniforms, from which all badges of rank had been removed. The imperial armed forces had ceased to exist but there were no civilian clothes for the former navy men pottering about the dockyard. They looked glum, dispirited, and spiritually drained, although the offer of a cigarette or a friendly smile activated the automatic politeness mechanisms built into every Japanese. What they really thought, I never knew. Probably nothing. Everyone in Japan that dreadful winter was numbed—and hungry.

Most of the men working in the dockyard were busy scrapping midget submarines. Kure seemed to have produced nothing else in the last stages of the war. A particularly large dry dock, the biggest I had ever seen, was packed so tightly with these odd little craft that they looked like sardines in a can. Surely a dock this big wasn't built to house midgets? I asked a young English-speaking workman. Certainly not, he explained, this dock was built for *Yamato*. For what? I hadn't the faintest idea. Isolated in our vicious little sideshow in Burma, we knew nothing about the Japanese navy and precious little about the Pacific war. I began to ask questions, setting off the processes, 34 years ago, which ended in this book . . .

It was not until I returned to Japan as correspondent for the London *Daily Express* in 1952 that I found time to delve deeper into *Yamato*'s sad saga. Public relations officers at the U.S. Navy base at Yokosuka were very helpful. Besides supplying background documents, including combat assessments, transcripts of interrogations, and translations of official Japanese war records, they introduced me to some of the protagonists in the drama, including ex-navy minister Admiral Mitsumasa Yonai; the former Commander-in-Chief, Admiral Soemu Toyoda; his chief of staff Vice Admiral Ryunosuke Kusaka; the commander of the Second Destroyer Squadron, Rear Admiral Keizo Komura; *Yahagi*'s commander, Captain Tameichi Hara; and others long since gone. I stored thousands of words of notes for future use.

The end of the occupation left the Japanese free to produce uncensored movies, many of which dealt, not unnaturally, with the Pacific war. I watched the true-life dramas of "Tiger" Yamashita, conqueror of Singapore, and the great Admiral Isoroku Yamamoto, reluctant mastermind behind the Pearl Harbor attack; and I saw a film devoted entirely to *Yamato*, whose heroic, hopeless sortie against the U.S. fleet off Okinawa was already part of Japanese legend. My interpreter on that occasion was Juzo Fukanaka, who later became a Japanese newspaper correspondent in London and is today a prosperous textile executive in Osaka. He was the first of many Japanese whose help and guidance made this book possible.

I happen to be blessed with a good memory. To this day I can remember entire scenes from that *Yamato* film, including the activities of a master gunner who was finally struck down on the deck while fetching ammunition. I made great face 23 years later describing this sequence to a group of *Yamato* survivors. The character in the film was portrayed by none other than the actual gunner Masanobu Kobayashi, who had volunteered to turn actor to inject a little realism into the production.

Unfortunately I had no time in the fifties to devote to this book. I was too busy chasing the news across Asia and the world. My notebooks were stored along with other souvenirs of an itinerant career in rusty old black tin trunks, relics of wartime India, and it was not until I began revisiting Japan in the mid-seventies that old memories revived. I was writing on defense matters for the *Far Eastern Economic Review*, and while making a call on one of Japan's leading naval historians and analysts, Commander Hideo Sekino, Imperial Japanese Navy retired, I noticed a picture of *Yamato* on his office wall. He was surprised to meet a *gaijin* who had even heard of the superbattleship; it was his generous encouragement and guidance which enabled me to pursue the very considerable research which went into this book. I would like to pay tribute to his patience, sympathy, and unfailing courtesy. Sekino-san is a true samurai.

I have done my best to be accurate despite a paucity of Japanese records, difficulties in translation, and the fading memories of men who are now grandfathers. Notes recorded immediately after the battle have proved surprisingly inaccurate. Recollections 30-odd years later are no better: they vary so alarmingly that in places I was forced to decide, somewhat arbitrarily, which was "probably" correct. Dialogue is recorded, however, only where participants were certain exactly what was said. No attempt has been made to gloss over the facts, unpalatable though they may be to either side. The result, I trust, presents more than the story of a ship or a sortie, but offers some insight into the agonizing dilemma of a misguided, courageous people who persisted in continuing a hopeless war.

Others who helped me beyond the call of friendship or duty include: my *Review* colleagues in Tokyo, Sasumo Awanohara and Koji Nakamura, both of whom got my early research off to a healthy start. Tracy Dahlby, John Lewis and his wife Naomi, and the bureau secretary, Kazumi Miyazawa, fixed meetings, interpreted for me, and performed endless little chores out of sheer goodwill.

Passages from Captain Hara's book *Destroyer Captain* are quoted gratefully.

Interviews were kindly granted by ex-gunner Masanobu Kobayashi (who allowed me to draw on his unpublished reminiscences), former Ensigns Sakei Katono, Shigeo Yamada, Mitsuo Watanabe, and Mitsuru Yoshida, Lieutenant Hideo Katori, and many others. Translations were provided by Margaret Nutt, Naomi Lewis, and Fumiko Naomi Nakamura. My wife, Rosemary, handled what seemed at times to be endless typing.

Research was conducted in the United States under the baton of Betty Yoklavich, who hunted America for eyewitnesses to the other side of the story. Special thanks are due to Rear Admiral

Arleigh Burke, Lieutenant William I. Graves of Rockville, Maryland, Lieutenant Dick Simms of Atlanta, Lieutenant Roy Gillespie of Bellingham, Washington, Rear Admiral Edmond Konrad, Captain Thomas Stetson, Captain Herbert Houck, and many other brave, modest, and generous U.S. Navy officers. The U.S. Naval Historical Center was unfailingly helpful, as were the U.S. Air Force, U.S. Marine Corps, and U.S. Submarine Veterans of World War II.

Maps were produced by David Osborne and his fellow artists here in Hong Kong.

Final thanks go to the literary editor Jean Highland, who labored heroically, and to Esther Margolis, whose perception gave me the break I needed.

PART
I

MARCH 28 – APRIL 3, 1945

PACIFIC THEATER, WORLD WAR II

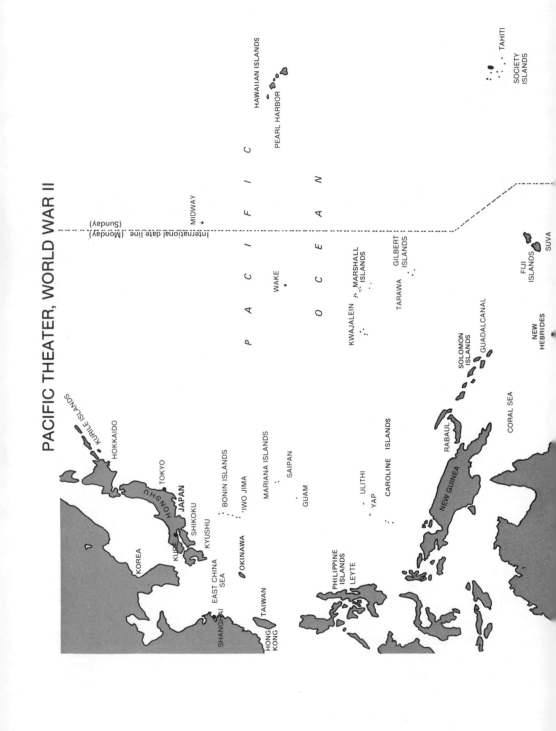

KURILE ISLANDS

HOKKAIDO

TOKYO

HONSHU

JAPAN

SHIKOKU

KURE

KYUSHU

KOREA

EAST CHINA SEA

OKINAWA

BONIN ISLANDS

IWO JIMA

TAIWAN

SHANGHAI

HONG KONG

PHILIPPINE ISLANDS

LEYTE

NEW GUINEA

RABAUL

CORAL SEA

MARIANA ISLANDS

SAIPAN

GUAM

ULITHI

YAP

CAROLINE ISLANDS

SOLOMON ISLANDS

GUADALCANAL

NEW HEBRIDES

P A C I F I C

O C E A N

WAKE

KWAJALEIN

MARSHALL ISLANDS

TARAWA

GILBERT ISLANDS

FIJI ISLANDS

SUVA

MIDWAY

International date line (Monday) (Sunday)

PEARL HARBOR

HAWAIIAN ISLANDS

TAHITI

SOCIETY ISLANDS

Kure Naval Base

THE BIGGEST WARSHIP in the world rose from the outer reaches of Kure harbor, a mountainous island of gray steel. *Yamato's* graceful curved bow, crowned by the imperial chrysanthemum, rose 60 feet above the oil-flecked waters of the bay. Nowadays she moored at orange-painted number 26 buoy, strictly reserved for flagships, with its underwater telephone and signal wires connected directly to Combined Fleet headquarters outside Yokohama.

No one quite got over the initial shock of seeing her. The first time Ensign Mitsuru Yoshida reported aboard, the great sweep of teak-decked forecastle looked like a rugby field. Even now, four months later, he could not help being impressed. He threw an awed glance at the towering superstructure, a profusion of guns, ladders, and antennas, while making the final adjustments to his uniform.

Yamato was a sharp ship. Even at this desperate stage of the war, her paintwork was spotless. Her officers and crew were expected to be better dressed than anyone in the fleet. A bosun's mate at the after companionway ladder respectfully held up a small mirror while Yoshida checked himself over. Cap straight, boots spotless, tie knotted to regulation size, sword belt suitably adjusted. He clipped off a smart salute before clattering down to the waiting launch.

One sharp blast of the coxswain's whistle, the motor roared, seamen fended off with their polished boathooks, and the bow swung out into the greatest naval anchorage in Japan. The launch carried *Yamato's* last shore patrol. It slipped smoothly across the mile of placid water from the main anchorage, around the islet which housed the miniature lighthouse and signaling tower, past a tree-topped rocky island honeycombed with ammunition tunnels. The steel tunnel doors were camouflaged light brown to match the rock face.

The coxswain dodged skillfully through tugs and lighters to come smartly alongside number one pier not far from the main gate of the naval base. The ensign sprinted briskly up the steps, sword clanking at his side. Behind him filed the petty officer and six men responsible for rounding up the remainder of the crew. The battleship was under sailing orders—"Prepare for action" was the word on board—and any man who failed to report could face a firing squad.

A careful search must be made for the last stragglers back from liberty. Patrols combed the town blowing their whistles and checking out addresses where officers and senior hands were known to be staying. There were some grim farewells. The navy had been steadily ground down by the American juggernaut through the appalling attritional battles of recent years. No one had any illusions about the future of the few surviving ships. The news had not yet been announced to the nation, but already the navy knew a full-scale invasion of Okinawa was getting under way next door to the imperial homeland.

The Kure navy yard hummed productively in the soft spring sunshine. Few bombs had yet landed among its workshops. The Americans were too busy directing their new fire raids at helpless civilian targets. Only two weeks before, the dreaded "Beeju-kyu" (B-29s) had gutted whole sections of Tokyo; although the censors tried to minimize the damage, horrific tales of carnage were being spread by terrified refugees seeking shelter all over Japan. Other great cities, Osaka, Yokohama, and Nagoya, were being systematically obliterated. It was merely a matter of time (six weeks, in fact) before the city of Kure suffered the same fate. Nothing would then be left of all these stores and homes except their incombustible chimneys protruding from the ashes.

Everyone was preparing frantically for the next raid. Ensign Yoshida watched squads of sailors, housewives, and schoolchildren burrowing into the soft sandstone mountain on the northern edge of the harbor to create protective galleries for instrument repair shops, irreplaceable electronic components, lathes and other semiportable machines. It was the same directly across the bay at Etajima, whose hilly spine was packed with explosives. Naval cadets of the class of '45 at the prestigious island academy did so much tunneling that colleagues called them "the moles." There was a standard joke that they were too busy digging to learn anything else. Hill slopes around the mainland base were simultaneously being excavated, although it was recognized that nothing could be done to protect the main workshops. Pessimists asked: "Whoever built a ship in a cave?"

Feeble attempts were being made to beef up fire precautions in the town. Orders had gone out from Second Army headquarters in neighboring Hiroshima, 12 miles along the coast, to tear down stores and homes to create firebreaks which should theoretically contain American incendiary attacks. But it was difficult to know where to start. Accommodations were scarce enough for the vastly expanded base work force without pulling the roofs from over their heads. The alternative was to bring in more fire trucks from the surrounding countryside, although there was scant gasoline to run them. Only an occasional staff car flitted through the streets; the pompous, whistle-blowing traffic cop outside the dockyard gate seldom directed anything bigger than a bicycle. Quite senior officers now cycled tinkling past, their swords hitched up on their belts, and the harassed officer suffered agonies trying to decide whether to halt them or salute them.

All Kure was drafted into some kind of war work. Schools only opened twice a week. The other five days, Sundays included, weary, hungry children joined their elders in chores around the yard. Tunneling was reserved for the bigger boys and girls. The younger ones carried buckets of rivets, sorted innumerable spares in dimly lit warehouses, or ferreted around for scrap.

Nothing was wasted. Nothing could be spared. The flow of

raw materials to the Japanese war machine was swiftly drying up. Temple gongs went to the smelters. So did the great iron gate of the Yasakuni shrine to the war dead. American submarines blocked the supply routes to occupied southeast Asia. Fuel supplies were so low that warships were immobilized and flying training halted. Attempts were being made to run some destroyers on soybean oil brought in by submarine from Manchuria. The effect on ships' boilers reduced their engineers to despair. Iron ore was still trickling in from Korea and north China, but the freighters were going down twice as fast as they were built. The Japanese merchant marine, once the third largest in the world, was reduced to little over a million tons—and most of this tonnage consisted of small wooden coasters. The surface warships still available for combat could be counted, precisely, on the fingers of both hands.

Kure had long given up hope of meeting the demand. The yard could scarcely keep pace with damage repair, let alone new construction. Over a million tons of warships were ordered under the Fourth Fleet replenishment program of 1940 with another million to follow under the emergency plans drawn up after the outbreak of the Pacific war. Less than 20 percent was ever completed. The Americans were producing 30 times the Japanese tonnage in 1944, besides a flood of other war materiél for themselves and their allies. During World War I U.S. air squadrons in France flew French and British planes; now it was the other way round. On every war front vast quantities of high-quality American equipment were swinging the balance against the Axis powers.

The Japanese suffered so many serious inadequacies. Important fields like electronics and optics had inexplicably been neglected. Radio had scarcely progressed since the thirties. There was a crucial shortage of adaptable manpower; the elitist education system turned out its share of geniuses but failed to produce the mass of educated manpower graduated by American high schools. Mechanical aptitude was confined mainly to workers in class-conscious Japan, whereas most American boys knew how to drive and tinker with an automobile, and became aviators and technicians far faster than the Japanese.

Efforts to mobilize Japan's limited industrial resources were constantly hindered by squabbles between the army and navy.

The army particularly resented the navy's insatiable need of steel. Little effort was made to adopt the American prefabrication techniques which filled the world's oceans with mass-produced freighters: the invaluable Liberty ships. Japanese design teams immersed themselves in whimsical experiment. At least 32 odd and unsuitable aircraft were built between 1941 and 1945 while the outdated Mitsubishi A6M2 Reisen Zero remained the mainstay of the naval air force. Two or three worthy replacements were in production, three years late, plagued by technical problems and constant demands for modifications.

Ensign Yoshida had graduated in 1943 from Tokyo Imperial University, which was (and still is) the most prestigious campus in Japan. Alumni were assured of automatic promotion into the upper ranks of government or business. But with war raging in the Pacific he volunteered for the navy. After a year's crash course in electronics he was drafted to *Yamato* as radar officer. Four months' service in the superbattleship convinced him that his beloved homeland was doomed. Japan had lost control of the air. Millions of soldiers and sailors still stood ready and eager to fight for the emperor, but without air power they were paralyzed.

The situation was so desperate, thought Yoshida, that the high command—indeed, the entire Japanese nation—was retreating into fantasy. People were hoping for a miracle like the heaven-sent typhoons which saved Japan from Mongol invasion in the 13th century. The suicidal activities of a small group of naval pilots in the Philippines seemed to provide that miracle. The selfless sacrifice of these brave young men, crashing their Zeros deliberately into American aircraft carriers, was confidently expected to turn the tide of battle. The Kamikaze, the Divine Wind sent by the gods to rescue the imperial islands, would blow again, not only from the air, but on the sea and underneath it too.

The key word in Kure these days, the ensign grimly noted, was *Tokko*. Top priority went to "special" operations, another thoroughly Japanese euphemism. No one openly spoke of suicide. Kamikaze pilots gave their squadrons poetic names like Cherry Blossom, Divine Thunderbolt, and Seven Lives for the Nation. This helped gloss over the grisly facts. The entire dockyard seemed devoted to *Tokko* projects: Kaiten (Divine Fate) human torpedoes, Koryu (Biting Dragon) midget submarines, and Shinyo (Ocean-Shaking) motorboats with explosive warheads. Regular work was at a standstill.

Over in the machine shops the chief engineer of *Asashimo*, one of the last serviceable destroyers, was begging in vain for an emergency overhaul. His boilers were fouled by improperly refined fuel oil. This was a common complaint throughout the fleet, particularly from ships which spent any time in southeast Asia. The gunnery officer of the newly built antiaircraft cruiser *Yahagi*, the last of its class still available for combat, found supply officers too busy to hunt for some of the new proximity fuse shells. Frustrated technicians sought new radar, sonar, and radio sets. They were brusquely ignored. Everyone was too busy limbering up for the last banzai . . .

Mitsuru Yoshida was prepared to die. He accepted the inevitable philosophically. Some of his fellow officers clothed their fate in mythological fancy. Their spirits would unite in some mighty cosmic force to destroy the enemy. This was far too fanciful. Yoshida simply hoped his personal sacrifice would contribute, in some obscure way, to the future of Japan. What that future was, he did not dare to guess.

Masanobu Kobayashi's furlough was almost over. The 19-year-old seaman first-class, youngest gunner on *Yamato*, had special permission to spend the night ashore with his parents. Now they knelt together around a black lacquer table making self-conscious small talk as the precious minutes ticked away.

"Masanobu, you look so fit," said his mother. The Kobayashis smiled shyly at their sailor son. He already had something of an adventurous reputation in the family. At 15 he went off to work in China as a junior clerk in one of the many Japanese economic enterprises exploiting the puppet kingdom of Manchukuo. Two years later he volunteered for the navy, acquiring new status as a servant of the emperor. The brutal months in boot camp were not enough to produce an experienced sailor—such men were in desperately short supply these days—but the savage discipline failed to damp his teenage enthusiasm.

The Kobayashis looked tired and threadbare, as did all civilians at this stage of the war. It had taken them over 24 hours to travel from their farm in Saitama Prefecture, close to Tokyo.

The overcrowded train stopped and started as sirens wailed along the route, warning of approaching bombers, or as work gangs cleared wreckage from the tracks. Every day now, somewhere in Japan seemed to be burning. Outside Osaka they glimpsed huge fires. At least they were safe in the countryside. And as farmers they were better off than the urban workers here in Kure where food rations were hitting starvation level. Men doing the toughest jobs in the shipyard received less than 2 pounds of poor-quality rice a week. Often it was mixed with sawdust. Pine tasted best, most people agreed. Women and children scoured the surrounding slopes for edible leaves and roots. Meat, fish, and fresh vegetables had vanished from the stores, and could be traded only for clothes, towels, or even watches with neighboring farmers.

Harassed, ill-tempered railway police searched the travelers' luggage for black-market food and nearly confiscated the small box of delicacies Mrs. Kobayashi had prepared for her son. These were his favorite *Yokin*, a kind of cake, and a sweetened bread called *Manchu*. They had saved up their sugar ration to make it, using a yeast substitute and boiled red bean paste instead of flour.

Mr. Kobayashi was a man of substance, a small landowner and the head man of his village. But the officers suspiciously scrutinized the travel passes which took so much trouble to obtain and ordered all passengers to draw the blinds on the seaward side of the cars as the train pulled out of the long tunnel through the mountain flanking the harbor.

The largest naval base in Japan had for years been jealously guarded. Foreigners were barred from Kure. Patrols across Mount Yasumi, now dotted with flowering cherry blossom, which overlooked the bay, ensured that no spy got a glimpse of the 3-mile crescent of belching foundries, workshops, docks, and jetties.

These efforts were wasted. Nothing could be hidden from the prying American B-29s, whose cameras were already mapping out the base and town for destruction. Antiaircraft gunners on Yasumi, on the upper slopes of Mount Haigamine farther north, and across the harbor on Etajima, the island site of the Imperial Naval Academy, no longer wasted their ammunition. They had no hope of hitting the high-flying intruders. Their task was to ward off return attacks by the U.S. carrier planes which had stormed across the port only a few days before.

Kure was a shabby, smoky blotch on one of the most beautiful places on earth. The scattered islands of the Inland Sea of Japan melted away into the misty distance like humpbacked monsters stricken down in some prehistoric age. They now lay cloaked in fir trees, fringed by small sandy beaches, picturesque rocks, and tranquil fishing villages. The base, by contrast, spread its pollution from Yoshiura Point, where an oil depot has been hollowed out of the hillside, past the submarine pens and gunnery school near Kawaraishi, through the great metal sheds and rows of elderly red-brick administrative buildings to the maze of slipways and drydocks stretching on past Miyahara.

All this lay south of the railroad behind the high brick wall and still higher bamboo mats which hid the base from unauthorized eyes. The city sloped up inland from the harbor, filling a shallow depression in the coastal mountains with dilapidated wooden houses. Five narrow streets fanned out from the station, each lined with tiny stores, many closed, the others showing the wear and tear of years of war. Woodwook was bleached and cracked from lack of paint, paper windows remained unmended, and there were gaps in the undulating sea of steel-gray roofing tiles.

There was virtually nothing to buy. Even the souvenir shops favored by the sailors were practically empty. A few bars and restaurants survived, some reserved for officers, but naval rations provided better meals aboard. There were still oysters, culled from their beds in nearby bays, but they were becoming expensive. Hungry fishermen were eating them themselves. The main attraction ashore these days was a drunken escape from discipline and etiquette, or a chance night with the family. Lonely men facing the prospect of imminent death found plenty of female solace for sale. Even the snobbish geishas from Kyoto were said to be migrating hungrily to Kure these days in search of a living. With inflation destroying the purchasing power of the yen, sailors bought themselves women for the night with gifts of soap and rice from the base canteen. Those with family obligations took rooms for their wives or parents, occasionally renting the bedrooms of men on night shift. Kure was entirely a navy town and most of its 140,000 inhabitants worked in or for the base. Many of the menfolk served in the dwindling imperial fleet.

Young Kobayashi was friendly with a boy whose parents owned a liquor store. Stocks were running low; the shelves were bare of bottled beer and locally made spirits, but there were plenty of rope-bound casks of sake. Workers just off shift lined up to buy it by the jugful. The owners rented spare rooms at something less than the extortionate prices people were beginning to demand. A few patriotic folk still refused to profit from the war. The Kobayashis knelt on the tatami floor of an upstairs bedroom, the parents facing their son across the low lacquered table and steaming cups of weak black tea. They had been chatting casually for hours about life back home. Yet it was obvious the older Kobayashi was uneasy. In traditional fashion he was saving unpleasantries until the end of their meeting.

"About the war," he finally said. "The Americans still do not seem to admit defeat. Their bombers are attacking the homeland. The Philippines and Iwo Jima appear to be lost. There are rumors in the town that Okinawa is about to be attacked."

Masanobu was still licking his fingers appreciatively. "Delicious cake," he told his mother. They bowed, smiling to each other. To his father he said: "There are always rumors."

He could not tell his parents the shipboard scuttlebutt that some islands of Okinawa were already occupied by the Americans and that some kind of counterattack was planned in the next few days. The Kobayashis seemed to sense that anyway. Perhaps that was why they had come. Japanese parents often seemed to know when their sons were about to die. He had heard many strange stories down on the mess decks of mothers with weirdly accurate premonitions. He glanced back at his mother. She sat stock-still, staring demurely down at the straw-mat floor.

"Of course," said his father, struggling to be cheerful, "the tide must turn. The glorious spirit of our nation will overcome the enemy. Our brave young Kamikaze pilots are sinking their ships and striking terror into their hearts. We shall fight on if 100 million perish."

He was parroting the standard nonsense churned out by the state propaganda machine. The truth was, nothing could save Japan from defeat; but the blinkered, overconfident militarists who had landed the empire in this mess could not yet bring themselves to admit it. They pressed an exhausted nation to continue the lost struggle in the vague hope that divine intervention would save them; if not, the entire nation would perish. Surrender was unthinkable.

Masanobu saw no reason to disagree with his father. He was not privy to the obstinate despair that haunted the high command. His duty was to obey—and to believe in victory. Like most loyal Japanese he accepted without question Radio Tokyo's inflated claims of American naval losses at the hands of the dedicated pilots of the Cherry Blossom squadrons. The newspapers had just published the haiku, the obligatory farewell verse, of a 22-year-old ensign who had sacrificed his life two months before:

> If only we might fall
> Like cherry blossoms in the spring—
> So pure and radiant.

It brought tears to his sentimental eyes. "A man must be prepared to die," he told his father gently. Not for him some flashing fireball ripping the guts out of a Yankee carrier. Death would come in surface action with the enemy, the great guns thundering, the shells crashing into the retreating fleet as the cowardly Americans fled for their lives. He often pictured himself dying heroically, ever loyal to the emperor.

Whistles shrilled in the street outside. There must be some emergency. Shore patrols were recalling the men on liberty. This might be the decisive battle the officers kept talking about. Chalked up on a blackboard behind B turret was the slogan "VOW TO DIE FOR THE EMPEROR."

"I have to go," said Masanobu Kobayashi. He paused, groping for words. There was still so much he wanted to say. He wanted to thank his parents for everything they had done for him. He might never see them again. But the stoic rituals of Japanese family life precluded any untoward display of feeling. All he could stammer out was: "I am proud to serve on *Yamato*." His parents bowed as he bobbed his way backward through the door. Halfway down the stairs he thought he heard his mother sobbing.

A petty officer was checking in a young seaman at the pier. He saluted and bowed to Ensign Yoshida and took his seat in the launch. Others were still straggling in. The patrol yelled at them to hurry. Some men were upset. There had been tearful scenes back home. One man bade a stiff, formal adieu to his wife and four-week-old son, then crept back aound the block to catch a last glimpse of them through the window. The emperor's sailors might be resigned to their fate but they were not emotionless robots. Most seemed to sense they would never see dry land again; they stared forlornly back as the launch headed into the outer anchorage.

A petty officer, suddenly brightening, remembered they would be showing an American film that night in the aircraft hangar. Such foreign cultural obscenities were banned in wartime Japan, but the navy made its own rules. The film was *A Hundred Men and a Girl* with Deanna Durbin. Everyone had seen it before and enjoyed it. But as someone pointed out, if they were sailing there would be no film show. He was right.

Yamato

THERE WAS HUBBUB aboard *Yamato*. Orders squeaked out of the mess-deck loudspeakers, whistles shrilled, men shouted, feet clumped up and down steel ladders. The boom of closing compartment doors echoed through the cavernous companionways deep in the battleship's hull. On the upper deck, crews were checking their guns, stowing launches, and huddling busily all over the forecastle in preparation for slipping the moorings.

She was a vast ship. Everything was conceived on the grand scale. Eight hundred and sixty-three feet of weather deck undulated gracefully aft without a break, a typical feature of Japanese naval design, sloping down from the bow, rising to a crest beyond B turret, the second of the two monstrous forward casements with their triple 18.1-inch guns, then falling away gradually toward the stern. The bridge tower soared 80 feet beyond this deck, topped by a 30-meter optical range finder and the primitive twin "bedstead" antennas of the type 13 surface radar. Inside the tower were two elevators and six decks for the officers who controlled the ship and its attendant fleet. The hull was divided into five decks, split into compartments so complicated that the eight divisional officers took nearly an hour completing

22

their inspection rounds last thing at night. Many compartments were air-conditioned—a revolutionary innovation in a navy where hardship was proclaimed a virtue—and accommodation was so roomy that envious outsiders talked of "Hotel Yamato."

Everyone agreed she was a beautiful ship. Japanese battleships grew increasingly ugly under the modernization and remodeling programs of the twenties and thirties. Bridge and fire control structures were combined into teetering "pagoda" towers which looked ungainly and top-heavy. But the years of hideous improvisation came to an end when the designers produced this powerful, aesthetic silhouette. The tower was free of clutter and carefully streamlined. The one monster smokestack raked back 25°. A crane and two catapults crowned the quarterdeck above an aircraft hangar with room for six floatplanes. The upper works bristled with guns ranging from the three giant triple turrets—two forward and one aft—and secondary armament of 6.1-inch guns to the amidships concentration of six dual purpose 5-inch turrets and 31 closely packed tubs of triple antiaircraft machine guns.

Japan decided to build five of these giants when it became obvious that sooner or later the Japanese navy would be forced to fight the Americans for mastery of the Pacific. The prototype was given the proud name *Yamato* after the district around the ancient city of Nara, the first permanent capital established by the imperial ancestors. The name has a special patriotic and religious significance: the Japanese still called themselves "the Yamato people." This gave the ship an extra sense of mission as the symbolic vanguard of the nation.

The effort of building such monsters strained Japan's industrial capacity. The country was already hard hit by the depression. Bankrupt farmers were selling their daughters into prostitution. Some rural prefectures, electrified in the twenties, went back to oil lamps and candles because the peasants could not afford anything else. But the army's reckless, unilateral interventions, first in Manchuria, then in the rest of China, whipped up nationalistic hysteria to such a pitch that reason became treason and no expense was spared to forge the tools of war.

These tools had to be all-powerful. The Imperial Japanese Navy maintained a healthy respect for its potential enemies. Many of the leading admirals had served as naval attachés in

Washington. They sensed the latent strength of this sleeping giant. But in the bankrupt thirties, when even the United States was prostrate, it seemed impossible that America would ever have the power or will to build a two-ocean navy.

This seems ludicrous today when American warships are deployed throughout the Atlantic, the Pacific, the Indian Ocean, and the Mediterranean. Japanese naval strategists of the mid-thirties saw only an isolationist Congress persistently blocking President Roosevelt's patient efforts to upgrade America's inadequate armed forces. The U.S. navy lacked the ships to dominate two oceans. If war broke out with Japan the U.S. would have to switch battleships to the Pacific through the Panama Canal. And here the Japanese believed they had found the formula for victory.

The canal locks were limited in size. The biggest battleships they could handle would displace 63,000 tons, according to Japanese intelligence estimates, with a maximum speed of 23 knots, and armament of ten 16-inch guns. Even that seemed fanciful in those days of treaty limitations: the largest U.S. capital ship built thus far displaced less than 34,000 tons. The *Yamato* class would be much bigger: superships, mounting guns of awesome caliber, massively armored and virtually unsinkable.

Design work began in earnest in October 1934. Strict secrecy was maintained from the outset. A hand-picked design team worked in total isolation at the chief naval test center in Yokohama. Such extreme secrecy was later criticized for failing to throw the project open to a wider range of expert evaluation. Less directly involved experts might have detected several fatal flaws. But secrecy was imperative because Japan was flouting her international obligations to restrict naval construction—the Washington and London treaties designed to prevent a worldwide arms race. Besides, the prevailing atmosphere of nationalist hysteria created an exaggerated need for security. Movements of foreigners were closely restricted. The police made it difficult for an overseas resident to obtain even a driver's license. The much-feared Kempeitai, the ubiquitous secret police, spent an inordinate amount of time dogging the steps of foreign attachés and newspaper correspondents. Large areas of the country were permanently off limits. Taking the most innocent snapshots was risky; in Japanese ports it was a criminal offense. No pictures were published of "superbattleship number one," as Yamato was furtively called—at least until after the war. It was not until then, when the surviving records were surrendered, that the Americans realized exactly what they had been up against. Even the efficient U.S. code breakers found out surprisingly little.

The initial blueprints were ready in five months. It was obvious at first glance that they were overambitious, even for the Japanese. They envisaged a monster battleship of well over 75,000 tons fully loaded, with 200,000-horsepower turbines giving a top speed of 31 knots. The strategists in Tokyo foresaw insuperable difficulties in docking anything this size in their shallow harbors. They also jumped to the inexplicable conclusion that a superbattleship did not need so much speed. A maximum of 27 knots would suffice because, in their erroneous view, the Americans were unlikely to build anything faster.

Here was a major mutilation of Japanese naval policy. The navy had always opted for speed, even at some sacrifice of protective armor. There would be no question now of the new ship keeping pace with the fast carriers. And when the golden opportunity came at Guadalcanal to tip the scales of battle against the Americans, Yamato's lack of an extra 5 knots prompted the naval command to commit faster, more vulnerable substitutes. The thin-skinned battle cruisers Hiei and Kirishima were thrown instead into the bloody night fighting of the third battle of the Solomon Sea. Both went promptly to the bottom.

Plans for the as yet unnamed superbattleship appeared final in July 1936, after long agonizing over the engines. The designers favored an unusual combination of turbines and diesels, each driving two propellers. Diesel engines offered attractive fuel economies for long-range cruising. The turbines would cut in under battle conditions. A total rethink was ordered a few weeks later, however, when fundamental faults were discovered in Japanese diesel design. The engine rooms were due to be sealed so tightly beneath 8-inch armor plate that any major alteration was precluded. So it was decided to revert to the old dependable turbines. The working blueprint submitted in March 1937, the 23rd in three years, was quickly approved and work began at Kure.

The specifications were staggering. The new ship would be

71,659 tons fully loaded, mounting three triple main turrets each weighing 2730 tons, as much as a heavy destroyer. The 18.1-inch guns fired a 1½-ton projectile 22½ miles. Their blast was so fierce that boats could not be carried on the open deck (they were stored aft in the aircraft hangar, along with the spotter planes). At each salvo antiaircraft gunners in exposed positions were likely to be scorched, stripped of their clothing, and knocked unconscious. This meant that as more and more light antiaircraft guns were added during the war they were packed in amidships. It was a major error. A single hit in this overcrowded space could create a shambles.

The secondary armament of twelve 6.1-inch guns in triple turrets was originally designed for *Mogami* class light cruisers. The two beam turrets were removed during a wartime refit to make way for twenty-four 5-inch dual purpose antiaircraft guns clustered in six twin turrets on either side. Point defense was assigned to antiaircraft machine guns which employed a slow-firing French Hotchkiss model that lacked real hitting power. The machine-gun count reached 98, mostly in triple mountings.

Armor was the heaviest ever installed in any warship. It formed a citadel, a kind of armored box around the vessel's vitals: the amidships section containing the 12 engine and boiler rooms, topped overall by 8-inch plate designed to resist a 2500-pound armor-piercing bomb dropped from a height of over 10,000 feet. Sixteen-and-a-half-inch plate formed a ledge along the outer hull tapering down to 3.9 inches at 20 feet below the waterline. More armor was built around the steering machinery aft and an auxiliary rudder was added. Perforated steel plate 15 inches thick guarded the mouth of the smokestack, which was sheathed in bomb-deflecting 2-inch armor. Protection against underwater explosions was provided along the triple bottom beneath the magazines. So much high-grade steel was needed for the job that the then considerable sum of $10 million was spent on expanding the Japanese steel-plate industry.

The hull, five decks deep, was divided into 1147 watertight compartments, most of them below the armored deck. Doors were snagged shut in action to prevent flooding—despite the danger to crewmen sealed inside. A double bulkhead divided the vessel from stem to stern; this was an ill-conceived design feature borrowed from the British. The designers also evolved a complicated arrangement of valves which pumped water into empty torpedo "blisters" overlapping the armor belt along the waterline. Compartments in these blisters could be filled to correct a list to the opposite side: if, for example, a series of hits set the ship heeling to port, water would be pumped into corresponding spaces on the starboard side. It was an ingenious idea—at least on paper.

The most practical innovation was a great bulbous bow to reduce water resistance to the hull. Many model tests were conducted in the experimental tank of the Naval Research Institute in Tokyo, the largest in Japan. The resultant design cut drag by 8.2 percent to achieve a trial speed of 27.46 knots. This gave a range of 7200 miles at an economic cruising speed of 16 knots. The same bow became obligatory on the supertankers built in postwar Japan.

Construction began on the first three superships at approximately yearly intervals. *Yamato* was laid down in 1937 at Kure, her sister ship *Musashi* at the Mitsubishi yard in Nagasaki the following year, and finally *Shinano* in the navy yard at Yokosuka outside Yokohama. Secrecy was maintained. *Yamato* took shape in a specially built dry dock behind screens of bamboo matting. She was commissioned without fanfare a few days after Pearl Harbor. *Musashi* was built on a traditional but heavily reinforced slipway behind a curtain of rope netting that was so large that Japanese fishermen complained for months of a rope shortage. Twenty-four hours before launching, police cleared the streets of Nagasaki and arrested people suspected of loitering to catch a glimpse of the huge hull as it splashed heavily into the water, creating a minor tidal wave. There were no bands, no flags, and, naturally enough, no reports in the Japanese press.

The remaining two ships of the *Yamato* class, numbers 111 and 797, never got off the order books. Two more (even larger) battleships, numbers 798 and 799, planned under the 1942 shipbuilding program were also canceled along with two type B-65 battle cruisers, numbers 795 and 796, which would have been faster, cutdown versions of *Yamato*. By this time aircraft carriers were more urgently needed than more of these expensive white elephants. It was one of the bitterest ironies of naval history that before *Yamato* was commissioned, the air attack on Pearl Harbor rendered the battleship obsolete. The destruction of the

U.S. Pacific Fleet's battle line by Japanese carrier-borne aircraft irrevocably altered the course of sea warfare. From now on, the carrier ruled the waves.

The battleship's demise was finally recognized in the decision to convert the half-built *Shinano* into an aircraft carrier. Her hull was completed up to the weather deck when the Japanese navy lost the decisive carrier battle at Midway. Valuable time was wasted while the planners haggled over conversion plans. The eventual compromise produced what was in effect an enormous carrier-support ship. The 70,755-ton hybrid boasted an armored deck, enormous fuel and ammunition storage, but only 47 aircraft for her own defense.

The ill-conceived project did not survive 24 hours at sea. While transiting from the building yard at Yokosuka for further outfitting in Kure on November 29, 1944, *Shinano* was waylaid by the U.S. submarine *Archerfish*, whose commander fired six torpedoes in the dark at his large, zigzagging target and dived to escape counterattack. All he heard was loud explosions as the torpex warheads hit home, enough to claim an important but unidentified kill. Exactly what he hit remained a mystery until after the war. Only then was it discovered that the giant carrier's main cargo was 50 "Ohka" Kamikaze flying bombs.

The subsequent inquiry in Tokyo concluded, with hindsight, that the carrier should never have been sent to sea. Civilian technicians were still working aboard. There was no way to seal many of the watertight doors. Untrained damage control crews were unable to cope with the extensive flooding on the starboard side. After floundering unnecessarily for seven hours, *Shinano* slowly capsized. It was agreed that this was scarcely a test of the original design, since the carrier seemed to be a victim of incompetence. But one thing was certain: the marine torpedo, correctly aimed, remained the greatest menace to anything afloat.

International Naval Rivalries

1918 – 42

THE JAPANESE EMERGED from World War I determined to become a major naval power. Their victory over tsarist Russia in 1905 had already established them as a force to be reckoned with in Asia. A minimal effort against the Kaiser won them a share of Germany's Pacific island empire which sprouted into fortified naval bases far from the imperial homeland. More ominously, the Japanese were given a free hand in divided, defenseless China. The European powers were too exhausted to continue their territorial encroachments upon the ruined Chinese empire. The traditional Russian enemy was convulsed by revolution. The Americans appeared more absorbed with jazz, a booming stock market, and Prohibition. The Japanese were able to take advantage of the power vacuum inside their great mainland neighbor. Militarists began to boast of a sacred Japanese mission to "liberate" China from "foreign exploitation." They reacted savagely when the Chinese failed to appreciate their altruism.

All the great powers were involved in ambitious and expensive shipbuilding programs when hostilities ceased in 1918. The five main Japanese yards contained the makings of an immense fleet. Eight *Kaga* class battleships were on the slips or on order, with eight *Amagi* class battle cruisers, intended to match the United States ship for ship. The U.S. had 16 still more formidable capital ships ordered under President Wilson's 1916 naval construction program, although work had temporarily halted to make way for more urgently needed convoy escorts. Construction of the bigger ships resumed after the armistice, threatening to make America the world's greatest naval power.

This was anathema to the British. Sea supremacy was the proudest part of their national heritage. But they could no longer compete in another construction race. The last one, in the immediate run-up to the war, had been costly enough. Britain was by now almost drained of its Victorian financial legacy: the Royal Navy was destined in 1924 for the first of a series of massive cutbacks which marked the end of Britannia's 150-year reign. But potential rivals must first be persuaded to cut back too. And that chiefly meant the Americans and the Japanese.

In 1922 the victorious Allied powers agreed in Washington to the fleet reductions advocated by the British. This undoubtedly averted a naval arms race. American navy lobbyists later blamed smooth-tongued British politicians for persuading the U.S. government to scrap so many ships. The British, Japanese, French, Italians, and especially the Americans sharply reduced the number of capital ships in their navies. Off to the wreckers' yards went six U.S. battle cruisers and seven battleships still under construction, along with two battleships already launched.

The most modern ships in the world, valued at a then astronomical $300 million, were written off in one magnanimous gesture. Two battle cruiser hulls were retained, more by good luck than good judgment, to be rebuilt as the *Saratoga* and *Lexington*, the first U.S. fleet carriers. The truth was that the starry-eyed Harding administration needed little British persuasion; a cynical domestic reaction to American intervention in "the war to end war" was fostering pacifism and isolationism. There was an added suspicion, encouraged by land-based air fanatics like Brigadier General Billy Mitchell, that a navy was no longer needed.

Harassed American admirals appreciated neither the extent nor the significance of the matching British cutback. A total of 657 Royal Navy warships, some 1,500,000 tons, were broken up for scrap. Four years after Britain's arrogant acceptance of the surrender of the German high seas fleet in the Firth of Forth, the politicians in London were abandoning the one precept which guaranteed British control of the world's oceans. The bulwark of British policy since Nelson's time had been maintenance of a navy big enough to match any two other navies combined. At the stroke of a pen that numerical edge was lost. Never again would Britain enjoy the total superiority once thought essential to the empire's existence. Gone too was the shield of worldwide British seapower most Americans subconsciously took for granted.

Militant Japanese condemned the Washington treaty as a national humiliation. The hard-line leader of the "fleet" faction within the Japanese delegation, Fleet Admiral Kanji Kato, loudly protested on his return home. He found ready listeners among hot-headed young officers and equally indignant civilians. Japan had been preparing what was called an 8-8-8 navy; that is, a fleet built around 8 battleships and 8 battle cruisers no more than 8 years old. But by the time the Japanese delegation to the conference reached Washington in 1921 naval expenditure was consuming one third of the national budget. The dovish Navy Minister Tomosaburo Kato recognized that cutbacks were inevitable and agreed to limit Japanese strength in battleships and aircraft carriers to 60 percent of that of the U.S. and Britain. This was the 5-5-3 formula which left the Americans and the British with about 500,000 tons of capital ships apiece while Japanese tonnage slightly exceeded the 300,000 mark.

The militants were unimpressed by their government's economic arguments. In their eyes, Japan was being treated as a second-class power. The fact that the Imperial Japanese Navy now outclassed its two potential rivals in the Pacific area was conveniently ignored. So too were other concessions won at Washington. The Americans were maneuvered into agreeing not to fortify major bases west of Hawaii—notably Guam and the Philippines—leaving the Japanese free to develop facilities at Truk, Ulithi, and elsewhere along the concentric rings of islands which projected their seapower deep into the Pacific. The Americans paid dearly for this concession during World War II. Equally important, from the Japanese viewpoint, was the Washington decision only to set limits on the tonnage of capital ships. Cruisers and destroyers were exempt. Japanese shipyards concentrated on these smaller vessels, proving marvelously innovative for a nation with brief experience in warship design. The *Fubuki* class destroyers, for example, outclassed all rivals in the late twenties. *Furutaka* class heavy cruisers gave Japan a lead in this class of ship well into the middle of the Pacific war.

But in 1930 Britain and America won an extension of the treaty limitations to all warships. The naval disarmament conference, held this time in London, touched off another outburst of nationalistic outrage throughout Japan. The Japanese delegation again agreed, however, to fall in line. It was the last splutter of compromise. Economic frustrations, jingoistic agitation and growing xenophobia were whipping up the irrational hysteria which finally propelled Japan to disaster. The 1931 invasion of Manchuria, seen in retrospect, was the opening skirmish of World War II. Japan's decision to seize all China, following an incident on the Marco Polo Bridge outside Peking in July 1937, drew agonized protests from the United States. When it became obvious that verbal complaints from Washington went unheeded the Roosevelt administration began planning economic sanctions. The U.S. and Japan were locked on a collision course.

The Imperial Japanese Navy did not relish war with the United States. Contingency plans had existed for years. Yet to many senior officers the idea was ridiculous. Men like Admiral Mitsumasa Yonai, later to become Prime Minister, and the then Rear Admiral Isoroku Yamamoto, eventually the mastermind behind Pearl Harbor, fought hard to respect the Washington and London treaties. Even restrictions on cruisers and other auxiliaries seemed preferable to a showdown with the Americans. But the national mood was against them. Intrigue mounted among staff officers as "fleet faction" hawks slowly overcame those who supported the treaties. When international disarmament negotiations were renewed in 1934 with the Japanese initially led, ironically, by Yamamoto, the decision had already been made to allow the treaties to lapse.

The rise of Hitler strengthened the militants' hand. Japan joined a tripartite pact with Germany and Italy. And when the Nazi blitzkrieg struck Europe, sweeping across Holland, Belgium and France and besieging Britain, the road was wide open to the oil- and rubber-rich colonies of southeast Asia. The Americans were not expected to put up much of a fight in defense of European colonialism.

The tragic inability of the more perceptive Japanese naval officers to restrain the militants seems inexplicable today. Yet the causes lie deep in national institutions and in the Japanese character. The navy itself was increasingly divided. Senior officers were reluctant to oppose an apparently patriotic consensus. There were undoubted fears of retribution at the hands of nationalist fanatics, particularly after the February 26, 1936, incident when mutinous officers seized temporary control of Tokyo and murdered leading figures suspected of opposing imperial expansion. The navy's failure was due above all to opportunism. The most sophisticated admirals joined the lemminglike dash to disaster once their gamblers' instincts convinced them they could get away with it.

But the Japanese were not the only ones who miscalculated. They themselves were dangerously underestimated by their Western opponents. The Zero fighter was a staggering shock to the white man's self-esteem, and so was the Imperial Navy— which, it is true, had more than its fair share of prewar teething troubles. Some of its new ships were overburdened with weaponry. The characteristic pagoda bridge towers piled onto reconstructed battleships gave the illusion of top-heaviness. On March 12, 1934, a new torpedo boat capsized outside Sasebo navy base in heavy weather. She was undoubtedly unstable. A typhoon hit Fourth Fleet the following year and two large new destroyers broke in two. The builders had not yet mastered the art of hull welding. Diesels also proved unreliable. Some Western naval attachés were tempted to the hasty conclusion that Japanese warships easily capsized, broke down, or split in half. The Western public tended to believe them. The Japanese were a joke. Nothing could have been more misleading. By 1941 most naval design faults had been corrected. Five years of war experience off the China coast had fashioned a superb fighting fleet.

The Imperial Japanese Navy opted for speed and firepower. It developed a 24-inch oxygen-driven torpedo, the famous Long Lance, which delivered a 225-pound warhead 24½ miles at 36 knots. The best the Americans could manage with their unreliable 21-inch Mark XIV was a 135-pound warhead and a range of less than 5 miles. In the first fleet actions in the Java Sea, Allied captains thought they had run into minefields when they were being picked off by torpedoes at an apparently impossible range. The Japanese concentrated on night fighting to reduce the odds against a potentially more powerful foe—a lesson well learned in the 1905 war with the Russians—and whenever possible they relied, as at Pearl Harbor, on the element of surprise. A "Day of Infamy" Roosevelt called it, but the preemptive strike was never used to more deadly effect.

Yet the Imperial Navy remained essentially a surface fleet dedicated to refighting the Battle of Jutland, the great naval showdown of World War I, the textbook confrontation between the mighty British and German battle fleets, which proved tantalizingly inconclusive. Admirals still dreamed of fighting a great sea battle which could win the war "in an afternoon." Despite early successes in the Pacific war with carriers and the sinking off Malaya of the British capital ships *Prince of Wales* and *Repulse* by land-based torpedo bombers, the Japanese clung to the belief, even when it was all too obviously nonsense, that the battleship was the final arbiter. Steeped in the doctrines of the American maritime prophet Admiral Alfred Mahan, and in the aggressive theories of such British masters as Lord "Jackie" Fisher and Admiral of the Fleet Earl Beatty, Japanese strategists persistently sought the classic "decisive" engagement which would win total command of the seas.

Japanese moviegoers a generation later savored the same simplistic fantasy, as the samurai unsheathed his doughty blade and settled everything in one short burst of climactic action. The Russians were beaten that way in 1905, it was argued, when at one blow Admiral Heihachiro Togo annihilated the tsarist fleet in the Tsushima Strait. In 1941, however, Japan faced a different foe.

World War I ended before two weapons destined to alter modern warfare had fully proved their effectiveness. One was the tank; the other, the airplane. The Japanese, unlike their future German allies, had scant need of tanks, but they seized avidly upon the airplane as a potent new weapon.

Standard Tokyo war games of the early thirties were aimed for a showdown with the Americans in waters around the Marianas in the west Pacific, with land-based attack planes supplementing the efforts of the defending Japanese fleet. The Mitsubishi 93M2 Type-96 twin-engined medium bomber (later code named "Nell" by the Allies) was developed for this role. Flying faster than any carrier-based fighter of the time and equipped with torpedoes, this remarkable aircraft proved in combined maneuvers to be worth an entire force of destroyers. Many Japanese navy aviators grew convinced that shore-based planes were the answer. Some went so far as to urge scrapping all carriers, relying solely on "unsinkable" island airfields. Their zealous arguments appeared fully justified on December 10, 1941, when near-obsolescent squadrons of torpedo-carrying Nells, flying from occupied airfields in French Indochina, sank the British capital ships *Prince of Wales* and *Repulse* off eastern Malaya. But by that time more potent lessons had been learned in China.

The brutal and unprovoked Japanese aggression against China was never called a war—even by the United States. The costly struggle was dubbed the "China Incident," which enabled neutrality-conscious Americans to supply both China and Japan with arms. Declared war would have invoked congressional prohibition of arms sales to either belligerent—and also the sale of oil and other strategic raw materials which fed the Japanese war machine.

Prewar Japanese warplanes were not given nicknames; nor for that matter were the Americans'. The idea caught on from the British. The Japanese listed their models under the last two numbers of the year they became operational. Since nationalistic fervor demanded use of the imperial calendar, dating from the mythical Emperor Jimmu in 660 B.C., the Zero, appearing in 2600 (1940), was designated "Type-00, carrier-based fighter." The Mitsubishi A6M2 Zero (and its superb pilots) initially outperformed anything the Allies could throw against it.

China was essentially the Japanese army's show, a simple mopping-up operation which bogged down into a quagmire. The navy was not seriously involved. Still, some supportive action was called for if giant naval appropriations were to be justified. Coastal bombardment in support of the invasion forces lacked the spectacular drama of long-range strikes against inland targets. So the navy sought to develop a unique ability to project its airpower ashore.

The Japanese had been experimenting for years with carriers, as had the Americans, who saw them as a valuable scouting force for their battleships out in the Pacific. China offered Japan an unexpected tactical option. Carriers provided convenient portable airfields for strikes along the lengthy Chinese coastline. There remained one apparently insolvable problem. Shore-based planes always outflew anything operating from a carrier. Elite navy aircrews flew the speedy Nells from fields in Formosa and southern Japan against inland targets as far away as Nanking and Nanchang. They flew without fighter escort. The Chinese beat them off with frightening Japanese losses. After this, the Japanese developed the Zero.

The value of air power at sea was still questioned. The exploits of the early elite Zero air groups, escorting a new breed of seaborne bombers, sweeping the skies over eastern China, did not shake the faith of the Japanese naval general staff in the battleship as the ultimate weapon. This faith was shared by admirals everywhere. Their myopic conservatism can easily be jeered at—even in this era of unproved missiles and nuclear submarines—until it is remembered that all navies had made immense investments in battleships, the dominant force in naval warfare since Henry VIII of England rearmed his galleons with heavy cannon.

The man who became Japan's greatest war hero, Admiral Yamamoto, was an exception. Although trained in the big-ship tradition, he recognized the aircraft as a potent extension of the cannon: a means of extending naval bombardment to ranges of hundreds of miles. But he had difficulty winning widespread support. Naval tactics had scarcely changed in centuries. Heavy ships still slugged it out in line of battle, admittedly with more sophisticated guns and shells, but seldom out of sight of each other. A spell at the Kasumigaura Aviation Corps teamed up the diminutive admiral with the pioneers of Japanese naval aviation—men like Vice Admiral Takijiro Onishi, who later became famous as "the father of the Kamikaze," and his brilliant deputy, Vice Admiral Matome Ugaki.

Their determined lobbying failed to dissuade their seniors

from diverting the bulk of Japan's limited resources into white elephants like *Yamato*. But they were able to take the bold step as far back as 1938 of organizing the first fast carrier attack force. Orthodoxy still clouded their thinking, however, thanks to their experience in China, because their carriers remained primarily shore-bombardment weapons. The Pearl Harbor attack was only the first of a number of spectacular Japanese strikes against land targets in the early days of the war. The Australian port of Darwin, Surabaja in Java, and the Indian Ocean ports of Vishakhapatnam and Colombo were among First Air Fleet's first and last battle honors.

The Japanese were busy bombing American military installations on Midway Island on June 4, 1942, when Raymond A. Spruance's diminutive U.S. carrier task force sank the cream of the Japanese carrier fleet, together with its irreplaceable aircrews, and sent the full supporting might of the Japanese navy, including seven battleships, scuttling home in ignominious retreat.

Admiral Yamamoto sat weeping in his cabin aboard flagship *Yamato*. Midway was the battleship's inauspicious first action. It was also the fatal turning point in the admiral's career. The charismatic little commander, a compulsive gambler and a calculating tactician, was a disastrously inept strategist. His surgical strike against Pearl Harbor touched off one of the most audacious offensives in history. In three months the Japanese overran territories half the size of the U.S. Yet they triumphed over minimal opposition: the only remaining antagonists, the British, were already fighting for their lives in the Atlantic and the Mediterranean. And in their eagerness to humiliate their old mentors—the Imperial Japanese Navy had, after all, been closely modeled on the Royal Navy—the Japanese wasted valuable time establishing temporary supremacy over the British in the Bay of Bengal off eastern India, when they should have been pressing home their attacks on the Americans. While the Japanese were sending the aged remnants of the British Eastern Fleet scuttling for safety to east Africa, the U.S. Navy was preparing for the showdown at Midway.

Admiral Yamamoto seemed to lose his confidence after that disaster. His tactics verged on the timid. When the battle began for Guadalcanal he hesitated to counterattack or follow through with overwhelming force. Ships were committed piecemeal. Their veteran crews won battle after battle against the inexperienced Americans without achieving the elusive "decisive" victory. The last elite aircrews were similarly expended, uselessly. But Yamamoto was incapable of restoring the naval balance. More carriers were ordered and battleship production was halted. Only halfhearted efforts were made, however, to provide the intensive, large-scale training program which might have revived the First Air Fleet.

The American offensive in the Solomons forced the burden of air defense on the navy—the Japanese army's own undistinguished air force was tied up supporting land operations from China to Burma—and Midway survivors who should have been training the thousands of urgently needed replacement aircrews were killed off, gradually and heroically, in the long attritional battle. Yamamoto himself died there, caught in an air ambush over Kahili on April 18, 1943. The main Japanese battle fleet, bereft of air cover, grew increasingly impotent. The expanding U.S. carrier force became the mightiest naval weapon the world had ever seen, striking with impunity at land and sea targets alike, until the United States dominated the entire Pacific.

Yamato *Sets Sail*

DOCKYARD WORKERS PAUSED to watch as the familiar flag signals
fluttered from the battleship's halyards. She was putting to sea.
There were rumors of some impending operation. A launch
crew unshackled the slip hawsers from the buoy, a puff of white
smoke blossomed from the great raked funnel. Slowly and
majestically *Yamato* headed for the Inland Sea, dwarfing her two
escorting minesweepers. It was risky to move, even here, now
that the B-29s were mining the Inland Sea. People on the dockside stood and waved. This was *their* ship. Many of them had
helped build her here in Kure, in the cavernous dry dock especially excavated for the purpose. Nowadays the dock was packed
with midget submarines, an indication of Japan's desperate new
priorities.

Crews of the remaining warships lined up silently on deck.
The trill of bosuns' calls echoed in salute across the harbor.
Officers stood stiffly at salute. It was the traditional navy send-
off. To some onlookers ashore it smacked of a final farewell.

The great ship majestically gathered way down the center of
the mile-wide channel separating Etajima from the mainland.
Kure vanished beyond Yoshiura Point and now there was noth-

ing but wooded hills on either hand, with a haze of factory smoke far ahead betraying the location of the garrison town of Hiroshima, an unremarkable place spread out across the estuary of the Ota River. The navy gave it a wide berth; the bars were too crowded with rowdy soldiers just waiting to pick on outnumbered groups of sailors. There was no love lost between the rival services. Soldiers made cracks about the American naval victories in the Philippines. The sailors sneered at the army's latest defeat on Iwo Jima. Brawls inevitably followed.

Seaman First-Class Masanobu Kobayashi stood to at his gun position wearing the helmet and flak jacket he was determined to discard in action. He had only once fired a shot in anger. That was on March 19—just nine days before—when the U.S. carriers struck for the first time at Kure. The Americans went for the warships. Two of the last surviving battleships, *Ise* and *Hyuga*, would never be repaired. The damaged battleships were moored close inshore festooned with camouflage foliage, under the lee of Etajima's powerful antiaircraft batteries. Scores of pine trees were hacked down by naval cadets to transform the damaged ships into miniature islands, but this subterfuge was soon detected by the snooping B-29s. The Americans were said to have dropped leaflets impudently advising that the camouflage was wilting and needed to be changed.

Yamato caught the tail end of the raid that day in Hiroshima Bay. Hellcats and Curtis Helldivers attacked the battleship as she maneuvered slowly in open waters near the Nasami channel. It was all over in three minutes. Bombs sent up fountains of water off the starboard bow, thrusting a sharp shock wave through the hull; every gun that could be brought to bear filled the sky with tracer and shell bursts. At least two of the attackers were seen to crash in flames, but whether they had been hit by *Yamato*'s antiaircraft armament or nearby shore batteries was not clearly established.

The whole thing had been wildly exciting and the young gunners looked forward to their next action. Many of them were new to the ship; most had never seen action. The fuel shortage prohibited frequent visits to the firing range. Some officers criticized the shooting. They were heard to say there was a desperate need for intensive gunnery practice. But Kobayashi and his friends felt they had proved themselves. It only went to show, they all agreed, that a well-defended warship could beat off any air attack.

The cherry blossoms were late this year. It had been a bitter winter. The past two days' sunshine now brought the blossoms out in all their glory. Fisher girls waved sprigs of blossom from the shore. Cherry blossom was the emblem of the Imperial Japanese Navy. Anyone with an excuse to get on deck crowded the guardrails for a nostalgic look at the trees and rocks and wooden hamlets parading slowly past. Etajima ended in a thin finger of weathered granite. The bow began a slow swing to port and they were heading into the Osu channel and out of Hiroshima Bay.

"Amidships!"

Yamato's commanding officer, Rear Admiral Kosaku Ariga, was conning the ship himself. He sat on the high wooden stool in his open-air command post, barking orders into a speaking tube.

"Amidships!"

"Wheel amidships, sir," answered old Koyama, the most experienced quartermaster in the fleet, entombed with his small electrically operated steering wheel in the armored cockpit inside the tower.

"Starboard ten!"

A little more correction needed here among these tricky islets.

"Starboard ten." Koyama's voice snapped up the tube. "Ten degrees of starboard wheel on, sir."

The helm orders were directly derived from the British. Until recently they had even been delivered in English.

The commanding officer took a quick azimuth bearing. "Amidships!" he growled.

"Amidships! Wheel amidships, sir," came the voice from below. It had the sound of a ritual incantation.

"Steady as she goes."

"Steady as she goes. Course 230, sir."

Ariga sat back humming to himself. He always hummed when concentrating. The Ando shoal was passing on the port beam and another correction would be needed in about five minutes if they were to take the southern side of the Nasami Strait. The navigating officer stood at his elbow ready to take over, but the rear admiral ignored him. He'd had little enough experience handling this great beast since assuming command four months before. Some of the more supercilious officers in the Navy Ministry had publicly questioned the appointment of this admittedly distinguished 48-year-old destroyer skipper to the largest warship in the world.

It was, of course, understandable; the chunky, hyperactive Ariga lacked the elegance and polish so dear to the men in the ministry. He was "a bulldog of a man," in the words of his own subordinates, "more like a stout country farmer than a samurai." But he had all the warrior's courage and plenty of the sailor's savvy. He was going to need it all in this last week of his life.

A telephone squealed on a nearby bulkhead. It was the gunnery officer, seated 12 feet higher up beneath the great optical range finder.

"Radar reports unidentified aircraft bearing 010. Range and height uncertain."

Ariga thanked him and cursed the wretched equipment. The ship's bugler blew general quarters. The executive officer at his damage control center close to the wheelhouse intoned, "Secure watertight integrity," over the internal address system. Crouched in the gloom of the main radar room at the base of the main mast, Ensign Yoshida irritably watched the operators fiddling with their inadequate 8-inch scopes. Something was up there, very high, undoubtedly another snooping B-29. But how high and at what range could only be guessed at. The type of radar still operating in *Yamato* at this late stage of the war provided little more than early warning.

Ensign Sakei Katono struggled through the crush to reach his action station. More men than usual seemed to be passing this way today. They were pausing before the ship's shrine, a 3-foot-long reproduction of a Shinto temple roofed with thatch and furnished inside with a miniature altar and a sacred rope hung with paper prayers. Men stopped and bowed before it; sometimes they clapped their hands to attract the attention of the gods.

Katono pushed his way aft to Eighth Division damage control center. It was a complicated, time-consuming journey through the endless companionways of number one deck; yet it was the quickest way, he had discovered long ago, because the compartmenting became still more intricate farther below, beneath the waterline. Even at this level, above the great armored box that protected the ship's innards, there were steel doors to be opened and snagged shut behind him. He came at last to the hatchway and clambered one deck down the steel communications ladder to find his men already assembled.

There were eight damage control divisions like this throughout the ship, each linked by telephone to the bridge, to adjacent control teams, and to the main control center immediately below the tower. A petty officer checked off the roll call amid mounds of splinter matting, bales of canvas, assorted lumber, coils of rope, and an impressive collection of fire-fighting equipment: asbestos suits, breathing apparatus, hand pumps, hoses, foam extinguishers, and sand-filled buckets ready to fight the sailor's oldest enemy: fire at sea.

A brief order and squads of men fanned out through the after decks checking doors and hatches from the steering compartment to the rearmost starboard engine rooms and down to the bilges. On the port side of the great central bulkhead dividing the ship the Seventh Division team was following an identical routine. It was no job for anyone claustrophobic, the ensign told himself, still adjusting to these unaccustomed duties deep inside the gray steel catacomb. He much preferred his old job in charge of lookouts high up on the bridge tower. An exposed position, admittedly, but at least you knew what was going on. Here you were entombed below with only a telephone link to the real world of sunshine and fresh sea air. If there were worse places to fight a battle, he couldn't think of any. Even the engineers were better off, slaving away over their boilers. They had plenty to keep them busy. Damage control teams could only sit and wait.

It was especially unnerving to know that the job was still not taken seriously in the Japanese navy. Emphasis was traditionally on attack, not defense, and the value of repairing damaged ships and rescuing their crews had never been fully accepted. *Yamato* carried neither life rafts nor life belts. Her medical facilities were incapable of dealing with heavy casualties. The wounded were expendable—or so it seemed—and there was indifference even to the fate of the irreplaceable pilots, who had only lately been issued parachutes.

Japanese ships were relatively combustible. Designers shared the national fondness for woodwork and installed shelving and partitions on a generous scale. Crews were loath to rip this lumber out, despite the fire hazard. *Yamato*'s teak decks remained, coated with inflammable gray camouflage paint. American ships were stripped to the bare metal.

The bulkhead telephone shrilled.

"Eighth Division damage control," Katono reported.

"Secure action stations," squeaked the earpiece. "Stand down damage control. All hands to cruising watches, readiness status two."

Katono repeated the order to his party and headed back, still thoughtful, to the junior wardroom. He paused briefly before the shrine, bowed, and clapped his hands in prayer.

The top staff officers crowded into the conference room, the command plot, back of number one bridge, six decks up the main tower. Officers wore regulation green battle dress with white shirts, black ties, and rank tabs on their lapels. Some of the older, more senior officers wore white cotton gloves. Together they stared moodily at the charts littering the great central table as if somewhere among the beautifully engraved coastlines, shoals, and now extinguished lighthouses there lay the answer to their problems. At one end of the table stood a large and expensive globe, made in London, a present to *Yamato* from the late Admiral Yamamoto. At the other end was the Second Fleet commander, Vice Admiral Seiichi Ito, a tall stooping veteran of 54, only recently appointed.

Most of Ito's war had been spent chairborne at Combined Fleet headquarters helping to plan the increasingly desperate improvisations which passed for a national strategy. Some said Ito felt personally responsible for the trail of recent defeats. He had lobbied hard enough for a risky sea command. Now he could pay for the defeats with his life. Friends sadly argued that no single person could be blamed for the mounting miscalculations, but they recognized the natural samurai reaction to feelings of shame and guilt that cried out for personal atonement.

Like so many of his senior colleagues, Vice Admiral Ito had strongly opposed the war with the United States. He had spent two years studying there in the late twenties and although he admitted, like many Japanese, that Americans were baffling, he sensed their untapped power. The U.S. humiliation at Pearl Harbor was greeted with contemptuous Axis cartoons of a disconcerted Uncle Sam uncorking a giant samurai warrior from a magic bottle. The implication was that Perry's "black ships" should never have opened up Japan in 1854. But it was the Japanese who pulled the wrong cork. Their preemptive strike at Pearl launched onto the world stage a vengeful, self-righteous superpower destined to dominate international affairs for decades to come.

Today, March 28, 1945, the Americans were breathing down Japan's neck. The flag officer reminded his staff that this morning's landings on some offshore islands close to southwestern Okinawa had brought the war to the imperial doorstep. A full-scale invasion of the strategic Okinawan island chain could come at any moment. The assembled officers nodded glumly. These islands, so close to the homeland, would provide the enemy with the final means of isolating, crippling, and eventually invading Japan. The garrison would fight to the death, of course, but if past performance on other islands was anything to go by, the invaders would prevail. The only hope was that the Americans would be so exhausted by the Okinawa battle that the ailing Roosevelt would sue for peace. At least that was the story peddled to the ignorant Japanese public. Those in the know knew better.

There was a lot the nation had not been told. Few people knew, for example, that the Imperial Japanese Navy was a spent force. In the first few months of the war the navy had carried all before it. Personnel could be forgiven for imagining themselves invincible. Then came the long, costly Solomons campaign. Despite splendid initial victories, growing American air and naval strength ground down Japanese opposition. The American counteroffensive in mid-1943 brought a trail of disasters that were concealed from the Japanese public.

The emperor himself seemed barely aware of the catastrophe which had overtaken the fleet at its last great battle five months ago in the Philippines. *Yamato* had seen no action since Midway. Throughout the first three years of the war she had never fired a shot in anger. Her undistinguished war service was spent mostly at moorings in southern waters punctuated by occasional supply runs to scattered island garrisons. The U.S. submarine *Skate* managed to get one torpedo into the battleship's armored waistline on Christmas Day, 1943. It penetrated the apparently impenetrable hull, causing ominous leakage. It was not until October 1944 that *Yamato* came face to face with the enemy.

The scheme of attack was complicated—Japanese naval staff officers were notorious for their intricate planning. They depended too often on the enemy doing what the planners expected. If the foe failed to oblige, chaos was probable. From the start it was obvious that this "decisive" battle stood little chance of success. A twin pincer thrust by the bulk of the surface fleet was supposed to push through the Philippine Islands and converge on the American beachhead at Leyte Gulf. A decoy force from Japan commanded by Vice Admiral Jisaburo Ozawa would, it was hoped, draw away the deadly American carriers. Land-based air cover would theoretically be available to shield the Japanese battleships while they blasted defenseless enemy transports.

Yamato was brought up from Singapore along with the bulk of the southern-based Third Fleet. With her was her sister ship *Musashi*. It was a magnificent sight, survivors recalled, as the two giant ships headed the last great battle line. No one would ever see that sight again. They bunkered in Brunei, where the oil was reckoned just pure enough to be pumped aboard without refining. The engineers griped. Enough impurities remained to foul the boilers; the oil was also dangerously volatile. But there wasn't much choice. B-29s had damaged the two main regional refineries at Singapore and at Palembang, a Sumatran oil center.

The fleet now split into the twin arms of the pincer. They hoped to sandwich the unsuspecting enemy between them. The southern arm headed through the Mindanao Sea hoping to break into Leyte Gulf through the Surigao Strait, but it was almost completely annihilated. The other arm, including the two superbattleships, took a northward route through the Sibuyan Sea toward the San Bernardino Strait. The expected air cover never materialized. The American carriers were destroying planes faster than they could be flown down from Japan. The U.S. quickly turned on the advancing surface task force. Every attacking ship was sunk or damaged. *Musashi* went down with 13 torpedo hits in her port side and seven to starboard. Her massive forecastle gradually dipped under the smooth blue sea until the forward turrets were awash. Speed dropped off and she straggled 20 miles behind the main force. Suddenly her bulkheads gave way under the weight of water and before she could be beached the superbattleship capsized.

Yamato took two bomb bits. One pierced the port bow anchor room, let in 2000 tons of water, and caused a slight list which the pumping system soon corrected. The ship's gunners claimed they had fought the Yankees off. In fact the American pilots were concentrating on *Musashi*. Before they could turn their full attention to *Yamato* their impulsive task force commander, Vice Admiral "Bull" Halsey, dashed off to attack the decoys, which included four almost defenseless carriers that had been sent into battle with less than 50 aircraft.

That subterfuge worked the way the Japanese planned it. The Leyte landing beaches were left lightly guarded. *Yamato* burst through the San Bernardino Strait under cover of darkness, accompanied by 2 older battleships, 8 cruisers, and 14 destroyers. The first thing the Americans knew, shells were raining down on the small force of escort carriers and destroyers patrolling the gulf. *Yamato* was firing at last at an enemy surface target. The battle she was built for had begun.

There is a story that when Napoleon was preparing to promote new marshals he impatiently exclaimed: "Don't tell me which man is good. Find me the man who is lucky." Luck was and still is the incalculable element in war. Japanese luck had long run out. At this supreme moment, when the Americans lay like lambs at the slaughter, the force commander, Vice Admiral Takeo Kurita, broke off the action and headed home.

The wretched Kurita was still suffering from tropical fever. Two nights before, his flagship, the heavy cruiser *Atago*, was torpedoed from under him. He was plucked out of the water, sick, shaken, and desperately tired. Out in the gulf with a carrier force within range, squally weather obscuring the battlefield, and facing persistent air attacks from the enemy's lightly armed aircraft and three defiant destroyers, he decided his force was too much at risk. Several of his ships were already damaged. *Yamato*'s great batteries had not yet scored a hit (and never did), although shells from another battleship and an escorting cruiser sank the light carrier *Gambier Bay*. The original objective, the

American troop transports, had already departed. Kurita pulled back into the strait, pursued by aircraft, and returned to lick his wounds in Brunei.

No one aboard *Yamato* challenged Kurita's decision: it would have been an unimaginable breach of discipline and etiquette. Not until after the war was Kurita publicly castigated. But officers who had watched the entire course of the operation tended to sympathize. They too were numbed by the confusion. They were convinced—and historians would agree with them—that the entire force would have been wiped out if it had dallied much longer in Leyte Gulf. As it was, a third of the ships were sunk; most of the others were too badly damaged to fight again. Some critics complained, on the other hand, that Kurita should have completed the massacre of the Americans even at risk of his own fleet.

Yamato returned to Japan as flagship of a fleet which existed mainly on paper. No one could quite decide what to do with her. Some officers felt the battleship should be moored in Kure as a floating antiaircraft battery. A few went so far as to suggest she should be demobilized, her guns mounted ashore for mainland defense. Others lobbied for a last banzai. Today, with Kure far astern in the misty spring sunshine, the superbattleship was heading into the Inland Sea to shelter from air attacks among the myriad islands.

There was an element of risk even in this sheltered area, Vice Admiral Ito told his staff. B-29s were mining the Inland Sea, concentrating on the Shimonoseki Strait, which had until now provided the safest, speediest route to Korea and Manchuria. Several freighters had been sunk in the past two days, blocking the channel and halting all seaborne traffic.

The operations officer handed Ito a folder of rice paper signals covered with neat vertical columns of characters. The vice admiral shuffled through them to find the latest instructions from Combined Fleet. With black-rimmed reading glasses perched on his nose he announced to his respectful audience that plans were being considered for a sortie. *Yamato* and whatever else could be scratched together from Second Fleet would sail out into the Pacific through the Bungo Strait, skirt southern Kyushu, and run for shelter in Sasebo naval base. Ample air cover was available from land-based planes; the Americans would be unable to resist the temptation to attack. Massed Kamikaze attack squadrons would hit the Yankee carriers as they chased the Japanese task force.

Several officers scowled disapprovingly. Fancy using the pride of the fleet as a mere decoy! But what alternative was there? Playing hide and seek around the Inland Sea was equally chastening. They had fought off attacks before by U.S. carrier planes. No doubt the Americans would be back. Better to face them in the open sea than to lose face skulking here in their own backyard.

"I must state in all honesty that I have doubts about this plan." Ito was never known to mince words, contrary to the national tradition of reticence. "Still, if those are the orders," he went on, looking his men in the eyes, "we will naturally do our best."

Vice Admiral Ito made no secret of his distaste for suicide tactics. Hard-liners only believed the Kamikaze advocates' inflated claims because they longed to believe them. The Japanese were grasping at straws. The claims were hard to refute for lack of reliable intelligence. There was a time when nothing moved in vast areas of the Pacific without alerting the navy. Now they had only the vaguest picture of enemy movements, even in waters close to Japan. Reconnaissance planes seldom returned. The most accurate information about the American fleet off Okinawa was radioed back by shore stations. The main U.S. carrier fleet, Task Force 58, which had rampaged all over eastern Japan in mid-March, seemed to have vanished back into the wastes of the Pacific. It was thought to be cruising somewhere to the east of Okinawa.

Kamikaze attack planes were supposed to have sunk or crippled at least half of this task force. The slaughter was so effective, Radio Tokyo boasted, that the Okinawa invasion would be set back three months. Yet there were the carriers strong as ever less than two weeks later, strafing and bombing Japanese defense positions on the embattled island as troopships gathered for a major landing. Apart from sporadic suicide raids there would be no concerted Japanese counterattack during the next few days.

Ito produced the top secret schedule for Operation Kikusui— "Floating Chrysanthemum," the heraldic device of the 14th-century martyr Masashige Kusunoki, the personification of gallant failure, who committed *seppuku* by the Minato River, where Kobe now stands, after losing a hopeless struggle to restore power to the imperial throne. Reverence for this loyal warrior blossomed into a cult 500 years later when the more successful Meiji Restoration broke the long-established system of government by shoguns, or military dictators, drawn from a dominant feudal clan. Kusunoki's selfless conduct was seized on as an example of total devotion to the emperor. Generations of Japanese schoolchildren memorized his exploits. It was no coincidence that he became the patron saint of young men determined to sacrifice themselves for Japan. The legendary hero's slogan "Seven Lives for the Nation" was quickly adopted by the Kamikaze attack corps.

Most senior naval officers considered suicide attacks criminally wasteful. Not because they were afraid to die in battle: that was their proud right, as samurai. But the steady, macabre loss of promising young men and irreplaceable aircraft was draining the nation's resources without appreciably weakening the enemy. The end of the European war was in sight. A great flood of American reinforcements must be expected. The devious Stalin was preparing to come in at the kill. Any thought of surrender was still taboo, but the more orthodox military thinkers were beginning to argue that Japan should be husbanding its resources for the defense of the homeland.

The final word still lay, however, with the superpatriots, mostly hotblooded young officers brought up on a diet of emperor worship and the Bushido warrior's code. They believed in miracles. They were determined to wreak miracles with Kamikaze attacks. Operation Kikusui was their plan to cripple the U.S. fleet. Beginning April 6 and spread over the following six weeks, ten main assaults by over 2000 suicide aircraft would be directed at the U.S. naval forces off Okinawa. The plan had imperial approval. It was confined almost entirely to aircraft; no mention had yet been made of any initiative by the surface fleet.

Okinawa

APRIL 1

THE AMERICANS WERE EXULTANT. They had scarcely been ashore four hours on the southwestern coast of Okinawa, and had pushed forward so unexpectedly fast that the Yontan and Kadena airfields were already overrun. The coral-edged Haguchi beaches and the cornfields beyond were carved up and reshaped by the clutter of invasion. Hundreds of landing craft maintained the unending shuttle from the armada of ships offshore. Jeeps, trucks, and tanks spewed out onto the dusty tracks the bulldozers were still carving through the sandy loam. Stores, dumps, casualty stations, command posts, and small villages of attendant pup tents blossomed all over the bridgehead. Shells still whined overhead from the bombardment force of battleships and cruisers steaming tirelessly offshore. Carrier planes swooped in with rockets, bombs, and napalm. But targets on Okinawa were becoming difficult to find. The Japanese seemed to have vanished.

So far, so good. Yet the Americans were worried. They had expected more resistance. Memories of the Iwo Jima bloodbath were all too fresh. Troops hastening toward the coast to bisect this narrow part of the island glanced anxiously at the moutains on their flanks, scarred and defoliated by bombs and shells but eerily silent in the misty sunshine. An occasional mortar bomb or sniper's bullet whined in from nowhere, to be countered by a disproportionate barrage of shellfire. The only visible challenge sprang from sporadic Kamikaze attacks off nearby islands upon the tempting concentrations of shipping, although so far the pilots had proved amateurish and erratic. The defenders were obviously staying their hand ... the vital question was when, how, and where would they strike?

Lieutenant Goro Matsuoka knew most of the answers. The 22-year-old signals officer of the 24th Division, formerly in Manchuria, chuckled to himself as the Americans prodded forward into a void. Beside him in their cleverly camouflaged spotting post in the hill country fringing the southern edge of the Okinawa beachhead, radioman Tanaka was openmouthed as he watched through his binoculars. It was an incredible spectacle. The sunlit sea was alive with toy ships. First the never-ending ranks of landing craft of all shapes and sizes, charging like cavalry across the rolling blue water. Then the fire support ships puffing clouds of yellow smoke, followed as much as a minute later by the crump of their guns. Way out on the hazy horizon were dozens of gray or dazzle-painted transports and what looked like aircraft carriers. The lieutenant passed sporadic reports down the field phone to regimental headquarters, calculated numbers, plotted positions, and made copious notes.

The whine of aircraft overhead set the two men sliding cautiously back into their bunker. Matsuoka moved a metal plate across the embrasure. He was confident their hideout had not been spotted—the Americans were strafing wildly at random— but the new petroleum bombs the U.S. was now using in the Pacific threatened instant incineration. He sat back, smoking a cigarette, checking over his notes. As far as he could see there must be well over 1000 landing craft: 60 warships, 10 of them battleships; and several hundred transports. More seemed to be concentrated in the lagoon at Kerama-retto, the small group of offshore islands 10 miles to the west and clearly visible from his observation post. The Americans had surprised everyone by seizing this lightly defended group four days ago. Now they'd moved artillery onto nearby Keise Island, still closer to the Okinawan coast. Their 155-mm guns were ranging in on Naha, the island capital and military command post.

The bunker shook with the thud of bombs. Small showers of earth spurted from the ceiling. Radioman Tanaka calmly covered his open can of salmon with a signal pad, paused, and resumed eating. The Americans were probably having another go at the group of ancestral tombs farther down the hillside. They seemed obsessed with the idea that the Japanese were converting them into strongpoints.

But the defenders were doing nothing so obvious. Despairing of further reinforcements and specifically ordered not to slug it out on the beaches, Lieutenant General Mitsuru Ushijima, a capable officer who had distinguished himself in China, was husbanding his resources for an all-out attack once the Americans were fully ashore. His garrison of 100,000 men was larger than the enemy estimated; it was not to be committed prematurely. Split into two unequal groups in the northern and southern ends of Okinawa it stood poised to crush the invading forces—as the general's order of the day made clear. The Japanese planned to hit back on April 6 in coordination with a massive Kamikaze blitzkrieg against the U.S. fleet. Until then they had to watch, wait, and keep out of sight in the least likely, best-concealed positions.

Lieutenant Matsuoka reopened the embrasure. A cloud of smoke poured in. For a moment he thought it was poison gas. The lick and crackle of flames down in the valley told him the bombardment had set the grass afire. It was a wonder there was any grass left around these parts; five days of incessant shelling had left the landscape pockmarked and denuded. It seemed impossible that anything could survive. Yet north of him, in the dead ground falling away to the nearest landing beach, advance pickets were dug into deep bunkers ready to resist when the Americans began their inevitable drive toward Naha. Further back toward the capital in another bombed-out wilderness lay batteries of artillery, tanks, trucks, and regiments of troops in well-protected caves and bunkers. When they sprang into action the Yankees were in for a shock.

The lieutenant smiled grimly as he adjusted his small spotting scope and latched the telephone under his helmet. His khaki uniform was thick with dust. He felt in need of a bath and shave. He wondered how long it would be before he was relieved. Several days, probably, judging from the amount of rations dumped in the bunker. The telephone earpiece crackled into life. It was Yoshida, the intelligence major back at headquarters.

"What's your figure so far for the numbers of troops landed?"

"About 50,000 I'd reckon, sir."

Yoshida gave an admiring whistle. "They sure mean business," he said.

The lieutenant felt his stomach knotting with fear. He'd been so absorbed by the spectacle he'd omitted to appreciate its lethality. He resumed his watch on the teeming beachhead. Another wave of tanks arrived south of the Bisha River. Artillery was coming ashore. The supply of hardware appeared endless. The radioman seemed to be reading his thoughts. "Don't worry." He grinned. "We'll crush them."

A red light twinkled down on the plain. With some difficulty Matsuoka centered it in his scope. The Americans were using flamethrowers.

U.S. Fifth Fleet,
Off Okinawa

APRIL 1

THE 14-INCH TURRETS of the battleship *New Mexico* exploded in flame and smoke every three minutes, jolting the elderly hull, numbing the ears, and clouding the upper works in acrid cordite fumes as another broadside hurtled into oblivion. Fountains of earth and dust erupted from the scarred mountain slopes as ship after ship lent its impersonal cover to dusty, sweating foot soldiers a dozen miles away. Spotters radioed their corrections. Gunnery officers plotted fresh coordinates. Dials spun and wheels turned, the hoists whined, breechblocks slammed, and gun barrels belched flame again.

Admiral Raymond A. Spruance neither looked nor paused. The ringmaster of this colossal circus kept pacing the quarter-deck with two breathless aides. It was time for his after-lunch constitutional. Nothing was going to interrupt his routine, or this afternoon's lecture. One thing they'd learned at Tarawa Atoll, he was saying, "you must never skimp on shore bombardment." He still had nightmares of those corpse-strewn beaches. A mere eight hours of concentrated shelling seemed quite enough for that insignificant speck of coral. But in those early days they were relearning the lessons of amphibious warfare discredited since the futile Allied invasion of World War I which petered out on the Turk-defended cliffs of Gallipoli. The bloody Tarawa assault was an unavoidable but costly first step in the long island-hopping campaign across the Pacific which had brought the United States to the doorstep of the imperial homeland.

Operation Iceberg was the penultimate act of American retribution against Japan. Okinawa, the largest of the Japanese-owned Nansei Shoto, a range of 140 drowned volcanic peaks trailing out into the East China Sea from the southernmost main island of Kyushu, was the final stepping-stone to Tokyo. It offered a convenient base for the B-29s, still making 1000-mile round-trip raids on Japan from the remote Marianas. Better still, it provided the jumping-off point for the invasion of Kyushu scheduled for November 1, 1945, already three months into the planning stage.

Spruance had argued doggedly for Okinawa. Equally passionate advocates favored Taiwan or even Shanghai. But the man who was masterminding the Pacific sea war, Admiral Chester W. Nimitz, supported his favorite commander. The first staff studies began on October 25, 1944. British observers described the operation as "the most audacious and complex enterprise yet undertaken by the American amphibious forces." And they were right.

The U.S. Navy's lack of Pacific bases had in a sense proved helpful. The fleet was forced to operate independently for long periods and longer distances at sea. Necessity mothered the invention of the "fleet train," an accumulation of increasingly specialized fast supply ships which kept warships operational for months at a time across the vastness of the Pacific. The Okinawa invasion stretched supply resources to the limit. A total of 287,000 troops had to be transported, maintained, and supported by over 1400 ships of all types, 1200 miles from the captured lagoon at Ulithi, which served as an assembly area, and about the same distance from newly liberated Guam, where Nimitz had recently moved his command headquarters away from the distractions of Hawaii.

The operation demanded a thoroughness once ascribed to Teutons, to say nothing of resources that would have beggared Croesus. It put a cruel strain on the new breed of planners and administrators recently emerged from the already formidable ranks of American admirals, the greatest assembly of naval talent since the days of Nelson. Men like beetle-browed Commodore Augustine H. Gray, "the oil king of the Pacific," responsible for supplying a total monthly consumption of 6 million barrels of fuel oil; or Rear Admiral Donald B. Beary, commander of the main support group, who helped coin the word "logistics." They supplied replacement aircraft from the United States, frozen beef from New Zealand, oil from the Middle East, and everything else from explosives to Baby Ruth bars. The still expanding industrial plants of the world's biggest workshop lavishly filled the oceans with ships, the skies with aircraft, and the battlefields on two continents with an incredible range of hardware. The imminent defeat of Nazi Germany was releasing still more men and materiél for the day of reckoning with the perpetrators of Pearl Harbor.

U.S. intelligence analysts believed the Japanese were incapable of recognizing the overwhelming force bearing down on them. None of the experts had any idea of the extent of the economic crisis paralyzing Japan. The few who claimed to understand Japanese psychology quarreled among themselves over the enemy's state of mind. The majority believed the samurai spirit would prevail. They cited the Kamikaze example. There would be a fight to the finish—a view shared by most American servicemen, who had no hope of an early, easy end to the war. They thought it would be another three years before they got home; then they feared another depression.

Admiral Spruance seemed infected by the general pessimism. It was a sunny spring afternoon. Everything was going smoothly, but he chose to hark back to the black days of Tarawa. There'd been many brilliant victories since then—islands stormed, defense lines breached with minimal loss of life—but his pioneering assault on that one insignificant atoll was something he never let himself forget. How could he have known the place was so stoutly fortified?

The Japanese bunkers on Tarawa had survived the shelling. The men inside survived too. Amtracs jammed on the coral because someone had gotten the tide tables wrong. Heavily burdened marines sank without trace in the potholes. Those who reached the beach were cut down by machine gunners who had been presumed pulverized under the debris. Casualties were so severe that embarrassing questions were raised stateside about the feasibility of the U.S. Navy's victory drive.

Much of the criticism was, of course, political. The navy had never lacked enemies since Brigadier General Billy Mitchell launched his mad, sad crusade for air power soon after World War I. Every naval vessel was obsolete, Mitchell declared, except possibly the submarine, following his questionable test in Chesapeake Bay where six U.S. Army bombers sank an abandoned battleship. His claims for the potency of air power proved prophetic, if exaggerated; his selective emphasis on land-based airpower was insane. Mitchell would have abolished aircraft carriers and everything else afloat if he'd had his way. As it happened, he preached to a ready audience. Isolationists leaped to applaud him. They dreamed of a Fortress America insulated from the squabbles and corruption of the outside world, defended, cut-price, by long-range bombers.

The infighting persisted throughout the interwar years. Echoes of it still rang through the American press, notably in the pages of the arch-isolationist *Chicago Tribune*. But now old parrots were learning new slogans. President Roosevelt was urged to give priority to the Pacific war; fortunately he spurned a policy that could have brought the Russians to the English Channel. Europe's priority affronted the egotistical General Douglas MacArthur, who was determined to regain face after his humiliating flight from the inefficiently defended Philippines. There came a time when Spruance and Nimitz felt they were fighting not one but three main enemies: MacArthur, the U.S. Army, and the Japanese—in that order.

Such rivalry was unavoidable. The original American defense effort in the Pacific was by now split into separate campaigns. When the Japanese were sweeping the Java Sea, the Indian Ocean, and the approaches to Australia, all forces combined to block them. Contending strategies only emerged once the tide turned after the crucial battles for the Solomons. MacArthur began advancing back through New Guinea toward the Philippines. He had promised to return and by God he would. But it was painful, unspectacular work. Not even the general's skilled and sycophantic public relations staff could drum up headlines to compare with the navy's exploits as it raced relentlessly westward across the central Pacific.

The Nimitz plan was to breach the rings of fortified Japanese islands which provided a protective cordon across the Pacific, far from the imperial homeland. First the Gilbert Islands, scene of the Tarawa trauma, then the Marshalls and Kwajalein, a tougher but less costly battle, and on to the Carolines and Marianas. MacArthur derided this strategy and demanded priority. The U.S. Navy won out, thanks to the active support of that former navy secretary, President Franklin D. Roosevelt. His patronage automatically antagonized Roosevelt's frustrated opponents. Somehow or other they had to get back at this political superman who had won an unprecedented fourth presidential term. MacArthur found plenty of politicians willing and eager to support his complaints of neglect. They echoed the future shogun's demands for a less costly route to victory. The pro-MacArthur faction seized on the general's plan for hitting the enemy "where he ain't." That worked well enough in southeast Asia, where the Japanese were thinly spread over hundreds of thousands of square miles, but would not work at the heavily defended approaches to Japan. And it was here, the navy knew, that victory would have to be won. The liberation of the Philippines brought the two rival forces temporarily together, but the costly marine attacks on Iwo Jima and now Okinawa revived the squabble. The situation could have been resolved by the appointment of an overall commander in the Pacific. But it was such a hot political potato that even Roosevelt hesitated. The feud kept simmering right up to the Japanese surrender.

Another salvo jolted *New Mexico* as Spruance clocked up his second mile along the quarterdeck. Flames and smoke sprouted from the superannuated battle line of Task Force 54. Every one of these ships was "old enough to vote." *Arkansas*, a 33-year-old patriarch, was the last capital ship on active service with 12-inch guns. Astern of her the remodeled *Tennessee*, her humiliation at Pearl Harbor long avenged, wore the flag of acting task force commander Rear Admiral Morton L. Deyo. Next the *Nevada*, another Pearl victim, then the elderly *New York* and *New Mexico*'s sister ship *Idaho*.

Lack of speed disqualified these venerable battlewagons from joining the fast carrier task force which dominated the war at sea. But amphibious operations gave them a last lease on life as mobile artillery batteries, able to throw heavy loads of concentrated shellfire whenever the troops ashore required it. The valuable if boring routine varied only when a flag signal from *Tennessee* ordered a 180° turn back across the target area. As the flags whipped down and each bow began to swing, Spruance and his companions automatically crossed to seaward and continued their pacing.

The Fifth Fleet commander missed his regular flagship. There were plenty of faster, smarter, more comfortable ships available than the 12-year-old *Indianapolis*. But he always hankered for a closeup look at his amphibious operations. The cruiser was old enough to risk inshore, yet fast enough at sea to keep up with the carrier strike force. A stray Kamikaze had clipped her fantail, exploding in the sea, the night before the main landing. The salvage crew attempting to repair number four propeller shaft dropped the loosened screw into the depths. *Indianapolis* sailed back to Marcus Island for repairs—all the expertise of the fleet train couldn't tackle this kind of job—and Spruance reluctantly transferred to *New Mexico*.

Spruance was an odd man, even his admirers agreed: a rather shy, introverted intellectual, different from his more flamboyant contemporaries, he spurned emotion and shunned publicity. War correspondents probed in vain for the sharp quotes, the boastful racist rhetoric of men like bluff "Bull" Halsey who vowed to blow "every one of those little yellow bastards back to their ancestors." Bombast offended Spruance. Wars should be fought with mathematical logic. Emotion upset the calculations and obscured the issues. Cool decisions won him the day at Midway, against seemingly impossible odds, and every other action he'd fought thereafter.

A practicing hypochondriac, he restricted his starving staff to salad lunches for fear they might get sluggish in the afternoons. A newcomer to the staff gave the cook a selection of his wife's favorite recipes but after one meal of steak and selected vegetables (which everyone but Spruance enjoyed) the menu reverted to normal. Lately the admiral had been eating a side helping of raw onion to ward off colds. The odor still cut through the cordite fumes as he finished his third mile and prepared to go below. No one would disturb him now, unless on matters of crucial importance, as he took his regulation cold shower, changed into fresh, stiffly starched suntans, and relaxed for an hour over some profound book. Classical music ground out of his portable phonograph. Nothing too heavy: he enjoyed Dvorak, Tchaikovsky, and other late 19th-century romantics. Phonograph needles were in short supply—a machinist's mate kept honing the worn ones on a whetstone—and the warped shellacs were getting chipped and cracked as the incessant gun-fire juddered the sound arm. But Stokowski and the Philadelphia played on and on, defying the din of battle . . .

Spruance was not quite the ice-cold genius he appeared. He had lately been sleeping badly, he confided in letters to his wife, waking in the small hours to complete some signal or memorandum already buzzing through his brain. The strain of almost continuous operations, broken only by pauses to plan the next ones, with rare breaks for leave with the family back on the West Coast, was taking its toll. Secretly he fretted and worried.

Fleet meteorologists were forecasting a storm (incorrectly, as it turned out) which could hamper landing operations. The army air force was being awkward. Their new whiz-kid commander, Curtis LeMay, was fighting tooth and nail to block orders from Nimitz to divert some of his precious B-29s from fire-bomb raids over Japan to more mundane tactical operations in support of the Okinawa operations. Replacement carrier planes were not arriving fast enough. The withdrawal of two damaged carriers after the softening-up of Kyushu threw an intolerable burden onto the rest. Crews were tired after weeks of unbroken action; some had been at sea without a break for nearly two months. And the Kamikaze threat was stretching men's nerves beyond the expected limits of endurance.

Richmond Kelly Turner clattered aboard at dusk with cheering news. The hard-drinking, hard-driving vice admiral had been growing increasingly irascible as his responsibilities mounted, but tonight he was positively beaming. It was all going according to the book. The commander of the Joint Expeditionary Force (Task Force 51) entrusted with the invasion of Okinawa had worked for months on his meticulous plans. They were now paying off. The masterstroke for which he could claim full credit was the preliminary seizure of Kerama-retto, the small group of islands just off the southern tip of Okinawa. The Japanese had neglected to defend them. Today the islands offered a haven for a host of auxiliaries including ammunition ships, oilers, transports, tugs, and repair vessels. Two squadrons of Martin Mariner flying boats were allocated a 1-mile stretch of water for takeoffs and landings in the Aka Channel. Occupying troops discovered over 250 "suicide boats" in camouflaged caves and hangars ready for attacks that would never be launched.

"So far, so good," said Turner, raising his glass in silent salute. A pity he had to drink iced tea.

"Bald Eagle" knew the real threat was yet to come. He sat for hours pondering the problem, hunched in his special chair out on the island catwalk, staring directly aft. Thirty feet below, the flight crews watched curiously. "The Old Man sits up there all day, riding backward," they would say. "The bow could drop off this ship and he wouldn't look around." Every time the vice admiral broke his flag in a new carrier—in this case the comparative newcomer *Bunker Hill*—a metalsmith was sent up to "flag country" to weld down the four-legged upholstered chair which gave him a clear view across the ranks of parked planes all the way to the stern. Staff officers thought he wanted to check out his flying boys as they set off on every mission. The truth was, he preferred to keep the wind off his face. It made his eyes water.

The ornithological code name suited Vice Admiral Marc Mitscher. There was a predatory birdlike look about the commander of Task Force 58, the most powerful carrier fleet the world has ever seen. The merest wisps of gray hair protruded from under the peaked blue cap which shielded his watery blue eyes from the Pacific glare. The cap was another one of his little peculiarities; it became regulation navy issue after the war. The beaky, wizened face beneath it glowed alternately sweet and sour. Mitscher was an airman through and through, the only one of the original Pensacola Pioneers to reach flag rank. Other founder alumni of the famous flying school who struggled so fiercely to develop U.S. naval aviation in the face of implacable opposition had long since fallen victim to flying accidents, political infighting, or sheer frustration. Only the fittest survived those bitter interwar years and none emerged unscathed.

The air pioneers were swiftly vindicated. The loss of those battleships, squatting ignominiously on the mud at Pearl Harbor, forced the U.S. Navy to fall back upon its carriers. Mitscher first commanded *Hornet* (code-named "Shangri-La"), from whose deck Lieutenant Colonel James H. Doolittle launched his impudent raid on Tokyo in April 1942. He later plotted the aerial ambush which killed Yamamoto. Mitscher earned the reputation among those who knew him least of a maverick, an eccentric, a sourdough. He made few close friends. He regarded newcomers to his staff with suspicion, especially if they were nonflying regular fleet officers or "black shoes." Mitscher harbored the devoted aviator's dislike of the battleship sailors who had dominated U.S. naval thinking (and procurement) throughout most of his career. Spruance fell into that category. It was ironic that Spruance, with his big-gun background, had won his greatest victory commanding an all-carrier force at Midway. Mitscher's feelings were reciprocated at first. Spruance believed his carrier commander had fumbled at the height of the battle. Still, that was years ago and Mitscher's subsequent performance had long dispelled the admiral's prejudices—except that the old aviator defiantly wore brown shoes.

Chester Nimitz was anxious to avoid these internecine tensions. He had enough trouble on his hands with MacArthur and the air force. He sought a cross-fertilization between aviators and sailors by drafting hand-picked black-shoe men into the carrier task groups. Captain Arleigh ("31-Knot") Burke arrived fresh from heroic action as a destroyer commander at Guadalcanal to become Mitscher's chief of staff. The gruff eagle was skeptical. Carrier operations were a highly specialized field. You couldn't teach an old sea dog new tricks. But he was wrong. Burke soon proved himself. The two men made a superb team, though it was not always apparent to outsiders. Mitscher seldom passed up the chance of a salty wisecrack. Whenever a destroyer came alongside he would advise the flag plot to "tie Captain Burke to a stanchion until that bucket shoves off."

The sun dipped into the Pacific. The flagship's bugler sounded general quarters. *Bunker Hill* sprang to life as men in flak jackets and helmets dived into the gun tubs where skeleton crews had spent a weary day waiting for something to happen. The squawk box shrilled: "Pilots, man your planes." Youngsters in nylon flying suits rushed on deck from the ready rooms. Crewmen in multicolored overalls milled round their machines. Engines burst into life and soon the grimy blue Hellcats were roaring through the exhaust smoke, down the deck, and into the air. The radio filled with incomprehensible chatter as the fighter pilots reinforced the combat air patrol, the perpetual protective umbrella over the fleet and landing force.

The eerie twilight was a favorite time for sneak attacks. Enemy pilots from airfields on islands farther to the north approached at extreme altitude, ready to scream down in a death dive onto the American ships, or wave-hopped toward their targets out of the symbolically setting sun. Blobs began appearing on the radar screens of the combat information center, one deck below Mitscher's flag plot where he stooped over the charts with Burke, planning fleet dispositions for the night. The carriers were lying way over to the west of Okinawa, 100 miles from the invasion beaches, and reckoned on moving farther out under cover of darkness. Down in the darkened information center at least five bogies were identifiable on the softly glowing radar tubes. Staff officers at the admiral's elbow began barking orders into the bulkhead battery of radio phones.

Mitscher never ceased reminding his men how much things had improved. "You've got it good," he would grunt in those rare bursts of public speech. Back in the Solomons in 1942 the few available carriers were hoarded like gold. The briefest withdrawal for damage repair was a major setback to the war effort. Overhauls were indefinitely postponed. Machinery worked way beyond design limits, a credit to the men who designed and built it. Ships' engines regularly worked double the prescribed hours before overhaul. Aircraft flew on a wing and a prayer. So, too, did the crews. Ammunition and spares were in perpetual short supply.

The U.S. Navy had such a lot to learn. Few American pilots could outfly the Japanese veterans in their Zeros. The art of air control was in its infancy. The top brass were still groping for new tactical concepts suited to the unfamiliar power of naval aviation. Experience at the Coral Sea proved the need to group carriers together for mutual protection instead of scattering before aerial counterattacks. At Midway they learned it was suicidal not to concentrate and coordinate their air strikes before defending Zeros hit the attacking squadrons.

Things would have been a lot worse if the United States had been attacked earlier. The 27 months between the outbreak of war in Europe and the Japanese raid on Pearl Harbor won the navy valuable time. Training and construction programs were well under way. The U.S. forces had perfected and standardized their weaponry. The navy was able to produce the prototypes which became the backbone of the fleet. Chief of these were the *Essex* class carriers—although it was not until December 1942 that the first of these remarkable ships was commissioned. They quickly proved how far American naval aviation had moved ahead of the rest of the world. Typical of this class was *Bunker Hill,* named after a heroic skirmish of the Revolutionary War.

These enlarged versions of the prewar *Yorktown* class were packed with aircraft. Four full squadrons could be accommodated. The Americans were devotees of firepower. Displacement fully loaded topped 33,900 tons. The original complement of 2171 men rose to 3500 as more guns and radar were crammed aboard. Four shaft-geared turbines gave a top speed of 33 knots. Armament included twelve 5-inch antiaircraft guns, with dozens of Bofors and Oerlikons bristling out from transoms just below the 870-foot flight deck. A later version, the long-hull *Essex* class, extended the bow and made room for still more antiaircraft guns.

The great square superstructure which rose from the starboard side of the flight deck, dubbed "the island," contained everything necessary for controlling operations. Here was the large, bustling room known as the flag plot (if a commanding admiral was aboard), where all vital decisions were taken. One deck below lay the combat information center, crammed with radar and plotting boards as well as a small cubbyhole for Japanese-speaking radio monitors. One deck lower were the intelligence and radio rooms where reports were received, decoded, evaluated, and dispatched. The hull contained crew space, engine rooms, a vast hangar, ammunition stores, and tanks full of diesel fuel and aviation gas. It was a vulnerable combination. Only the strength of the bulkheads, the intricacy of the compartments, and the skill and bravery of the fire fighters and damage control parties could save a hard-hit carrier from blazing disaster.

The fire danger was taken so seriously after the loss of two irreplaceable carriers in the first crucial months of the war that the U.S. Navy turned for help to the New York City Fire

Department. Deputy Chief Harold J. Burke, commissioned into the naval reserve, introduced atomized water sprays which proved more effective than hoses and a foamite system for smothering flames every hundred feet of a carrier's deck. Mobile pumps were installed, in two sizes, with all couplings standardized. Whenever an attack was imminent, the aviation gasoline still in the fuel lines was pumped back into storage and the pipes were filled with inert gas.

Twenty-four *Essex*-class carriers were built during the war. Each was being completed in a record 15 months and still there were never enough to go around. The Kamikaze pilots were taking a worrisome toll. No fleet carrier had been lost lately, Tokyo claims to the contrary, but the recent raid up the Japanese coast had finished the *Franklin*, gutted by fires and explosions after a conventional bombing attack that cost over 700 lives. Thanks to heroic efforts by her skipper and crew the crippled ship made it back to a stateside repair yard. Fires like that would have destroyed her earlier in the war. *Enterprise* and the new *Yorktown* were also damaged. The force was fleshed out with *Independence*-class light fleet carriers of some 11,000 tons, built on surplus cruiser hulls.

The fact remained that U.S. carriers were not designed for the kind of punishment they were now getting. They were big, well armed, long-range, and unusually thin-decked. The designers could scarcely be blamed for failing to allow for madmen who deliberately crashed their planes into the deck elevators. Task Force 58 would be withdrawn the moment airfields were operational on Okinawa, if Mitscher had his way, and the job handed over to land-based air. Spruance thought otherwise.

An alarm klaxon warned of imminent attack. A babel of voices rose inside flag plot. Mitscher put on his helmet with the two white stars. He hated that helmet, but orders were orders. Out on the catwalk he peered into the lowering darkness, ignoring the pleas of his staff. The chief danger, they kept pointing out, was from friendly flak. Every ship was hit at one time or another as excited gunners blazed away at suicide pilots weaving through the task force in search of a suitable target. Streams of red tracer rose lazily into the darkening sky from the destroyer screen way out on the port quarter. Others joined in. *South Dakota* opened up just off the port beam. The flash of her secondary armament silhouetted the battleship intermittently.

Shell bursts flickered low over the water. A fireball flared, fell, and vanished. One bogie splashed. The firing slackened.

Reports coming into the combat information center indicated that sporadic attacks were being made elsewhere. The combat air patrol had splashed two Judy bombers way out beyond the early-warning cordon of radar pickets encircling Okinawa. Another carrier had been attacked, unsuccessfully, out of sight across the horizon. The 80-odd ships of Task Force 58 were strung across 25 square miles of ocean, subdivided into task groups, each attended by its protective shield of high-speed battleships, cruisers, and destroyers. Damage losses since the departure from Ulithi on March 14 had temporarily forced Mitscher to reduce his four task groups to three, but now he was back to four—still the greatest carrier attack fleet ever created: 15 carriers with over 1000 aircraft, protected by 8 fast battleships, 18 cruisers, and over 60 destroyers. Squadrons were mainly composed of Grumman F6F Hellcats, although there was still a sprinkling of the older F4F Wildcats and Vought F4U Corsairs. The Japanese could no longer match their speed, armament, and durability. The Grumman TBMF-1 Avenger had replaced those old death traps, the misnamed Devastator torpedo bombers. The reliable Dauntless dive-bombers were also largely replaced, with some reservations among their pilots, by Curtis SB2C1 Helldivers.

It was men as much as machines who had swung the balance in America's favor, Mitscher always insisted. Many of his fliers had two years' combat experience and over 300 hours to their credit. Their Japanese opponents, with a few notable exceptions, were obvious greenhorns. Fuel shortages and the demands for replacements cut short their training. The Japanese now made amateurish mistakes like failing to keep tight formation and falling for the simplest lures. The last big carrier confrontation during the invasion of Saipan became known throughout the U.S. fleet as the Great Marianas Turkey Shoot because it developed into a massacre. The Japanese carriers were denuded of aircrews (a total of 445 planes lost) without inflicting appreciable damage on Task Force 58. Recognition of their pilots' inadequacies, and the increasingly desperate war situation, forced the Japanese to resort to suicide tactics five months later in defense of the Philippines.

Kamikaze Headquarters, Kanoya Air Base, Kyushu

APRIL 2

THE ZERO BANKED in a little too sharply, a little too fast. Anti-aircraft gunners watched critically. Another half-trained replacement. The pilot hesitated when he saw the bomb-pocked runway, cut his throttle, and bumped heavily along an emergency track just cleared by the repair gangs. Ground crews swarmed out of their slit trenches to hustle the plane under camouflage netting. A grizzled old chief mechanic anxiously checked the landing gear. The pilot climbed out as the two flag officers strode over. Everyone froze to attention.

"You've been reposted from Korea?" asked Vice Admiral Matome Ugaki. Small, slim, with the physique of a youngster, only his lined face betrayed Ugaki's age. At 54 the onetime chief of staff to the great Yamamoto was feeling the strain of sending men to their death. As commander of the Fifth Air Fleet he made a special point of greeting all newly arrived pilots. His headquarters at Kanoya Air Base in the southernmost Japanese island of Kyushu was the attack center for Kamikaze raids against Okinawa, almost 400 miles to the south.

The Fifth Air Fleet was less than two months old. It was formed on February 11, 1945, when the battle for Okinawa appeared inevitable. Its 600 aircraft were dispersed among 36 airfields on Kyushu. The army air force with about half as many planes occupied another 19 fields. These bases were kept operational in spite of constant U.S. raids. Some bases were disguised as farmland, some as country roads. There were few hangars or identifiable military installations. Nearby civilian buildings became barracks and repair shops. Aircraft were hidden beneath high earth banks under camouflage netting; antiaircraft gun positions were similarly concealed around each runway. The soft rock made tunneling easy.

Most though not all pilots belonged to Kamikaze squadrons. A handful of experienced men were retained to fly escort and reconnaissance. Most, though not all, of the Kamikaze pilots were volunteers. The number of draftees was lately rising, which caused some worries at first among the staff until it was found that the young men quickly accepted their fate and began volunteering eagerly for their fatal missions.

The newly arrived pilot saluted. "Ensign Hayashi," he reported, overawed at the sight of so much brass. "Ichizu Hayashi, Genzan Air Group."

Ugaki detected the telltale accent. His face softened.

"You're a Kyushu man. You come from around here?"

"No, sir. From Fukuoka. To the north."

Ugaki smiled. The atmosphere thawed appreciably.

"Then you'll be able to visit your parents."

The pilot shook his head.

"I've already written my mother goodbye," he said. "I think that is enough."

The other flag officer bit his lip. There was an embarrassed silence. Far off an air-raid siren wailed.

"There should be five of you," said Ugaki. Suddenly he was his old hard-bitten self.

"They'll be coming, sir. The usual breakdowns. Two landed at Iwakuni. The others failed to get off."

Ugaki turned to the other flag officer and shrugged. That was just what he'd been telling him. Replacement aircraft were either clapped-out wrecks or unreliable new production. Maintenance even on the Kamikaze bases was proving a major headache.

"But you navigated here yourself?" he asked the pilot. "How many hours have you got?"

"Sixty-three flying hours, sir."

Ugaki walked away, impressed. That young man had the makings of a first-class pilot. Too bad he wouldn't live long enough. Ugaki said as much to his fuming companion, Vice Admiral Ryunosuke Kusaka, chief of staff, Combined Fleet.

Kusaka had been sent on a tour of Kamikaze air bases in Kyushu on the eve of the massive Kamikaze air assault against the Okinawa invasion force, code-named Operation Kikusui. It was pure sadism, he sometimes told himself. The commander in chief, Admiral Soemu Toyoda, a prominent bitter-ender, knew that his top planning executive detested this kind of warfare. Or maybe he just wanted to get him out of the way? Headquarters was riddled with factional intrigue.

Kusaka is credited with being the first officer to advocate a preemptive air strike against Pearl Harbor. He brought up the idea at a staff lecture as early as 1927. He had long been connected with naval aviation, had commanded two carriers and served as chief of staff, First Air Fleet, when his original idea— later code-named Operation Z—was put into devastating effect. He afterward saw his carriers destroyed in the Midway massacre and his best pilots dissipated in the southwest Pacific. Today he was stuck at a desk job where his experience was ignored and his word carried no weight. Applications for a transfer were so often refused he had long since lapsed into sulky compliance.

"It was unfortunate," Kusaka reflected years later. "I should have spoken out sooner. And so should many others. But it was difficult to go against the tide. I blame it on the system as much as myself . . . especially over this Kamikaze question."

"We don't do this lightly," Ugaki was explaining again. It was Monday, April 2, and Kusaka had been here two days, braving the air raids and politely ignoring his illustrious colleague's self-justifying lectures. The Japanese naval air force only resorted to Kamikaze tactics, Ugaki insisted, when it became obvious that conventional attacks had no hope of success.

The man who began it all, Vice Admiral Takijiro Onishi, the finest naval aviator Japan ever produced, admitted that although men had been called upon to risk their lives from the 1905 war onward, they had always been given some chance of survival. Even the five midget submarines which attacked Pearl Harbor were expected to get back to their mother ships. But crisis conditions called for crisis methods. When it came to the type of pilot the naval air force was getting today the flag officer was bluntly honest: "These young men with their limited training, outdated equipment, and numerical inferiority are doomed even by conventional fighting methods."

"We only intended to launch crash attacks for one week in the Philippines," Ugaki explained. "They were so successful that we naturally continued."

Kusaka had doubts about the successes. Enemy strength was apparently unimpaired. He might have been mollified if he had known the amount of worry the Kamikaze were causing the Americans. But the Kamikaze faction was in the ascendant these days. It even had the emperor's approval. Open criticism could be dangerous.

He could have pointed out that the wastage rate of men and aircraft was unjustifiable. Not one plane in ten was hitting a target. Even a hit was not guaranteed to do much damage unless an aircraft carrier was caught with a deckload of parked planes. Only the smaller, more expendable warships suffered irreparably. Kamikaze pilots often picked on escort vessels in the excitement of the moment, instead of seeking juicier prey. Kusaka could have said plenty to knock down Ugaki's arguments. Instead he maintained his guilty silence.

The two vice admirals threaded their way back to the command post beneath cherry trees and painted netting. Air fleet headquarters here in Kanoya had taken a terrible pounding, but out in the nearby rice fields peasants were busy transplanting the spring seedlings. There was an extraordinary proportion of young men among them, Kusaka noticed; looking closer, he could see from their shaved heads that they must be Kamikaze pilots, filling in their final days helping sow a crop they would never harvest.

Living conditions were appalling. Worse in some ways, Kusaka thought, than in New Guinea. The 721st Air Group, part of the Fifth Air Fleet based in Kanoya, was billeted in an old, bullet-riddled primary school. The windows were gone, the roof leaked, the floors were filthy. Men slept on the floors without beds. One blanket apiece was available to fend off the chilly April wind. Not that they got much sleep, since regular nightly raids forced everyone on base to spend hours in the nearest slit trenches.

U.S. Task Force 58's barnstorming attacks up the Japanese coast two weeks before had dislocated Vice Admiral Ugaki's plan for a Kamikaze assault as soon as the Americans hit the Okinawa beaches. He lost 65 planes in Kamikaze attacks and about 50 more on the ground. The Kikusui attack schedule was set back six days, which was just as Mitscher planned it. Replacements were still being scraped together from as far away as Manchuria and Korea, with a trickle starting to arrive from Tenth Air Fleet, the reserve of tyro pilots based on the main Japanese island of Honshu. Some of these men had less than 40 hours of flying. They could scarcely take off and land, let alone engage the Americans in combat. Few had been given gunnery practice, apart from loosing off a burst or two while in the air. Navigation was such a mystery to most of them that guide pilots led them to their target, fought off American opposition, and lingered, if possible, to observe the results. The reports they brought back tended, naturally, to be sketchy.

Kusaka had his first opportunity that afternoon to watch replacement pilots learning suicide tactics. Among them was Ensign Hayashi, fresh from Korea. The instructor told them there were two things they would have to practice: fast takeoffs and formation flying. It was essential to get off the ground quickly before some marauding American fighter caught them. They must then cling together in flight for mutual protection. Two forms of attack were recommended. The first began at high altitude and ended in a steep dive. The attacker overflew American fighters but risked tearing his plane apart on the way down. A better tactic was to go in at sea level under the American radar and unnoticed by the combat air patrol. The problem here was holding the aircraft steadily at wave height in the face of distracting flak. The bombload was not armed at takeoff.

"We don't want any damage to the airfield," the instructor emphasized. "Just in case you crash on takeoff."

The pilots nodded and made occasional notes. None looked the least bit troubled. They might have been sitting in on a weather briefing.

" . . . so you'll find a toggle inside your cockpit," the instructor went on. "Pull this to activate your bombs. Don't do it prematurely. You may not find a target and you may be forced to return. You don't want to ditch valuable ammunition. Pull the toggle as you close your target."

Wherever possible they should go for a carrier. The carriers of Task Force 58 were the most potent weapon in the U.S. naval arsenal—and also the most vulnerable. Aim for the deck elevators, if not the "island." One hit there would knock out all controls. Battleships were only secondary targets. Again the maximum damage would be inflicted by a hit on the bridge tower. The same went for cruisers and destroyers. Smaller ships like landing craft would break apart if hit amidships, though an attack should not be wasted on anything so insignificant unless in exceptional circumstances.

Someone asked: "Should we strip unnecessary instruments from the planes? It would be a pity to waste them."

The instructor advised the pilots to check with their aircrews.

It was a cool day, but Kusaka was sweating. He needed fresh air. He walked out into the garden, a tall elegant figure in his smartly cut uniform. The pale sun glinted on his gold staff officer's aiguillettes. All around him the cherry blossoms were slowly falling.

Assembly of Japanese Fleet, Mitajiri Anchorage, Inland Sea of Japan

APRIL 2

"SO THIS IS WHAT we've come down to," thought Captain Tameichi Hara. He felt understandably depressed. Japan's task force assembling round the anchored *Yamato* was a shadow of its former self. There was a time, not so long ago, when the roadstead would have been filled with battleships, cruisers, and destroyers trimly moored in lines as far as the eye could see. Today there were just ten ships, all that could be scraped together, some showing signs of the wear and tear of over three years of unremitting warfare. Their battle honors included every action since Pearl Harbor.

Hara's own ship, the light cruiser *Yahagi*, was a relative newcomer. Like all Japanese cruisers, she was named after a river. Battleships were given the names of ancient provinces. Fleet carriers were mythical birds or dragons.

Hard on *Yahagi's* port bow lay the elderly *Hatsushimo* (translated poetically as "first frost of the season"), which was built in 1933. After fighting all the way from the invasion of Java through the Aleutians campaign to the Marianas to Leyte Gulf, she was lucky to have survived. All other ships of her class had been sunk.

74

The slightly larger *Kasumi* (meaning "spring") was commissioned in June 1939. Although there were initial design problems with her steering, she had been part of the Pearl Harbor raiding force, screened the carrier strike into the Indian Ocean, covered the Darwin attack, watched the Japanese carriers blown apart at Midway, and fought in the Solomons.

Then there were three wind-class ships, all commissioned a year before the outbreak of the Pacific war. They had taken part in almost every important action. With their quadruple quick-loading torpedo tubes they were the ultimate in Japanese destroyer design. The three were *Isokaze* ("shore breeze"), *Hamakaze* ("breeze off the beach"), which stood by the sinking superbattleship *Musashi* in the Sibuyan Sea, and *Yukikaze* ("snow wind"), survivor of so many battles that the men who served in her believed she was unsinkable.

Yet another destroyer, *Asashimo* ("morning frost"), came limping in with engine trouble. She was long overdue for overhaul. Built a little over two years before in Osaka, topping 3400 tons, her machinery still suffered the shock of near misses incurred during the surprise breakout near the Leyte Gulf landing beaches.

Suyutsuki, whose name translates vaguely as "moon sounds like a bell," lost her bow and stern in torpedo attacks on January 16, 1944, but still made port. She also had a reputation for survival. Her sister ship *Fuyutsuki* ("winter moon"), only nine months old, was a later version of the moon class. These were antiaircraft destroyer escorts equipped with the new 3.9-inch, .65 caliber high-velocity antiaircraft gun capable of firing 25 rounds a minute. Their single-trunked smokestacks made them look surprisingly like a scaled-down version of Captain Hara's *Yahagi*.

The captain had spent most of his war as a destroyer commander. According to the casualty rate among officers of his seniority he should already be dead. He was proud to be on *Yahagi*. There had admittedly been considerable sacrifice of armor to give her a top speed of 35 knots. How much punishment she could take was a question mark. Since joining the fleet early in 1943 she had taken part in two major actions, off Samar and in the Marianas, but had not really been put to the test. Weighing 8534 tons fully loaded, she was equipped with two catapult planes, two sets of quadruple torpedo tubes, six 5.9-inch guns in double turrets, and fifty-nine 25-mm antiaircraft machine guns. Two type 13 radars gave early warning of approaching aircraft and little else.

Yahagi was designed as a destroyer flagship. The captain's old friend Rear Admiral Keizo Komura, officer commanding the three divisions of the Second Destroyer Squadron, was beside him on the lightly protected bridge watching Asashimo come to anchor. The bridge was extraordinarily exposed. Everything was lightweight steel. The overhead canopy "just about kept the rain off," one officer recalled. Still, there was no question of conning the ship from the safety of the armored wheelhouse. Japanese commanders had scorned protection ever since the example of the great Admiral Togo. His refusal to take cover from Russian shells bursting over the open bridge of his flagship at the decisive 1905 battle in Tsushima Strait was part of navy folklore.

Captain Hara recalled the words of Sun Tzu, a Chinese military sage who lived about the time of Alexander of Macedon: "One who has few must prepare against the enemy . . . sally out when he does not expect you." What a hope they had of preparing anything! They should be out now on the open sea practicing fleet maneuvers. But the supply clerks told them there was scarcely any fuel. The ration for March allowed a total of 1½ days' steaming at 12 knots. It was bad enough lying here, the boilers half fired, eating up oil, with anchors ready to slip at a moment's notice. They should be doing something—anything. Hara wondered how Ariga, the new captain of Yamato, would ever get the feel of his giant command. He'd had scant chance to put the superbattleship through her paces. The first time Ariga got around to handling her might very well be in action. It was the same story everywhere. Communications staff, sonar and radar technicians, torpedomen, and, above all, gunners were desperately in need of practice. Too many new and inexperienced hands were being drafted to the fleet. There hadn't been a training shoot in the past three months.

As for sallying out when the enemy least expected it . . . this force could never escape the eyes of the patrolling B-29s or of the American submarines clustered round the Bungo Strait, the only practical exit from the Inland Sea. It was the route they would have to take if they were to get through with their projected sortie around southern Kyushu to Sasebo. Hara shook his head sadly. Whoever thought up such an imbecile scheme? If Combined Fleet headquarters was determined to throw away all that was left of the navy it would be better to send the ships out singly as ocean raiders to harass the Americans' supply lines. That way they would have an outside chance of helping the defending forces on Okinawa.

Rear Admiral Komura was staring contemptuously around the anchorage. The small fishing village of Mitajiri lay half a mile on the beam, hedged in by fir-covered hills. Boats were drawn up on the beach where women in head scarfs sat mending nets. Behind them, the huddle of gray houses was relieved by splashes of cherry blossoms. Komura seldom said much; now he snorted.

"Hiding," he said.

Captain Hara agreed. Their scraped-together force was doing just that. They should be moored at the regular Hashirajima fleet anchorage in Hiroshima Bay. Instead they were sheltering 25 miles farther west along this godforsaken stretch of coast, hoping the Americans would not spot them. Fleets normally formed up in the Hashirajima roadstead on leaving Kure but this was now too obvious, too open—and possibly mined.

"What's wrong with *Asashimo?*" barked Komura. "She's taken 20 minutes anchoring."

The wretched skipper was interrogated by signal light. "Engine trouble," translated the signals officer, scribbling on his pad.

"Tell them to fix it," shouted Komura and stamped off below. The man who sent off the first search planes over Pearl Harbor (from the heavy cruiser *Chikuma*) was not his ebullient self.

The officer of the day saluted the captain. He was Lieutenant Kenji Hatta, one of the handsomest and smartest men in the ship.

"Launches approaching, sir," he reported. "It must be the cadets."

Twenty-two cadets were due aboard, straight from graduation at Etajima Naval Academy. The captain automatically reached for the big 16-power binoculars mounted at his elbow. These glasses had proved more effective than radar in the early days off Guadalcanal.

"There's more than 22," said Hara.

"Naturally, sir," the lieutenant reminded him respectfully. "Most of them are being posted to Yamato."

Hara nodded. He was already worrying about the extra paperwork.

Masanobu Kobayashi was looking forward to his bath. He would need it after completing his chores on the deck of Yamato. He loved to relax each evening in the 30-foot tub full of steaming water assigned to his division. The designers had thoughtfully provided 20 of these very Japanese installations on Yamato. Bathers washed themselves clean before sinking into the water and quietly unwinding. It was just like the village bathhouse back home, except that there were no women. Sometimes the young seamen fooled around; tying a towel around their heads and sticking a lump of soap in it, they swam about the bath in line, with only the soap protruding above the surface. They called the game "submarines."

The bath master waited patiently for them to finish. As they climbed out he charged each man a few sen for a clean towel and a bucket of fresh water. The bath itself was filled with heated seawater which left the body sticky unless you doused down afterward with fresh water.

"Hey, you!"

A petty officer awoke Kobayashi from his reverie. He scrubbed the deck with renewed vigor. Any sign of slacking could earn him a boot in the ribs. Superior officers never hesitated to slap or kick errant juniors. Worse still, he might be taken off tonight's bathing roster. Section chiefs had a nasty habit of grabbing you just as you were about to put your feet up in the mess deck and demanding an instant, word-perfect recitation of the Emperor Meiji's Rescript to Soldiers and Sailors. "If the majesty and power of our empire be impaired, do you share with us the sorrow . . ." Everyone had to know it by heart because it was, in effect, the oath that bound them all to die, if necessary, without question at the emperor's command. Those who fumbled their words got no bathing either.

It was a long day, especially for junior ratings. They were on deck at 0500, doing calisthenics and exercising at their guns in the predawn darkness. All hands formed up forward for colors. A bugle call brought the ship's company to attention, the officers saluting, as the chief signal yeoman raised the ensign, a rising sun with extended rays. Beside it flew fleet commander Vice Admiral Ito's flag, a sun with fewer rays and topped by a red bar.

There was an hour's break for breakfast at 0700 followed by training and chores like scrubbing the deck from 0800 to noon. The one-hour lunch break was followed by three more hours of exhausting gun drill and two hours of sumo-style wrestling and similar toughening-up exercises. Bath time, dinner, and a brief rest were fitted in between 1700 and 1900, before gun crews went back on deck for night training and lookout practice. At 2200 the seamen stood beside their bunks for final inspection by their divisional officers. Kobayashi's bunk was second from the bottom in a tier of five. Cigarette ash and candy wrappers were apt to land on him from above, but as a young junior seaman he could hardly expect anything better.

At least the food was good. Menus changed daily. Eighty cooks worked in the main galleys deep on number four deck. Meals were brought up to the mess decks in large stainless steel canteens. The crew ate ample portions of frozen fish, fried beefsteak unobtainable ashore, a variety of vegetables, pickles, and of course plenty of glutinous Japanese rice. The three officers' messes had their own cooks and the pick of the food supplies.

Japanese ships were far from dry. Ratings could draw a ration of rice wine in the evenings with their dinner, or a bottle of beer. There was no restriction on the officers, who frequently caroused in port; out here, on the alert, they were noticcably more abstemious. Not that it bothered Kobayashi: he neither smoked nor drank.

Commotion broke out around the after gangway. Two launches were approaching. They carried 71 cadets, 22 of them for *Yahagi*, the remainder posted to *Yamato*. The executive officer, Captain Jiro Nomura, hurriedly joined the side party, hitching at his sword belt and glancing through the personnel list. He had tried vainly to dissuade the Manpower Bureau from sending any more unskilled hands aboard. There were enough already. His appeal was ignored. The Etajima Academy graduates urgently needed sea training. They must be rushed in to fill the gaps in the decimated officer corps.

The exec regretted his initial inhospitableness as the youngsters stumbled up the long ladder. Their faces glowed with awe at the size of this ship and with pride at joining her. Two years of intensified training had hardened their bodies and imbued them with fighting zeal. Any one of them would dive immediately over the side, Nomura thought, if he cared to give the order. It was from dedicated material like this that the navy selected its captains courageous. If only the academy put a little less stress on obedience and taught more of them to think . . .

The cadets formed a double line on the after deck and sharply answered roll call. The executive officer handed the newcomers over to the president of the gunroom, a cadet with one year's service, and watched them march away along the undulating deck, gawking at the towering superstructure, the giant turrets, and all the mysterious accouterments of a mighty man-of-war. Later in the day Nomura would be giving the first of his lectures: "Yamato contains 6,153,030 rivets. A total of 7,507,536 welding rods were used to complete 463,784 meters of welding. The largest welded block is 11 meters high and weighs 80 tons." It never failed to impress.

Ensign Mitsuo Watanabe was watching from the wing of number one bridge. There were extensions like this on either side of the tower, some 40 feet up, where the signalmen prepared and hoisted their flags. The 24-year-old communications officer shook his head in disbelief. Where were they going to put these cadets? Yamato was designed to hold a complement of about 2000. The addition of extra guns and other equipment brought the present crew to 3332 (the paymaster had shown him the figures), and spacious as this ship was, there wasn't room for all of them. Watanabe himself slept in a hammock slung in the main companionway between the ship's shrine and Vice Admiral Ito's in-port cabin. Ito was unusually tall. He occasionally bumped his head on the ensign's hammock, apologizing profusely for waking him.

The young officer went back to work inside number one bridge. It was a large circular affair with the elevator dead center and big bulletproof glass windows which were never closed in action. Officers could hardly enjoy protection when gunners were fighting, fully exposed, on the open deck. Seeking safety bucked the samurai tradition. The forward part of the bridge was studded with high-powered binoculars, a magnetic compass, and a variety of monitors giving information on engine speed, propeller revs, and gyro heading. A large brass clinometer revealed the degree of list. At the moment it registered zero.

This was strictly "admiral's country." Ito and his staff took up their action stations here. Watanabe handled the VHF radiophones. The TBS ("talk between ships") was mounted on the elevator wall between a chart table and the safe containing the code books. Most of the books had weighted covers for easy emergency disposal overboard. The ensign used a simple memorized code whenever he transmitted orders to the rest of the fleet. He chatted with the VHF radio room on number four deck well below the waterline, and made test calls to *Yahagi* and several of the attendant destroyers.

He strolled around the after part of the bridge to the command plot. Vice Admiral Ito had held his staff conference here when they left Kure two days ago. Technicians were at work in the radar cabins on either side of the plot. These housed the type 22 surface warning sets which ranged on large surface targets up to 21½ miles away. There was no radar capable of directing guns against aircraft. Through the wide-open windows he could see the massive adjacent bulk of the smokestack, the inverted tripod of the mainmast, an intermediate clutter of antiaircraft guns, and, way aft, the twin catapults, each with a floatplane ready for launching.

There was plenty of activity. Antlike figures were swabbing down the decks, oiling wire ropes, and chipping away at the first traces of rust. Gun crews were stripping and cleaning the weaponry. They were just as busy, he knew, down in the depths of the ship where technicians were checking the ammunition hoists, and the electrical circuits; in the four main engine rooms, engineers were at work on the great Tanpon geared turbines. The order had gone out to get everything in tip-top shape while they awaited operational orders.

The main after turret swung ponderously to port. The three big gun barrels lifted to maximum elevation. This did not give them much antiaircraft capability, but a new shell, the *San-Shiki*, nicknamed "the Beehive," supplemented the regular armor-piercing ammunition. The projectile was packed with layers of incendiary pellets, Watanabe was told, which exploded at set ranges like the blast of a shotgun. The only drawback, apparently, was that the copper drive bands of the "Beehives" were poorly machined. Constant rapid fire seriously damaged the rifling of the 18.1-inch gun barrels. The gunners were loath to use them. *Yamato* was, after all, designed for surface combat.

The Navy Ministry, Tokyo

APRIL 3

TOKYO STILL STANK of burning. The soot and dust from a quarter of a million gutted buildings coated the stricken city. It blackened the early blossoms in Ueno Park, left an inky layer across the Imperial Palace moat, and caked the windows of the Navy Ministry. Twenty-four days before—on the never-to-be-forgotten night of March 10—the B-29s changed their tactics, abandoned their ineffective high-level attacks, and came in low with nothing but incendiary bombs. The raid did more damage than any air raid in history; more even than the atomic blast, four months later, over Hiroshima. Sixteen square miles were burned out of the heart of the capital. Official, probably conservative figures put the dead at 83,783, wounded 49,918, and homeless over a million. Today army volunteers wearing face masks and rubber coveralls were cremating the last piles of blackened corpses beside the Sumida River.

Americans who once had condemned the Nazi bombings of civilians in Warsaw, Rotterdam, London, and Coventry hailed the raid as a triumph. In a sense they were not far wrong. It gave grim force to those who argued that the war was lost. Admiral Mitsumasa Yonai, minister for the navy, could scarcely walk up the gray granite steps of his headquarters without an agonized glance at the soot-caked statues, the blackened brick and grimy paintwork. The stone-floored entrance hall clacked to the click of heels as the hefty, round-faced minister negotiated a flurry of salutes and climbed the ornamental central staircase where the steering wheel of a Russian warship captured at Tsushima hung prominently on the wall. He hurried along the picture-filled corridor leading to his stylish Victorian office. Portraits of former ministers stared down in resplendent full-dress uniform. Puzzled aides and secretaries glanced at their watches. The usually precise Yonai was three minutes late. They did not know (and would not be told) that the minister had been meeting urgently with men who were determined to end the war.

Admiral Yonai settled down behind his handsome oak desk, a present from the lords of the British admiralty. He shuffled through signals and dispatches stamped "IMPERIAL JAPANESE NAVY, TOKYO" in English. There was nothing odd about this use of an alien language. The Japanese modeled their navy after the British at the height of Britannia's power, and secretly admired these haughty barbarians, sprung from a class system as hierarchical as their own. The subtle nuances which fixed each Briton's place in society appealed to the Japanese. The system contained an arrogant, ritual element any samurai could understand. This ministry, the Etajima Naval Academy, and the Tokyo railroad terminus were all built with bricks individually wrapped and shipped all the way from England. Shipboard commands were given in English until the early thirties. Then xenophobia began to spread, fanned deliberately by the militarists, until foreign words were expunged. Baseball fans had to learn new terms for "umpire" and "pitcher." But the navy stuck to rugby football.

Yonai's intelligence summary from Combined Fleet claimed a Royal naval task force had joined the Americans off Okinawa. As if the Americans needed reinforcements! What would it be like, Yonai wondered, when Germany surrendered? The Russians were nearing Berlin. The Ruhr was overrun. And still those stupid Germans fought on. They were simply encouraging the idiot militarists in Tokyo.

There was little other signaled information. Admiral Toyoda told him nothing. The commander in chief, Combined Fleet, paid little attention to the Navy Ministry, which he dismissed, in his usual sarcastic manner, as the "red brick faction." The place was packed with bureaucrats and politicians, as far as Toyoda was concerned, well suited to the menial tasks of mundane administration. And a bunch of peacemakers, at that.

Factionalism and rivalry were eating away the ramshackle command structures at the apex of Japanese politico-military life.

The founding fathers of modern Japan, the handful of provincial samurai who masterminded the modernization program carried out under the nominal leadership of the "restored" Emperor Meiji, were anxious to import Western technology. They were less enthusiastic about democracy. Their privileged past left them wary of the mob. Commoners did not have family names before the 1870s. A samurai could hack a peasant to death with his sword at the slightest sign of disrespect. No one questioned his right to do so. The babel of Westminster and Capitol Hill seemed far too freewheeling to these paternalistic disciplinarians. The authoritarian atmosphere of Bismarck's Germany held more appeal for Hirobumi Ito, the most influential of the early Japanese statesmen who traveled abroad in search of a governmental system.

Japan was saddled with a constitution which worked well enough during the elders' lifetime. The emperor was enshrined as the Confucian father figure to whom his people owed full allegiance. The revived cult of imperial divinity preserved the convenient seclusion which left the throne a prey to manipulation. Important rescripts published in the emperor's name were drawn up, in practice, by his advisers. Men died in battle, apparently, at the behest of his Divine Majesty. But it was the militarists who were giving the orders. Answerable to though by no means guided by the emperor were three contending groups: the elected government, headed by a prime minister, and the two armed forces. Neither the army nor the navy was subject to civilian control. As in imperial Germany the military had a direct line to the throne. They also exercised an automatic veto over the cabinet through the ministers for the army and navy. Both ministers had to be serving officers. If one or both resigned the government fell.

Mitsumasa Yonai was perfectly at home in this jungle. He

considered himself a consummate politician. Others had their doubts. When someone asked Yamamoto his opinion of Yonai, the late admiral had pointed to his head and his stomach. He meant that his old friend was "all guts and no brains." It was an unfair judgment. Yonai was a marked man, regarded, like Yamamoto himself, as pro-Western and antiwar: a dangerous combination in these neurotic times. Yonai was no coward but he enjoyed life. The red veins in his pouchy face betrayed his taste for fine whiskey. And, like Yamamoto, his frequent appearance in the geisha houses drew delighted giggles from a score of expensive young entertainers.

It was in the red-light district of old Edo that the admiral-turned-politician conducted much of his intrigue. Discreetly, of course, in the Japanese fashion, never appearing treasonably obdurate, especially if army officers were around. The military police, the dreaded Kempeitai, had been dogging his footsteps for two years waiting for his first false move. Yonai moved much too carefully to give the police any excuse to arrest him. His behavior was typical—and regrettable. Caution and conformity did almost as much damage to Japan as militarism. In a land where a passive public took orders from a mere handful, it was the duty of eminent leaders to speak out; yet the bandwagon was packed with responsible men who could not bring themselves to reach for the brake. They seemed more absorbed by infighting . . .

A prime example was the joint army-navy staff, formed to advise the emperor on the conduct of the war. The rival services appointed staff chiefs who pointedly ignored each other. There was more squabbling than interservice consultation. Things were not much better inside the navy. The chief of staff, Admiral Koshiro Oikawa, ostensibly the emperor's adviser, found himself ignored by Combined Fleet. The command headquarters under Admiral Soemu Toyoda was in sole charge of fleet operations. It had in the past enjoyed direct access to the Emperor. Oikawa's role of imperial go-between was greeted by a surly lack of cooperation. The only person who commiserated with him was Yonai, equally isolated and uninformed in his ministry.

This was no way to run a war, the admiral agreed. Oikawa had dropped around to Yonai's office for one of his periodic chats. He was late as usual. He had the harassed air of a man who never stopped running to catch up with his next appointment. Still, there was plenty to gossip about. The government was tottering. General Kuniaki Koiso, who had replaced Tojo as prime minister in July 1944 after the fall of Saipan, was about to pay the price for defeat in the Philippines and Iwo Jima. It was a heaven-sent but risky opportunity to install someone who might lead the way to an honorable peace.

Yonai favored Admiral Kantaro Suzuki. The 80-year-old hero of the war with Russia still carried a bullet lodged close to his heart. Mutinous soldiers who hated his moderate views had tried to kill him during the muddle-minded February 26, 1936, army revolt in Tokyo. Plenty of fanatics were ready to try again if he attempted a "Badoglio"; in other words, if he imitated the marshal who surrendered Italy unconditionally to the Allies. Oikawa wondered whether the old man wasn't senile. He was extremely doddery. Granted, he favored peace, but would he accept the unacceptable and urge the emperor to support unconditional surrender?

Why, Yonai often asked himself, had well-informed navy men like himself not opposed the war more strongly? He and a handful of others, including the late Admiral Yamamoto, had opposed the army's insane ambitions to the eleventh hour. Then they gave in, throwing themselves heart and soul into a conflict they knew Japan could not win. The cruel truth was that at heart they were opportunists. The rising strength of Germany and the persistent irresolution of the United States allowed them to be convinced that the gamble might just come off, that the Americans could be persuaded to negotiate instead of fight, once Japan had established a dominant position in east and southeast Asia. The army firmly believed this. Men like Yonai were more doubtful, but they went along with the militarists, fearfully but hopefully, in a miscalculation as disastrous as Hitler's invasion of Russia. Now they were searching desperately for a way out.

Oikawa was speaking of his recent imperial audience. Air-raid sirens were wailing on March 29 when he drove through the inner palace gates. A court official ushered him into the damp, dimly lit shelter adjoining the imperial library. His Majesty appeared a few minutes later from behind the gold ornamental screen covering the steps down from the palace. The admiral and his staff bowed deeply, then seated themselves at the checker-cloth conference table. They sat sideways in their chairs, carefully averting their direct gaze from the divine countenance. The 44-year-old emperor, a slight bespectacled figure in field marshal's uniform, flipped through the schedule for the Kikusui Kamikaze attacks, asking occasional questions. Oikawa, back on his feet, did his best to answer.

"Two thousand aircraft will be used throughout these operations?" The high-pitched imperial voice was sharply interrogative. "Is that all?"

"There will be an additional 1,500 army aircraft," replied the admiral, bowing reverently.

Hirohito put down the file. He looked puzzled.

"But where's the navy? Have we no ships?"

The embarrassed Oikawa hung his head in silence. Should he tell the emperor the truth? Should he admit there was only a handful left?

He repeated the story to Yonai and other senior colleagues, little knowing that Hirohito's question had sealed *Yamato's* fate.

PART
II

APRIL 5, 1945

SOUTHERN JAPAN AND OKINAWA
WITH LOCATION OF JAPANESE AND U.S. FLEETS,   APRIL, 194

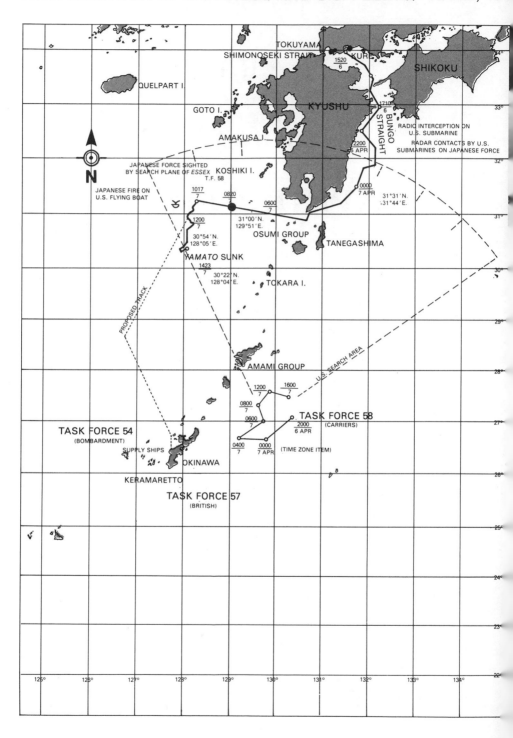

TOKUYAMA
SHIMONOSEKI STRAIT
KURE
1520
6
SHIKOKU

QUELPART I.

KYUSHU

1710
6

BUNGO STRAIGHT

RADIO INTERCEPTION ON
U.S. SUBMARINE
RADAR CONTACTS BY U.S.
SUBMARINES ON JAPANESE FORCE

GOTO I.

AMAKUSA I.

2200
6 APR

JAPANESE FORCE SIGHTED
BY SEARCH PLANE OF ESSEX   KOSHIKI I.
T.F. 58

0000
7 APR

31°31'N.
131°44'E.

JAPANESE FIRE ON
U.S. FLYING BOAT

1017
7

0820

0600
7

N

1200
7

31°00'N.
129°51'E.

OSUMI GROUP

TANEGASHIMA

30°54'N.
128°05'E.

YAMATO SUNK

1423
7

30°22'N.
128°04'E.

TOKARA I.

PROPOSED TRACK

AMAMI GROUP

U.S. SEARCH AREA

1200
7

1600
7

0800
7

0600
7

2000
6 APR

TASK FORCE 58
(CARRIERS)

TASK FORCE 54
(BOMBARDMENT)

SUPPLY SHIPS

0400
7

0000
7 APR

(TIME ZONE ITEM)

OKINAWA

KERAMARETTO

TASK FORCE 57
(BRITISH)

Japanese Combined Fleet Headquarters, Hiyoshi

APRIL 5

COMBINED FLEET HEADQUARTERS crowned an inconspicuous knoll on the grounds of Kieo University at Hiyoshi, halfway between Tokyo and Yokohama. There was little to indicate that this unpretentious huddle of camouflaged buildings concealed the nerve center of the entire naval war effort. A single strand of barbed wire fenced off the center from the rest of the campus. A single sentry guarded the single entry road, now devoid of vehicles because of the gasoline shortage. The two double-story concrete buildings smeared with green and brown paint were lecture halls and dormitories which the navy had taken over on the eve of the Pacific war. A series of underground tunnels cut into the soft limestone hillside sheltered the communications equipment which transmitted operational orders to warships all over the Pacific.

The volume of signal traffic had dropped sharply since the Leyte battle in the Philippines. But so had the number of ships. It was a matter of vast concern—and irritation—to the American code breakers. Throughout the war, unsuspected by the enemy, they had been cracking Japanese naval codes. Now, gradually, the airwaves were falling silent. Surviving warships and submarines operated mainly from home waters, where they received their most important orders by landline. Just what were the Japanese planning to do with these ships? The subject aroused intense speculation among Admiral Nimitz's intelligence experts. It seemed inconceivable that even in its present, weakened state the Japanese navy would resist the temptation to disrupt the Okinawa landings.

Precisely the same view was held by one of the squabbling factions in Hiyoshi. A creeping paralysis, broken only by irrational bursts of action, had overtaken Combined Fleet since it became apparent after the Marianas massacre that the navy was no match for the Americans. Underemployed staff officers formed rival cliques offering impractical, desperate solutions. Debates grew increasingly bitter. The commander in chief of the navy, Admiral Toyoda, swung one way, then another. In recent months he appeared to have lost all power of decision. A squat, square-faced man of 57, Soemu Toyoda had inherited the mantle of the late, great Yamamoto and his immediate successor, Admiral Mineichi Koga, whose aircraft disappeared in a storm on route to the Philippines. Toyoda's apologists—and there were many—considered him a brilliant man broken by insurmountable problems. His detractors thought him shallow, shifty, and a fool. His main weakness, all agreed, was a tendency to snap up the first piece of advice that caught his fancy.

Plenty of conflicting advice was available. One faction enjoyed rare support from the army. It argued that the navy should husband its resources for the coming battle for Japan. The last remaining battleworthy ships, called Second Fleet though they scarcely amounted to a naval division, should be held in reserve. Such a force could not possibly abort the Okinawa invasion with or without air support. Even the plan to sortie around Kyushu was crazy. Surely the navy had learned some lessons over the past three years? The wisest kept their counsel. They realized the war was lost but felt, like the red brick faction, that it was too dangerous to say so openly. The vocal, militant majority believed in action, no matter what the odds. To them the recent carrier raid on Kure proved conclusively that the fleet eventually would be sunk at its moorings. As it turned out, they were right. Far better to sally out in a last glorious banzai. The prospect of a crippled *Yamato* striking her colors to the enemy would forever stain the honor of the Imperial Japanese Navy.

Captain Shiganori Kami talked emotionally about honor and glory. He talked emotionally about everything. His arguments were seldom rational. Not that this mattered: the situation was so desperate that everyone was going out of his mind. "I think we were all a little unhinged," a colleague admitted years later. But Kami was worse than most. His closest friends felt he should never have been a staff officer. An unabashed admirer of the Nazis, he spent 18 months in prewar Germany. Instead of being given a sea command where his natural aggressiveness and impatience would have found a suitable and probably terminal outlet, he was kept desk-bound in Hiyoshi as chief of operations, a post for which he was temperamentally unsuited. He worked off his excess energies with sumo wrestling and vicious bouts of kendo.

The emperor's remark to Admiral Oikawa soon reached Hiyoshi. It left the patriotic Kami more emotional than ever. "His Imperial Majesty asks 'Where is the navy?' How can we evade our responsibilities?" he argued. The situation called for something akin to the soldiers' banzai charge. A wild swinging charge, naval fashion, aimed straight at the enemy's jugular.

"What would we have done in olden times?" cried Kami. "We would have thrown everything into a do-or-die attack! Risked everything on one momentous gamble! Have we all become women? Hark back to history! Evoke the spirit of Togo at Tsushima! Of Yamamoto at Pearl Harbor!"

It was stirring stuff. Hopeless to explain that the Bushido spirit could scarcely correct a crushing imbalance of power which faced neither Togo nor Yamamoto at their moments of triumph. Sheer courage could scarcely be expected to compensate for lack of air power, carriers, and escort ships. The navy could very well squander its remaining strength without influencing the outcome of the war . . .

"Irreligious nonsense!" thundered Kami. Such heresy left him red-faced and breathless with anger. Rumor had it he was drinking secretly these days in his office.

"A show of spirit! That's what we want! The spirit of our glorious ancestors! The spirit of the Yamato people! The gods will come to our aid!"

Opponents backed away from this sort of argument. Questioning the muddled tenets of Shinto metaphysics came dangerously close to treason. Instead they declared that a Japanese force heading for Okinawa stood little chance of survival. "Even if the odds were only 10 percent in favor, the effort would be worthwhile," Kami replied. "A true samurai doesn't ask whether his efforts pay off. He's not a Kanto merchant. He merely seeks the opportunity to sacrifice himself."

The Bushido code encouraged flamboyant gestures. Like all knightly guides to chivalrous conduct, it was constantly ignored. Treachery and cruelty flourished throughout the feudal struggles of the late 15th and 16th centuries. But a band of cornered samurai, despising capture, could seek an honorable exit from the world by throwing themselves hopelessly into the fray. It was dangerous anachronistic nonsense to emulate this example four centuries later when Japan's survival was at stake.

There were many who fumed with frustration as the Americans spilled effortlessly across Okinawa. The impudent Yankees taunted Japanese impotence as they fast established a foothold on the doorstep of the imperial homeland. The army was already complaining, as it had at Iwo Jima, of being forced to do all the fighting on its own. Granted, the Kamikaze were coming, but the emperor was right. The surface fleet should be there too. A sortie with all remaining strength could set *Yamato* slaughtering the American transports, providing the kind of shock that would abort the entire operation.

Nonsense, argued others. Without air cover even *Yamato* had no chance of making the 350-mile dash unscathed from Kyushu to Okinawa. Hadn't the navy already learned enough bitter lessons from the American carriers? Spruance and Mitscher could hardly be expected to let this plum target pass serenely beneath their noses. Even if they did, and that was a big "if" indeed, what could one battleship, no matter how formidable, hope to achieve in a running action off Okinawa? How many enemy ships could she hope to sink—10, 20, 30—out of an armada many hundreds strong?

Kami was impervious to argument. In his view, Toyoda was bound to support him. A true samurai had no alternative. Kami would even beg the admiral to let him join the sortie. No one could accuse him of preaching anything he dared not practice.

Combined Fleet held its staff meeting each morning at nine o'clock sharp. The meetings were a daily ritual. Today nothing important was tabled for discussion. Admiral Toyoda took his place at the head table. The battle maps stretched along the wall behind him were studded with colored pins and paper flags. The red pins were Japanese warships. The red flags were Japanese army units, many of them marooned on Pacific islands bypassed by the American advance. The blue pins and flags represented the enemy. The blues greatly outnumbered the reds.

Some 20 staff officers sat at scattered tables around the converted lecture hall. They included specialists of all ranks and ages: engineers, gunners, supply officers. The head of the intelligence section began his meager briefing. American strength on Okinawa was growing steadily. Over 100,000 enemy troops were ashore. The counterattack was scheduled for the next day. His nod gave the cue to Vice Admiral Takijiro Onishi, deputy chief of naval staff, better known as "father of the Kamikaze," who had overall charge of the first Kikusui assault in the morning. A tough, wiry little man, Onishi felt stifled in the politically charged atmosphere at Hiyoshi. He had never suffered fools gladly; here he made it disdainfully clear that he was surrounded by them. In clipped, dry tones he reviewed the operational status of Ugaki's Fifth Air Fleet in Kyushu.

It was at this point that Captain Shiganori Kami chose to drop his bombshell. He sprang to his feet and announced:

"Second Fleet will participate tomorrow in Kikusui One. The code name will be Operation Ten-ichi [Heaven Number One]. Flagship *Yamato* will sail with cruiser *Yahagi* and eight destroyers on April 6 to attack the American fleet and transports off Okinawa. After inflicting maximum punishment on the enemy, *Yamato* will be beached, using her main batteries as additional artillery to aid our defending forces. Surplus crew members will go ashore to reinforce the garrison."

Startled staff officers glanced at Toyoda for confirmation. The admiral sat, chin cupped in his hands, gravely nodding. It had been the hardest decision of his life, he later claimed. For the moment he exuded calm confidence.

Lieutenant Hideo Katori was horrified. He could not challenge the operational decision but, as a supply officer, he could question its practicality. The lieutenant was a specialist in oil supplies. He doubted whether there were sufficient reserves to fuel *Yamato* and her escorts without cutting down elsewhere. Convoy escorts would have to be reduced along the supply routes from Manchuria and Korea. He requested permission to check out the fuel situation with Kure.

"It won't be necessary." Kami brushed the objection aside. "Second Fleet will be redesignated the First Special Attack Force. This is a *Tokko* operation. Fuel supplies will be enough for one way only."

So that was it. *Yamato* was no longer to be risked as a decoy. The superbattleship and her escorts were doomed to die like other Kamikaze. It had all been decided, privately, during the night. Kami and Toyoda sat talking for hours in the privacy of the admiral's office. Both men had drunk a great deal of sake. Snacks were brought in several times while bleary-eyed aides sat dozing in the corridor outside. An air-raid alert at about 2300 sent staff pattering down to the shelters, but the admiral and the captain did not join them.

No record was kept of their conversation. Toyoda was reluctant to discuss it later. Perhaps he had qualms about the ease with which Kami was able to talk him into this ultimate operational gamble. For Operation Ten-ichi was the admiral's last combat order.

Members of the staff spoke afterward—with hindsight—of the inevitability of the decision. Both men were hard-liners. Neither could accept the notion of defeat. Obsessed with pride and "face," they were perfectly prepared to sacrifice the remnants of the fleet to avoid the stigma of surrender.

Toyoda was marginally more rational. His subsequent justification was that there seemed an even chance of the *Yamato* task force surviving the dash to Okinawa. Similar attacks on Guadalcanal early in the war had succeeded brilliantly. Men who knew they were on a *Tokko* mission would fight more fiercely than ever. They need only burst in on the moored transports, suspending all landing operations, providing the ideal opportunity for the Okinawa garrison to mount its counterattack and hurl the invaders back into the sea. Unfortunately, like all Japanese intelligence appraisals at this point in the war, the admiral's ambitious plan seriously underestimated American resources and strength.

Kami shared his chief's misguided optimism. He was, if anything, even more inclined to shrug off the obstacles. Fighting spirit, his inexorable catchall remedy, would swamp the productive and technological power of the enemy. It was an argument born of necessity; other Asians would shortly be adopting it, with varying degrees of success, in their forthcoming campaigns against the white man. Most of these later warriors would be Marxists preaching "peoples' war" and "men above machines."

The simple captain saw things in more mystical terms. He fell back on ancient, ill-formed superstitions long fed into the samurai subconscious: a mixture of half-digested Buddhist belief and animist legend. From it all emerged the sincerely held belief that an indefinable force, vaguely referred to as "the Japanese spirit," was destined to triumph over American "materialism." Sacrifice reinforced that spirit. It contributed to victory. The shades of the heroic dead, backed by sympathetic gods, would mass for a miraculous counterattack like the typhoons which saved Japan from the Mongols in 1274 and 1281. A gesture— even an apparently futile gesture—at this crucial stage could not fail to attract divine aid . . .

And what a glorious way to die! The light of revelation glowed from Captain Kami's excited face in the morning as with unexpected eloquence he outlined the details of the suicidal sortie. The last banzai! The conference room fell deathly quiet as he walked among the desks waving a crumpled handful of notes . . . the great ship and her escorts, hurtling forward at full speed in the predawn darkness, descending like a divine thunderbolt in the midst of the enemy host, spreading panic and disorder. The Yankees losing their heads, as they did at Savo Island, firing blindly at each other in the darkness . . . the sea littered with drifting, burning ships . . . The staff sat listening, astounded.

A flustered planning officer asked whether Chief of Staff Kusaka should be consulted. An operation of this importance required careful preparation. Ordinarily the process would take days, even weeks.

"Plans are being drawn up" Toyoda replied. As far as he was concerned the matter was closed. "Kami will shortly telephone Kusaka in Kanoya."

Katori slipped out to consult the supply department in Kure. The base had storage facilities for 3 million tons of oil, but as far as he knew the tanks were empty.

"What's this madness?" spluttered the depot superintendent

in the navy yard. "We've still got a long war to fight. Total reserves stand at 40,000 tons. That's more than enough for a round trip for the entire task force. But it'll be wasted. How are we going to operate after that?"

By the time the lieutenant got back, the meeting was breaking up. Kami was already on the telephone.

Kamikaze Headquarters, Kanoya Air Base

APRIL 5

THE PILOTS ROSE EARLY. Their sleep was disturbed by the nightly raid that pitted the runway. Some wanted to stay on in the schoolhouse instead of cowering in the shelter. They were going to die anyway, so what did it matter? Fellow officers sternly reminded them that they were destined to die destroying an American carrier. Not passively, here in bed. Dawn found them reasonably refreshed; after a frugal breakfast of hot black tea, rice, and pickles they spread out across the airfield in search of their hidden aircraft. Ground crews were already at work. It was the pilots' job to ensure that nothing went wrong on the morrow.

Ensign Ichizu Hayashi was surprised to see the cherry blossoms falling. They had not bloomed yet in the chilly north of Korea. He made his way along a small stream, south of the pilots' quarters, which wound through thickets of bamboo and wild roses. The water was red with fallen petals. He felt perfectly calm. Tomorrow he would be a god, his debt to the emperor finally repaid. The others felt much the same. Few showed signs of nervousness. One or two tried to quiet their fears with sake. Most were quietly resigned, freed of earthly

99

cares, savoring the extraordinary detachment of men already dead.

These were not the doped-up fanatics the Americans imagined. Records showed that the bulk of the pilots were quiet, studious boys, devoted sons who had reached their awesome decision after considerable reflection. The majority were college seniors. Postwar critics accused the navy leaders of killing off the nation's educated youth instead of first committing their regulars. The original Kamikaze in the Philippines were, in fact, regular officers; although many experienced men had been held back to train the flood of new volunteers, they too were being gradually committed as the campaign mounted in intensity.

Pilots who had not been assigned a mission in tomorrow's assault were cleaning up the schoolhouse. At least they no longer slept on the floors. Bedding had arrived from the stores depot at Kagoshima. It would be passed on to new arrivals as occupants went off to die. A mother and daughter were wandering around the billets asking for a certain officer. His colleagues hesitated to tell them he was gone. He had flown off against the U.S. carriers in March. They lamely explained that he had been posted to a forward island. The two women seemed to understand. The girl was the dead man's fiancée. She asked to see the bunk where he once slept. Her fingers caressed the bedding. Perhaps she sensed the truth.

Vice Admiral Kusaka felt out of place in these macabre surroundings. The chief of staff had been sent temporarily to Kanoya to oversee the initial phase of the Kikusui operation. He regarded the suicide attack with undisguised distaste. He was particularly shocked at the primitive conditions at the Kamikaze base and said as much to Ugaki, who was normally solicitous of his men, but the Fifth Air Fleet commander shrugged. It was worse still in other parts of Kyushu. On some of the newer fields aircrews did not have a roof over their heads. They slept under trees, wrapped in their ponchos. It would be getting warm soon; they only had to worry about the rain.

An aide marched down the long sandbagged corridor with a sheaf of meteorological reports. Phones rang all around the command post; officers scribbled notes for the air fleet commander sitting at his desk in the middle of the shelter. Morse signals chattered next door. A code machine spewed out punched tape. Ugaki examined the weather forecasts and allowed himself one of his rare, wry smiles. Tomorrow would be fine. The rain front moving in from the southwest would not reach them until the following day. Kikusui One was spread over the next two days; the major effort would therefore have to be launched in the morning.

One of Ugaki's desk phones rang. It was the safe line from Hiyoshi. "He's here," Ugaki said, handing the instrument to Kusaka.

"That you, sir?" Kami asked. He sounded excited.

"It's me," said Kusaka, icily polite. He loathed the firebrand captain.

"Admiral Toyoda requests me to inform you that Operation Ten-ichi is in force. Second Fleet is now the first special attack force. It will launch a *Tokko* assault against the enemy fleet at Okinawa. After firing off all ammunition, ships will beach on the island, where crews will join the defending forces."

Kusaka stood transfixed. The telephone trembled in his hand. When he failed to answer, Kami asked: "Are you still there, sir? What do you think of the plan?"

Spluttering with rage, Kusaka yelled: "What the hell am I supposed to think? I haven't even been consulted!"

The command post was suddenly silent. The occupants froze over their tasks, watching the white-faced Kusaka. Kami's voice ground on:

"Operational orders from Combined Fleet are under dispatch to you at this moment. The necessary fleet order is on its way to Admiral Ito. A further signal from the commander in chief requests you to fly immediately to Mitajiri and brief the fleet on its duties. Sailing time must be no later than 1500, tomorrow."

"Look now, wait a minute—" Kusaka was groping for words.

"I respectfully suggest you study the orders," Kami interrupted. "The commander in chief requests immediate action. He regrets the lack of notice. There are others to be advised. Thank you, sir, and goodbye."

The phone went dead. Kusaka replaced it softly and deliberately.

"Bad news?" Ugaki asked automatically. He had enough worries of his own right now. "It *will* be bad," said Kusaka, wandering off in search of the operational orders. Within ten minutes they were coming in over the teleprinter.

Now it was Vice Admiral Kusaka's turn to face the most difficult decision of his life. He felt outraged, insulted. The cruelest blow was Toyoda's insistence that he personally deliver *Yamato's* death warrant. It was pure sadism. Operationally, the enterprise was nonsense. The paucity of orders, six pages of vague instructions obviously composed with more haste than thought, offended his bureaucratic sensibilities. Combined Fleet was notorious for its detailed, often overcomplex battle orders.

The chief of staff weighed his options. He could fly straight back to headquarters and resign. Many people later criticized him for not doing so. But it wasn't easy to buck the national tradition of obedience, Japan's strength—and weakness. Kusaka wearily accepted the inevitable. He walked back to the command post to brief Ugaki.

"I call that good news," the air fleet commander commented. "The Americans won't know which way to turn."

"What about air support for the fleet?" asked Kusaka.

Operation Heaven Number One proved to be less of an attack plan than a pyramid of crude assumptions. *Yamato* and nine escorts were to dash out into the China Sea through the screen of lurking U.S. submarines, sail unchallenged down the Ryukyu Islands chain, and swing in toward the Okinawa landing beaches. There the ships would burst out of the darkness, all guns blazing, to massacre the unsuspecting American transports. No mention was made of air cover, but it was made perfectly clear that none of the force was expected back. Once the ships had inflicted maximum damage they would be deliberately beached to enable their crews to join the defending troops ashore. One lunatic addendum suggested that *Yamato's* great turrets might continue providing artillery support after the battleship wedged herself on the coastal coral. Just how power was to be maintained to operate those turrets was not explained. In less serious circumstances the whole thing might have been dismissed as a tasteless practical joke.

"I've no aircraft to spare," said Ugaki. "I'm already committing everything I've got. Even with a little advance warning I couldn't help much. But remember, your ships won't be within range of Task Force 58 until April 7. Our strikes tomorrow will knock out enough carriers to draw the enemy's sting. We'll throw in the rest of our force next day to keep the Yankees busy."

Kusaka admired his confidence. Or was it self-delusion? He ordered transportation to a nearby base on Kagoshima Bay where a seaplane waited to fly him to *Yamato*. Vice Admiral Ugaki went off to check his pilots. He liked Combined Fleet's death and glory gesture. He was determined to die himself before this war ended. But the surface ships would have to look after themselves. It was going to be difficult enough getting his half-trained aircrews on target.

The young men were practicing emergency takeoffs. They ran to their warmed-up aircraft, rolled them out of the revetments, and clambered skyward as quickly as possible. It was the only way to escape lurking enemy fighters. They had evolved this drill, after bitter experience, down in the Philippines. Quick thinking was required because the runway was still cratered by last night's raid.

Ensign Ichizo Hayashi joined in the scramble. He wanted to practice aerial gunnery and acrobatics too, but there was not enough gas. There would only just be enough in his tank tomorrow for a round trip to Okinawa. No extra for head winds or combat. It was his duty to bring his plane back safely if he failed to find a suitable target. Emergency landing strips elsewhere in Kyushu would help him back to Kanoya—provided, of course, that he could find his way.

The air group staged a farewell dinner for tomorrow's heros. The celebration fell flat. Few of the pilots knew each other. Most of them refused to drink. They excused themselves early, some going to bed, others writing farewell letters by the schoolhouse fire. Hayashi fondled the crucifix he wore beneath his shirt—it was not wise to profess Christianity too openly—but poured out his feelings to his mother:

> We live in the spirit of Jesus Christ, and we die in that spirit. This thought stays with me. It is gratifying to live in this world, but living has a spirit of futility about it now. It is time to die. I do not seek reasons for dying. My only search is for an enemy target against which to dive.

Hayashi was due to be disappointed. His mission on April 6 was canceled. Six more days would pass before he was allowed to die.

Japanese Fleet, Mitajiri Anchorage

APRIL 5

THE SIGNAL was stamped "TOP SECRET." The *Yamato* duty signals officer decoded it and delivered the sealed envelope personally to Vice Admiral Seiichi Ito, who was relaxing after an early lunch in the reception room of his in-port cabin. The officer looked pale and flustered. The admiral put on his reading glasses, tore open the envelope, and read the signal twice. His expression did not change. He might have been digesting a status report. When he spoke his voice was perfectly calm:

"Ask Morishita-san to report to me."

The chief of staff, Second Fleet, Rear Admiral Nobii Morishita, was leafing through charts on the number one bridge. He was unusually tall and well built, a chain-smoking, dynamic, articulate officer; one of the brilliant handful who defied naval orthodoxy and threw off occasional flashes of real inspiration. Fellow officers categorized him with Kami, Ugaki, and Onishi, though he differed from them profoundly. All were heroic mavericks.

Morishita was looking forward to a poker evening with members of the staff. He was a fearsome player. Few could equal him. He had learned his game facing up to giants like the great

Yamamoto. Officers who served as attachés in Washington or studied in the United States introduced poker to the Japanese navy in the early thirties. Gambling was very much a part of their samurai tradition. This tough-nosed foreign game required a degree of nerve and bluff that appealed to the martial spirit. Stakes were never high: what counted was winning.

Morishita clattered down the sets of steel ladders inside the tower. He seldom used the elevators. At the weather deck he slipped through the watertight hatch that led into the quartermaster's well-protected compartment. It was here that old Koyama spent his sea watches at the steering wheel, following the dim red strip of the gyro repeater. Nearby was the executive officer's damage control center. A watertight door led aft to the main starboard companionway, leading in turn to the ship's shrine, the senior officers' wardroom, and Vice Admiral Ito's cabin.

It was a splendid room, carpeted, partly paneled, and handsomely furnished. Morishita removed his soft peaked combat cap and came respectfully to attention. Following the British custom, Japanese naval officers did not salute below decks. Ito motioned his chief of staff to a chair and handed him the signal, adding that *Yamato's* commanding officer would shortly be joining them. Ariga arrived, slightly out of breath, while Morishita was still reading. The signal was from Toyoda at Combined Fleet headquarters:

OPERATION TEN-ICHI WILL NOW COMMENCE. SECOND FLEET WILL FORM THE FIRST SPECIAL ATTACK FORCE, FLAGSHIP YAMATO, WITH ALL AVAILABLE ESCORTS. THE FORCE WILL SORTIE FROM THE INLAND SEA AT 1500 APRIL 6, 1945, AND ATTACK THE ENEMY INVASION FLEET AT OKINAWA. COMBAT SHOULD COMMENCE BEFORE DAWN, APRIL 8. FUEL IS ONLY AVAILABLE FOR ONE-WAY PASSAGE. THIS IS A TOKKO OPERATION.

Morishita read it aloud for Ariga's benefit.

"Not giving us much time," remarked the phlegmatic rear admiral.

"Not much in the way of instructions," growled Morishita. At any minute he would explode.

"Kusaka's coming," said Ito. "Would you care for some tea?"

Ariga sat back, humming quietly to himself.

Vice Admiral Kusaka's seaplane reached the Inland Sea at Nakatsu and held its course, a few degrees east of north, toward the anchorage. A brisk wind whipped the shallow blue waters into tiny wavelets. Over on the port side, masts, funnels, and the partly submerged hulls of sunken ships sprouted from the approaches to the Shimonoseki Strait, the western outlet to the China Sea. Air-dropped mines had effectively blocked this vital route. The tiny biplane banked sharply as a huddle of warships came into view close to the Honshu coast. Even at that height *Yamato* looked impressive: a basking whale surrounded by minnows.

The pilot landed gently on the choppy water and taxied toward the warships. His observer called up the battleship by signal lamp: "SEND A LAUNCH, PLEASE, FOR VERY IMPORTANT PASSENGERS." Within five minutes Kusaka and an aide were scrambling awkwardly onto the floats and into the launch. The side party twittered its greeting as they reached the top of the long accommodation ladder. Everyone with business on the weather deck came stiffly to attention while the visitors hurried past to Ito's cabin. Word was spreading through the ship that something big was in the wind.

Ito greeted Kusaka courteously. They had been friends for years. Morishita bowed, glowering. Ariga smiled. Members of the Second Fleet staff watched curiously. They had never seen a serious operation launched as haphazardly as this. The chief skeptic, besides Morishita, was Captain Yuji Yamamoto, Admiral Ito's chief of operations. It was his job to convert Combined Fleet's latest fantasy into a coherent plan of action. Although he was not (as rumor had it) a distant relation of the late commander in chief, Yamamoto shared his small stature, sharp analytic brain, and addiction to cigarettes. On a trying day like this one, he got through three packs. He squinted coldly at the uneasy Kusaka from a haze of smoke.

They were not all hostile. The fleet gunnery officer, Commander Tadeo Miyamoto, felt *Yamato* should go down fighting. This much they owed to the nation. But the thought of setting off with only enough fuel for a one-way trip made him sick to his stomach. After all, they weren't piloting some flimsy airplane. This was a massive ship with over 3000 men on board. Every one of them was ready to die—that had been drummed into them since the day they joined the navy—but in the past there had always been some hope of survival.

Rear Admiral Keizo Komura, the destroyer commander, had just hurried over from *Yahagi*. A portly, square-faced veteran with unusually long arms, he had been nicknamed "Gorilla" by classmates at the Naval Academy. But it took a brave man to say it to his face. As far as Komura could see, Combined Fleet were out of their minds. The fact that Ito was taking it all so calmly did not make him any happier. He still had to pass on this idiot order to his escort skippers. It would be interesting to see how the headquarters bunch at Hiyoshi justified these antics.

Kusaka produced his slender sheaf of signals. Apologetically he explained that there wasn't much more to tell. The special attack force would sortie through the Bungo Strait, accompanied as far as the open sea by a maximum of four minesweepers. Two full minesweeping divisions were usually allocated to an operation of this size, but there wasn't enough fuel for more. Submarine attack was considered likely. At least four American boats were believed to be patrolling the mouth of the channel. This would necessitate a high-speed night dash close by the Kyushu coast.

The fleet navigation officer shook his head glumly. Those were tricky pilotage waters.

After clearing the strait between Kyushu and the Osumi Islands, course must be set due east into the East China Sea. Six hours later, the force would turn southeast, parallel to but about 160 miles distant from the straggling Ryukyu chain. At the appropriate moment (and here Kusaka made it clear there were several possible options) the Special Attack Force would swing southwest straight for Okinawa. The final turn would be timed to bring the force shortly before dawn into the middle of the American transport fleet off the Hagushi beachhead. After destroying all targets, ships would beach near Point Kazu. Those with ammunition would continue firing as backup batteries for the Japanese defending force. Sailors would make their way ashore to join the defenders.

Komura wondered if he was dreaming. Plans for a sea battle, code-named Ten-ichi, had been in existence since before the Okinawa invasion. Second Fleet was supposed to challenge the

American carrier force off the coast of Japan. Something along these lines was first discussed during the battle for Iwo Jima. But this latest concoction bore little relation to the original. Beaching a battleship, fighting ashore . . . This was the scenario from some improbable movie script.

Vice Admiral Ito peered over the top of his spectacles.

"You realize this commits us to about ten hours of steaming in broad daylight on approach course to the enemy." He spelled it out slowly and deliberately. "Experience in the Philippines shows that surface ships stand little chance against carrier aircraft. Remember what happened to *Musashi?* Presumably we can therefore expect adequate air cover?"

Kusaka shook his head. He found himself justifying policies he couldn't personally accept. There would be token air cover, he explained, until about 1000 on April 7. All escorts were required after that for the Kamikaze squadrons. The fleet could take comfort from the fact that the first wave of Kikusui One attacks, scheduled for the previous day, April 6, would have already damaged the American carriers so severely that the task force stood a good chance of getting through unscathed. They need only cover a mere 350 miles.

"A dash across out own backyard," one young officer remarked optimistically. Morishita glared at him.

Second Fleet had taken bigger risks in the Solomons, Kusaka pointed out. Immensely successful night attacks were pulled off over far greater distances.

"That was three years ago," said Morishita. "The Americans had two or three carriers. They've got six times that number today."

"And we have the Kamikaze," replied Kusaka. "This is to be a coordinated attack. Fifth Air Fleet and 32nd Army will strike simultaneous blows against the enemy."

Komura publicly admitted he was baffled. He had fought in every major action since Pearl Harbor. He wasn't a fool. He knew what was at stake. Nor was he a coward. He had been wounded twice. Two ships had been sunk under him. Would the chief of staff kindly explain the purpose of this enterprise? Was the attack force really supposed to get to grips with the Americans, was it just a decoy, or was it a bit of both?

Kusaka tried to improvise an answer while Morishita and

other staff officers clamored for meteorological data, signal channeling, code procedures, oil supplies . . .

Ito brought Kusaka up short by asking: "If our ships are irreparably damaged on the way, should we still proceed with the operation?"

For the first time in this embarrassing meeting, Kusaka admitted years later, he felt cornered.

"You'll have to decide that for yourself," he said.

Morishita lunged in with more unanswerable questions. Every point he raised appeared to ridicule Combined Fleet's hasty planning. Kusaka began to lose his temper. Orders were ultimately accepted in the Japanese navy, whether you liked them or not. This sort of interrogation was unprecedented.

"I think it is necessary to understand that *Yamato's* reputation is open to criticism," Kusaka told Morishita icily. "This ship's only action was a failure. People are wondering whether it has become a comfortable hotel for unemployed admirals."

Morishita had commanded *Yamato* at Leyte. He took Kusaka's remark as a personal insult. For a moment it looked as though Morishita was going to hit Kusaka. Operations chief Yamamoto drew himself up to his full five feet four inches.

"The failure of *Yamato* in the Sibuyan Sea was the Imperial Navy's failure. Combined Fleet sent us into action against the American beachhead without air cover. Now you are telling us to do it again."

"That was not the intention at Leyte," Kusaka retorted. "Air cover was planned. The Americans destroyed our planes on the ground."

"So this time you aren't even going to risk your precious aircraft?" cried Komura. "You're not even going to give us a chance?"

Ariga and Morishita nodded agreement. Ito sat staring at his notebook. Kusaka opened his mouth to reply.

"Since these orders have been sprung on us without notice," Komura interjected,"I respectfully request permission to consult my destroyer commanders."

Ito nodded absently. Kusaka shrugged. Komura bowed stiffly and left the cabin.

Ensign Shigeo Yamada watched all the excitement from

Yahagi's weather deck. He had come up for a breath of fresh air after a spell in the cruiser's main radio cabin. There he had been chatting in English over the intership phone with his colleague in *Yamato*, Kunio Nakatani, a nisei like himself, employed to monitor enemy voice communications. Neither was quite used to this word "enemy." The United States was their home. Yamada was born in Idaho and "raised on potatoes." Nakatani hailed from Sacramento. But both came from traditional Japanese families, with old-fashioned fathers who couldn't allow their sons to lose touch completely with their ethnic heritage.

The boys were bundled off to universities in Japan where the outbreak of war faced them with the agonizing choice of prison and possibly execution as suspected spies—or collaboration. Grudging agreement to enlist against the land of their birth did not save the nisei from being singled out for brutal harassment at the hands of navy drill instructors. They suffered everything from ribbing to outright hostility from fellow officers. The insular Japanese are quick to resent deviation from their exclusive social patterns.

Fortunately there was no such tension in *Yahagi*. Life aboard a cruiser was more companionable and compact. Nor was Yamada the only nisei aboard. A burly ensign named Kuramoto, born in Santa Monica, California, shared his intelligence duties. He had been captain of the American football team at Meiji University; his repatriated parents lived in Kure. Before this trip he had urged Yamada to leave all his belongings with his parents. But Yamada insisted on taking his ceremonial sword, his money ... everything. He was to regret it later.

Ensign Yamada was resigned to his fate. He was 24 years old, drafted straight out of Keio University where he was majoring in economics. His family had returned to Japan in 1941, shortly before hostilities began, and were now braving the raids on the home islands. Talk about jumping out of the frying pan into the fire! Now it looked like his turn to land in trouble, for it was obvious that something important was happening.

Real Admiral Komura was back from *Yamato* with a face like thunder. Boats were pulling alongside *Yahagi* from the surrounding destroyers. The side party was kept busy saluting the eight commanding officers and three division commanders, who climbed briskly onto the steel deck, swords held stiffly in their left hands at the precise parade ground angle, acknowledging the greetings of the officer of the day before disappearing into the senior wardroom. Overhead fluttered the hoist of signal bunting which summoned them.

Komura came straight to the point. Kusaka had flown from Kanoya Air Base with extraordinary orders. His audience listened tensely. "The high command wants the Second Fleet to sortie to Okinawa, without air cover, with fuel enough for only a one-way trip," Komura told them. "In short, the high command wants us to engage in a Kamikaze mission.

"No, this is not even a Kamikaze mission, for that implies the chance of chalking up a worthy target. I told Kusaka our little fleet has no chance against the might of the enemy forces and that such an operation would be a genuine suicide sortie. Ariga and Morishita agreed with me. Admiral Ito said nothing, so I do not know his opinion of the proposal.

"As you know, I was chief of staff to Ozawa when he went on the decoy mission to the Philippines and lost four carriers. I have had enough to do with the killing of our own men. I am not concerned with my own death, but I do shrink from wantonly throwing my own men into a suicidal sortie. Accordingly I asked Ito and Kusaka for a recess in order to get your opinions."

The rear admiral was close to tears. But as he admitted later, they were tears of despair rather than anger. Second Fleet prided itself on being the toughest fighting outfit in the Imperial Navy. It had always done its best despite the odds. Never before had officers and men been faced with a situation like this. The commander of 17th Destroyer Group, Captain Kiichi Shintani, broke the silence. "Has Kusaka come to cram these orders down our throats?" he asked.

It was an unprecedented remark. Orders were not questioned this way in the Japanese navy. Still, Komura had prompted a debate. Now he got one.

Shintani scathingly analyzed the Philippines action at Leyte the previous October. On that occasion Ozawa's decoy force from Japan had at least given the southern fleets an opportunity to get at the enemy. Admittedly the attack was broken off unsuccessfully, but now *they* were going to be the decoy. They would all be destroyed and no fleet would be left to defend Japan.

"I agree with Shintani." The speaker was Captain Hisao Kotaki, commander of 21st Destroyer Group. "The high command has been blundering now for many months. Why must we, who have been through so many battles, blindly follow a bunch of inept, inexperienced leaders?"

Everyone voiced agreement. Captain Hara of *Yahagi* found this rapidly becoming the liveliest naval conference he had ever experienced. He pleaded for a chance to head out into the Pacific and attack the enemy's long, unguarded lines of communications.

Captain Masayoshi Yoshida of 41st Destroyer Group supported Hara. His two ships, *Fuyutsuki* and *Suyutsuki*, were the most up-to-date antiaircraft destroyers in the navy. They would be ideal for a raiding mission. Commander Yoshiro Sugihara, the skipper of *Asashimo*, most powerful of the destroyers, demanded his ship be given a proper fighting chance. He declined to mention that with *Asashimo's* engines in her present state he stood little chance in any case.

This is the story as told by Captain Hara in his postwar book *Destroyer Captain*. Some of his recollections appear hazy and inaccurate—and are disputed by other sources—but his is the most complete eyewitness description of something close to mutiny. It was unprecedented because Japanese naval tradition and training demanded total obedience. Orders were sacrosanct since they stemmed, ultimately, from the emperor. But this was no longer 1905, or 1941. Every officer present had fought continuously for nearly 3½ years. The destroyer crews had made an outstanding contribution, escorting, transporting troops and supplies, and winning victory after brilliant victory over the U.S. Navy in the Solomons campaign. Despite their best efforts, the tide had turned against Japan. They noted with concern the high command's growing irrationality, culminating in the recent Philippines disaster and an eleventh-hour acceptance of the Kamikaze as the "decisive" weapon.

The navy's first suicide pilots went into action in October 1944, as the surface fleet prepared for its abortive and costly attempt to interdict the Leyte landings. Orders made it clear that suicide tactics were essentially a temporary measure. The results were so gratifying, however, that the Kamikaze won imperial approval. Regular navy officers could not agree. As Kusaka had been told aboard *Yamato*, it was idiotic enough to expend planes and pilots from the nation's dwindling reserves. To throw away the few remaining warships with their seasoned crews was criminal.

Yet morale was high in Second Fleet. Few crewmen realized the extent of disillusion among senior officers at the high command's impotence. The misnamed Operation Sho ("'Victory'") in the Philippines had created intense bitterness among commanders who objected to being used as gambling chips by reckless admirals. It was no use the men fighting like lions if, as Kaiser Wilhelm II once remarked, "they were led by donkeys." But nothing had shaken the ordinary sailor's belief in ultimate victory.

The way Captain Hara remembers it, Rear Admiral Komura returned to *Yamato* to put the destroyer men's case. He was given a polite hearing but was overruled by Kusaka. Others present at the meeting believe the final vote was cast by Vice Admiral Ito. He had asked searching questions but offered no comments. At last he said: "Gentlemen, we are being offered the chance to die. I have no regrets and am leaving willingly." Ariga supported him: "You can tell Combined Fleet we will do our utmost to make the operation a success." Sake was ordered. Toasts were drunk. Whatever doubts persisted were now suppressed.

Komura returned wearily to his waiting destroyer commanding officers. He told them the mission would go ahead as scheduled. Hara wrote:

> Komura bent his head low at these last words, as if apologizing. We sat in stunned silence. As the hourlike moments passed, I decided to face the reality of this most unreal situation.
>
> "We appreciate your stand on our behalf, Admiral Komura," I said. "But orders are orders. We must now make the best of the situation."
>
> The three destroyer group captains—Kotaki, Shintani, Yoshida—accepted the orders subject to the approval of their skippers. The eight destroyer skippers chorused their unanimous acceptance.

This abrupt change of heart may be hard for Westerners to understand.

The demands of duty, discipline, and tradition were accepted with a certain resignation. Fate decreed ... man agreed. They were now prepared for death.

Japanese Secret Fleet Signal 607, Tokyo . . . Okinawa . . . Hawaii

APRIL 5

SECRET FLEET SIGNAL 607 from the Combined Fleet commander at Hiyoshi arrived on Navy Minister Yonai's desk in Tokyo at 1507. He made a personal note on his memo plan. It advised the ministry that the surviving remnants of Second Fleet, all that Japan had left, were to be thrown away in a hopeless sortie against the American armada off Okinawa. The minister could scarcely believe his eyes. Toyoda must be completely mad! Yonai reached for the direct phone to Hiyoshi, then hesitated. Perhaps Combined Fleet had ganged up with joint staff? That would complicate the situation still further. Things were complicated enough already. Prime Minister Koiso had just resigned. The navy chief of staff was urging the appointment of old Admiral Suzuki. The council of former premiers, the *jushin*, would soon be debating the crisis in the Imperial Palace. As a onetime prime minister, Yonai would be among them.

Mitsumasa Yonai phoned Admiral Oikawa. The chief of staff was his usual flustered self. "Kido seemed impressed with Suzuki," Oikawa blurted out. "But he's still got to convince the army."

Marquis Koichi Kido, the lord privy seal, was emerging as a

115

vital force behind the imperial throne. He was thought to favor peace. It was his business to wring a consensus from the bickering factions on a successor to the unlamented general whose government had survived a mere nine months.

"I'm talking about *Yamato*," said Yonai. "Have you seen Toyoda's signal?"

Oikawa had seen the signal. He did not approve of the operation. But other senior officers appeared to back the plan.

"Kusaka?" asked Yonai.

"He's in Kyushu or somewhere," said Oikawa. "He's made no complaint as far as I know. But it's no use getting involved in a row with Combined Fleet right now. There are more important things to worry about."

Yonai put the phone down thoughtfully. The survival of the navy was threatened by those imbeciles in Hiyoshi. But Oikawa was right. The choice of a prime minister affected the very existence of Japan. Yonai had been the last navy man to fill the post when they were still struggling to avert war with America. Now they must struggle to find a way out of this war. If only they could struggle more effectively! Halfheartedly he called Toyoda. The Combined Fleet commander in chief was not there. Kami answered.

"It will be a miracle if they make it," said Yonai.

"But an inspiration," Kami replied.

"To whom? Who will be left?"

"Better to be sunk in battle than sunk without a fight," said Kami.

"What an end for the Imperial Navy!"

Yonai sat back in his worn leather chair. He braced himself for the imminent council meeting with a soothing nip of Scotch. It was useless to rage at a fool like that. Better not to lock horns with Hiyoshi until matters were settled in the palace. Why did they build that damned ship anyway? This was going to be a long, long night . . .

The secret signal reached Okinawa several hours later—there were the usual communication delays—and was handed to Lieutenant General Mitsuru Ushijima as he pored over the battle maps in his bunker deep below Shuri Castle. With the signal came a reminder that 32nd Army was expected to take advantage of the sortie next morning—and of the long scheduled Kamikaze assault—to counterattack.

The navy's gesture left Ushijima singularly unimpressed. He had a better appreciation of American naval strength than those people at Combined Fleet. They must be living in a dream world. He could climb up anytime to a coastal lookout and count the American warships. And there were plenty more over the horizon. What could one battleship, one cruiser, and eight destroyers hope to achieve against the largest fleet the world had ever seen?

His aggressive chief of staff, Lieutenant General Isamu Cho, automatically disagreed. A naval sortie at this moment would help turn the tide of battle. He always disagreed. Cho was pressing Ushijima to counterattack immediately. The Americans were starting to pile on the pressure in their drive toward Shuri. They had begun an intense bombardment of Kakazu Ridge, a physically insignificant but tactically vital barrier across the highway leading straight to the old royal capital of Okinawa.

Impatient and overconfident, Cho was all for catching the enemy off balance. His bespectacled eyes gleamed in the yellow lamplight as he advocated an irresistible banzai charge, lines of khaki-clad men flashing bayonets, swords, battle flags, swarming over the bemused Americans. It had worked well enough against the Chinese. The present defensive tactics were unnecessary—and unnatural. He thumped the map with nicotine-stained fingers.

Ushijima threw the naval signal contemptuously on the floor. He refused to be rushed by anyone. Conditions were not yet ripe for the counterattack. It would have to be postponed at least until April 14. As for the navy, they'd better think out a more realistic plan. The thought of a grounded battleship firing away in defense of Okinawa while its crew reinforced his troups . . . Ridiculous! He dictated a signal to Combined Fleet detailing his objections and demanding immediate cancellation of Operation Ten-ichi. The message seems never to have reached Hiyoshi; incoming signal logs were later searched in vain for any record of it.

Secret fleet signal 607 sparked a flurry of activity among the U.S. code breakers in Hawaii. Its contents were quickly deciphered by the large and highly expert staff which had operated since early in the war from the closely guarded two-storey headquarters, the joint intelligence center, on Makapala Hill overlooking the submarine base. Apart from an occasional hiccup when the Japanese changed their naval code, the U.S. Navy had for years been privy to the enemy's closest secrets. So sophisticated had the organization become lately that almost every Japanese radio message was quickly decoded. The submarine blockade, now strangling Japan, owed a measure of its success to detailed advance knowledge of Japanese shipping movements. Scarcely a warship moved without forewarning. Army deployments, reinforcements, and future plans were all revealed.

This Heaven Number One operation required the urgent attention of Chester Nimitz, now in Guam, and Raymond Spruance, his Fifth Fleet commander off Okinawa. An Ultra (short for "ultrasecret") signal went out with every possible priority. Senior officers were awakened from their sleep to learn that "the Japs are planning a breakout."

No one was greatly surprised. Aerial reconnaissance revealed plenty of unusual warship movement in the Inland Sea. A big battleship, undoubtedly *Yamato*, was anchored with about a dozen escorts in the eastern reaches, half a day's steaming from the Shimonoseki Strait. Intelligence officers doubted whether a ship of this size would try to transit the strait. The channel just touched 10 fathoms and was sown with mines. The sortie would have to come from the wider, deeper Bungo Strait between Kyushu and Shikoku. The submarines patrolling there were alerted. Nothing more could be done now except get back to bed. A little extra sleep would be welcome. The morning promised to be hectic.

Yamato, the biggest battleship ever built, in its final construction stage at the Kure navy yard in Spring, 1941, and at sea in April 1945. (Self Defense Force Archives)

The Japanese fleet on its way to Leyte Gulf, October 1944. Yamato is third in line. (U.S. Navy)

Attack by U.S. planes on Kure harbor, March 1945. (National Archives)

Masanobu Kobayashi, the youngest gunner on Yamato's last mission, 1945. *(Kobayashi)*

Mr. Kobayashi and the author, 1980. *(Kobayashi)*

Rear Admiral Kosaku Ariga, Captain of the Yamato. (Self Defense Force Archives)

Tameichi Hara, Captain of Yahagi. (Self Defense Force Archives)

Vice Admiral Seiichi Ito, Commander of the Japanese Second Fleet. (Self Defense Force Archives)

Captain Shigenori Kami, Chief of Operations of Combined Fleet Headquarters at Hiyoshi. (Self Defense Force Archives)

Vice Admiral Ryunosuke Kusaka, Combined Fleet Chief of Staff, assigned to Kanoya Air Base to oversee Kamikaze operations, April 1945. (Self Defense Force Archives)

Emperor Hirohito. (U.S. National Archives)

Admiral Mitsumasa Yonai, Japanese Minister of the Navy. (Self Defense Force Archives)

U.S. fighting fleet in December 1944. From foreground to horizon, Wasp, Yorktown, Hornet, Hancock, Ticonderoga, Lexington. *(National Archives)*

U.S. invasion of Okinawa at the time Yamato was leaving Kure harbor. Here a wave of LVTs moves past the bombardment line toward the beach. *(National Archives, Courtesy of Robert O. Baumrucker)*

miral Chester W. Nimitz, Commander in
ief of the U.S. Pacific Fleet, 1945. (U.S.
val Historical Center)

Admiral Raymond A. Spruance, Commander
in Chief of U.S. Fifth Fleet, aboard battleship
New Mexico, April 1945. (National Archives)

Rear Admiral Morton L. Deyo, commanding Task Force 54, aboard Tennessee. (U.S. Naval Historical
Center)

Admiral Marc A. Mitscher,
anding Carrier Task Force 58,
Bunker Hill. (National
es)

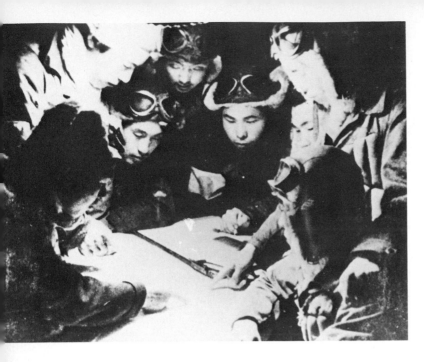

Japanese air grou
planning the next day
maneuvers. (U.
National Archives)

Japanese standby bomber crews at Kanoya Air Base. The "Betty" bomber in the background is carrying an ohka. (U.S. Naval Institute, Annapolis)

The carrier USS Hancock. *(U.S. Naval Historical Center)*

Torpedomen of USS San Jacinto bring a torpedo into place in front of a TBM. (National Archives)

The carrier USS Intrepid. *(National Archives)*

A Kamikaze pilot tightens his comrade's hachimaki, samurai symbol of courage worn by all pilots. (U.S. Naval Institute, Annapolis.)

mikaze pilots assem-
. (U.S. Naval Insti-
e, Annapolis)

Kamikaze pilot taxis his "Zero" to take-off position. (U.S. Naval Institute, Annapolis)

Ensign Michele Mazzocco in his cockpit before taking off from Belleau Wood. (*U.S. Navy. Courtesy of Michele Mazzocco*)

U.S. "Helldivers" flying in formation after takeoff from Yorktown. (*U.S. Navy*)

Two Japanese ships under attack by U.S. planes on April 7, 1945. *Yamato* in the background seems a sitting duck. Photo taken from plane from USS Intrepid. *(National Archives)*

Yamato maneuvers evasively at 15 to 20 knots prior to attack. One fire can be observed amidships from previous attack. But at this point she is not listing. Photo taken from plane from Yorktown. April 7, 1945. *(U.S. Navy)*

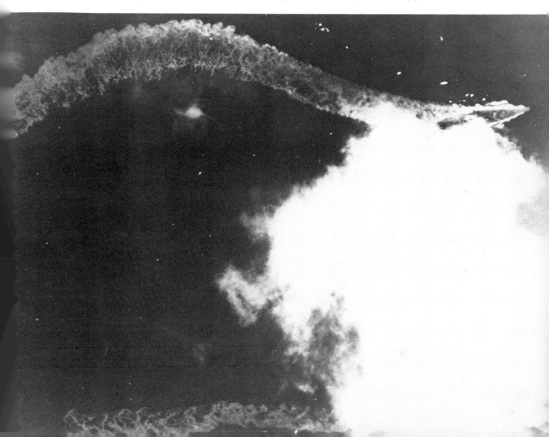

Yahagi, *leaking oil, lies dead in the water.* (National Archives)

American bombs narrowly missing Yahagi. (National Archives)

American planes literally surrounding the exploding Yahagi. (National Archives)

...ttered wreckage of Yahagi and a riddled ...ervation plane settle into a watery grave. April ...945. (National Archives)

Moments later, a close-up view of Yahagi sinking.

Yamato explodes and capsizes. The smoke cloud billowing thousands of feet was seen by coastwatchers in Kyushu more than 100 miles away. April 7, 1945. (National Archives)

Japanese Fleet, Mitajiri Anchorage

APRIL 5

YAMATO BUZZED WITH RUMORS. The battleship was going into battle. Just when or where wasn't certain. The flag signals mentioned Operation Ten-ichi. What was that supposed to mean? Some of the older hands nodded knowingly. "Heaven Number One now in force." Whenever the top brass sought divine blessings these days, a lot of sailors ended up dead.

The executive officer, Captain Jiro Nomura, wondered if his luck had run out at last. He leaned against the towering steel shell of the foremost main turret, the great gun barrels aiming straight into the setting sun. It was his favorite time of day. He paused deliberately to sort out his thoughts, pretending to check over the forecastle party. He guessed what was coming when the ship's commanding officer, Rear Admiral Kusaku Ariga, strode up with the signal.

"Shall I muster all hands, sir?"

Ariga nodded.

The executive officer took a microphone from a canvas-covered box welded to the outside of the bridge tower.

"Attention, ship's company. All hands not on duty watch will muster forward immediately. That is an order."

There was a rumble of feet as Nomura followed his commanding officer up the steel rungs projecting from the sloping side of the turret. Rear Admiral Ariga stood there panting on his lofty perch as the deck below filled with men. Soon it was carpeted with ranks of green uniforms, division upon division, stretching right up into the bow. The dying sun gilded the sea and haloed each upturned head. The shouted orders, the shuffling and expectant murmurs died away. Ariga stepped forward.

"My friends," he said. "The enemy is at our doors. Already he is trampling the sacred soil of Okinawa. Our gallant troops are fighting there to repel the invader. Our special attack aircraft, the Kamikaze are causing him terrible losses. The pilots are gladly giving their lives for the emperor. We have been chosen to help them. We are going to draw away part of the opposing forces. Our guns are going to sow destruction among our adversaries."

In a few words he outlined the details of the operation. He went on:

"The following signal has just been received from the commander in chief, Combined Fleet:

THE FATE OF OUR EMPIRE TRULY RESTS UPON THIS ONE ACTION. I HAVE CALLED FOR THE ORGANIZATION OF A SURFACE SPECIAL ATTACK UNIT FOR A BREAKTHROUGH OPERATION OF UNRIVALED BRAVERY SO THAT THE POWER OF THE IMPERIAL NAVY MAY BE FELT IN THIS ONE ACTION IN ORDER THAT THE BRILLIANT TRADITION OF THE IMPERIAL NAVY'S SURFACE FORCES MAY BE EXALTED AND OUR GLORY HANDED DOWN TO POSTERITY. EACH UNIT, REGARDLESS OF WHETHER OR NOT IT IS A SPECIAL ATTACK UNIT, WILL HARDEN ITS RESOLVE TO FIGHT GLORIOUSLY TO THE DEATH TO COMPLETELY DESTROY THE ENEMY FLEET, THEREBY ESTABLISHING FIRMLY AN ETERNAL FOUNDATION FOR THE EMPIRE.

A great cheer rose into the bloodred sunset. Cheering echoed across the water from crews on other ships being told the same news. Tears came to Nomura's eyes as he watched the sea of eager faces. The Japanese sailor still had plenty of fight in him. Most of these men's hometowns were bombed to ashes. Countless families were missing. "We'll show the bastards!" they seemed to be shouting. The exec stepped up beside his skipper.

"Let *Yamato* strike the enemy like a Kamikaze!" he shouted.

Another great roar. Three banzais for the emperor. Then spontaneously they broke into "Kimigayo," the national anthem, followed by the Navy March. Ariga saluted and made his way below. Before dismissing the assembly, Nomura issued final orders. Divisional officers should report to his cabin. Preparations would be made to remove all inflammable materials, including ship's boats, spotter planes, aviation gasoline, spare stores, furniture, and signal books. He drew himself to attention.

"Ship's company, *dismiss!*"

A crash of feet as more than 2000 men turned right, paused while their officers saluted, and doubled away in the darkening twilight. A hum of animated chatter arose in defiance of repeated calls for silence.

"Great news," someone cried to Kobayashi as they tumbled back into their messdeck. "About time we taught those Yankees a lesson." The young gunner agreed. He couldn't wait to get a Grumman in his sights. "Rat-a-tat-tat. Rat-a-tat-tat," stuttered one of his gun crew, aiming from the top of his bunk. The divisional officer momentarily halted the clowning. Reluctantly, but with lots of lighthearted horseplay, the teenage sailors began hunting out combustible materials. "Waste of time," one lad remarked. "Anyone would think *Yamato* was about to sink."

A small group pestered the petty officers for rifles and bayonets. They were supposed to make their way ashore at Okinawa to join the defending forces. How could they do that unarmed?

"Just take a weapon off a dead American," an old hand said grimly. "There'll be plenty lying around."

"One salvo from our main battery can wipe out a whole division," someone said. "How many divisions have the Americans got? Five, six? Boom! Boom! Boom! That'll be the end of them!"

"We've got to get there first," one cautious soul remarked. The scornful gunners cheerfully emptied a collection can of combustibles over his head.

The junior wardroom was equally exuberant. The younger officers were spoiling for a fight. They were less optimistic than the enlisted men about the outcome. "What's the betting we don't make it halfway?" One ensign asked. "No takers," another said, laughing.

"How many torpedoes do you reckon we can absorb? They say *Musashi* stopped 19."

"Depends where they hit us. *Musashi* was hit on both sides. Now if they all hit on one side, 10 should be enough to finish us."

"Can't we beat them off with antiaircraft fire?"

"Not with our guns," said a young man who seemed to know what he was talking about. "Battleships have been a sitting duck ever since we sank the *Prince of Wales* and the *Repulse*. We'll be helpless without air cover."

"But surely they'll send a few planes? The Kyushu airfields are close enough?"

"You heard the orders," said a lieutenant (jg.). "We're a decoy. No one protects decoys. Whoever armor-plated a worm before putting it on the hook?"

Some went to bathe, shave their heads, and collect new uniforms. Some wrote last letters home, enclosing nail and hair clippings. Since their ashes would never reach Japan, these meager souvenirs were better than nothing. Others sat smoking, playing cards, or reading philosophical books. There was a great vogue for Tolstoy.

Ensign Sakei Katono, released from his vigil in the bowels of the ship, was deep in *War and Peace*. He scarcely heard the debate. *Yamato* stood some chance, in his opinion. No matter how small that chance, they ought to try. If they failed . . . he tried not to think of the dim steel tomb awaiting him below. Besides, Napoleon was at Borodino. He licked his finger and turned the page.

"You only die once," a radar officer shouted. "Steward! Drinks! Let's celebrate!"

The nisei ensign Kunio Nakatani sat quietly sobbing in a corner. He had been the object of the usual cruel cracks. What a way to die, at the hands of his fellow Americans, among men who treated him as an outcast. He tore up his last letter to his parents. What did there remain for him to say?

Senior officers sat in the clublike quiet of their exclusive wardroom, discussing the mission with almost inhuman detachment. Would it not be interesting to see how the hull structure stood up to the effect of near-misses? No one had seen a detailed analysis of the loss of *Musashi*. The engineers felt that somewhere the designers had slipped up. In producing the most heavily armored ship in the world the designers had overlooked the need for sufficient lateral flexibility. The engineers' highly technical arguments suggested that under sufficient stress *Yamato* could shake herself to bits.

Some expressed doubts over the choice of a central bulkhead. The Americans had done away with this feature in the interest of stability. Others wondered whether the pumping system would work under heavy pressure.

"*Yamato* is a well-built ship. None better," mumbled the senior engineer. "But the whole nature of naval warfare has changed since she was designed. I believe she can take plenty of punishment. The question is, how much?"

The navigating officer sought comfort from the weather reports. A high-pressure area was building up southwest of Kyushu. The present fine spell would be broken by the time they reached the East China Sea. Given enough low cloud and rain squalls, they might make the dash undetected.

"You forget the Americans' radar," said the assistant gunnery officer. He was seated close to his particular charge, the emperor's portrait. The revered picture was displayed only on ceremonial occasions. It was now strapped safely to the bulkhead in a heavy teakwood case. His duty was to transfer the portrait to another ship if *Yamato* was in danger of sinking. If this proved impossible, "all measures" must be taken to prevent its capture.

"The Americans have a new aircraft radar that produces a map of the terrain," said the chief electrical officer. "It's incredibly accurate. Far better than anything we've developed. I've seen a captured set. Fantastic."

A steward served Scotch in cut glasses. The whiskey and the glassware were part of the leftover loot from Singapore. The liquor stocks of the captured fortress were so vast that the Japanese navy was still drinking them more than three years after the British surrender. *Yamato* carried so much liquor, in fact, that her supply staff swore the fish would be drunk for miles around if ever she were sunk.

Executive officer Nomura was determined to foil the fish. His final orders of the day were for a monumental party. It might be the last one most of them would ever have. Cooks had already been instructed to break out the best rations for a symbolic last supper. But the supply officers were worrying, as usual, about the paperwork. A bespectacled lieutenant commander was whining about his monthly returns. How would he account for all these extra rations?

"What's it matter?" Nomura snorted. "We aren't coming back!"

Most seamen had already bathed and changed into their white pajamas when the welcome order came over the intercom: "Open the canteens." White is the mourning color in Japan. Kneeling at the low tables in the messdecks, the sailors seemed to be attending a funeral feast. As the sake bottles began circulating they laughingly drank to each other's death.

"Meet you at Minatogawa."

That was the site in Kobe of heroic Masashige Kusonoki's shrine. Their spirits would meet there after they left this world.

"But we'll kill some Yankees first!"

"*Shichisei Hokoku!* If only I had seven lives to give for the emperor!"

They gulped the warm sake with magnificent bravado. Few of the younger seamen believed they would die, anyway. If they did . . . well, that was the way it would be. Their deaths would never be in vain. They were destined to become demigods, still fighting for the survival of Japan. The few who survived spoke later of their sense of inner calm once they had accepted the inevitable. They enjoyed the clarity of mind that comes only to one who assumes he is already dead.

A neurotic pyramid of obligations piled up on every Japanese from early childhood—first to members of the family, then to the outside world. Personal debts and duties gradually accumulated toward fellow citizens, career associates, and above all toward the emperor. No Japanese could ever fully repay that sacred, secluded figure for cementing and preserving the fabric of Japanese society through the revolutionary changes which followed the Meiji Restoration in 1868. Even the supreme sacrifice was insufficient.

Death was especially welcomed by warriors. Buddhism engendered fatalistic resignation. The Zen cult adopted and adapted by the samurai in the 13th century cultivated a stoic self-discipline. Shinto offered divine status for the heroic dead. The knightly Bushido code pointed to the unerring path to duty. Death became a refreshing release.

The one great fear was shame. Few other ethnic groups have created as self-conscious a society as the Japanese. Few feel such a weight of hierarchical burdens. Few are so minutely regulated by ritual. Such is the lack of privacy that every individual's action is publicly and constantly appraised. Ridicule becomes a fearsome weapon, as Allied war prisoners discovered when they dared to laugh at their Japanese guards.

It was this fear of shame that was sending *Yamato* off on a questionable mission. Captain Kami's strongest arguments played upon Toyoda's unwillingness to see this great ship, the pride of the navy, fall intact into enemy hands. The very officers who argued with Kusaka did so only on tactical grounds. They were unwilling to squander what was left of the fleet. But they would rather die than reenact the German navy's humiliating surrender at the end of World War I.

Rear Admiral Ariga thrust aside his paperwork. He was determined to join in the fun. Usually he dined alone in his cabin: a ship's captain's lonely privilege. Tonight he invited himself to the main wardroom. Two hundred officers rose to attention as their paunchy little commander entered the door. The mess president welcomed him, pledging full support for the mission. A steward ushered him to a seat at the head table. The initial embarrassment over his august presence evaporated with the sake.

The cooks had outdone themselves. Special dishes appeared, suitable for the eve of battle. There was *sekihan*, made of red bean paste, and *okashiratsuki*, a kind of sea bream, served complete with the head of the fish. And more, lashings more, of the warm rice wine that brought a flush to their faces. Ariga drank with the best of them. Legend had it that he could drink any man in the navy under the table. They said that about Morishita too . . .

"Speech, speech," yelled a claque from down the table. Ariga grinned, shook his head, and raised his cup in another toast. Every officer followed suit and downed his drink in a gulp. Some of the younger men linked arms in a corner of the room, swaying from side to side as they sang the old Academy song. Like the cherry blossoms, they would fall in battle. Others took up the refrain. Ariga nodded benignly.

A drunken party was in full swing in the gunroom when Ariga

appeared in the doorway holding a large bottle of sake. The boisterous cadets grabbed their commanding officer unceremoniously and tossed him in a blanket. Down on the messdecks there was more loud singing. Young Kobayashi joined in, though he did not drink. Two cups of sake were enough to make him sick.

The atmosphere was more businesslike on *Yahagi*. Members of the crew were crowding into the machine shop to sharpen their bayonets. One man kept working on a generator. He had given his sake ration to a buddy. "Got to make sure everything is ready," he told the tipsy carousers who dropped by from the messdecks. Rear Admiral Komura entertained his senior officers. Their recent objections were forgotten, but the party never got going. Everyone drank hard without the slightest effect. Captain Hara went up on deck to clear his head. The black shapes of ships stood silhouetted by the waning moon. A ghost fleet sailing a silver sea . . .

"*Nippon banzai!*" yelled Hara. "*Yahagi banzai!*"

U. S. Fifth Fleet, Off Okinawa

APRIL 5

EVERYONE WAS BORED but Admiral Spruance. Six days after the first troops stormed ashore on Okinawa, there were serious doubts about the Japanese willingness to fight. The marines pressed north into the waist of Okinawa against token resistance. Army units plodding warily south toward Shuri reported much the same. The enemy appeared to have concentrated some of his forces in this southern area, although no serious opposition had been encountered apart from small groups of skirmishers. Jocular marines asked the army to send them a dead Jap since "most of us have never seen one." This was obviously no Iwo Jima.

The U.S. bombardment force dutifully maintained its daily barrage until the paint peeled off the overheated gun barrels, but it seemed to be firing at nothing. Carrier pilots complained about the dearth of targets. The fleet was continuously heckled by lone Kamikaze, probably from nearby islands; the planes seldom got past the combat air patrol or, after that, the warships' antiaircraft defenses. Gunnery coordination had greatly improved since the first surprise suicide attacks in the Philippines; the greatest danger these days came from overexcited gun crews ignoring their prearranged arcs of fire and hitting neighboring ships. Several sailors had been killed by erratic shooting.

127

The flood of false reports made everyone trigger-happy. Identification equipment (IFF) on friendly planes was supposed to distinguish them from foes when their blips appeared on the radar, but so many aircraft were aloft that it was often difficult to be certain. There were also grounds for believing that some enemy intruders used IFF sets salvaged from downed American planes. Naval radar had developed by leaps and bounds since the start of the Pacific war. The first tentative steps were being taken toward what later became electronic warfare. Ships got together and threw out powerful signals to jam the enemy's radar. Equipment was still plagued, however, by inexplicable bugs like the "galloping ghost of Nansei Shoto," a series of mysterious contacts which kept appearing on the scopes but never materialized.

"Sightings" like these kept gun crews on edge. Endless misinformation coming in over the ship-to-ship (TBS) radio was fed into gunners' headsets, particularly at night. Friendly planes attracted most of the flak, although on at least one occasion an approaching destroyer was mistaken in the darkness for an incoming Kamikaze and met with a barrage of fire. Luckily, the shots missed.

Raymond Spruance knew the lull would not last, and so did Nimitz. When Vice Admiral Richmond Kelly Turner gleefully signaled, "I may be crazy, but it looks like the Japs have quit the war," Nimitz sarcastically signaled back: "Delete all after 'crazy.'" News that the remnants of the Imperial Navy planned a sortie was the least of their worries. If this Heaven plan went off as scheduled, they would have ample time to meet it. The real threat was the Kamikaze. Aerial photographs from high-flying B-29s indicated a continued buildup at some 50 airfields in Kyushu. The Japanese were cleverly concealing their activities. It was difficult to spot widely dispersed aircraft in scattered revetments well back from the runways. Constant bombing of these runways made them look unserviceable, but repair gangs filled the craters as fast as they appeared. Daylight fighter sweeps were the answer, though that would mean sending Task Force 58 on another marauding raid off the Japanese coast. Just now the task force could not be spared.

The weather was breaking up. Friday, April 6, was misty and overcast. A freshening northeast wind stirred up a growing swell. White wave caps dappled the heaving waters. Landing craft shuttled ashore with spray bursting across their bows and seasick soldiers retching on their decks. The battleships rolled ponderously along the bombardment route. They were not firing so often now. Some 8000 tons of shells had already been pumped into the island. Vast areas were devastated. Whether the enemy had suffered much was doubtful.

The Fifth Fleet commander's morning conference aboard *New Mexico* emphasized the need for vigilance. Tired gun crews were ordered to stay alert. Radar pickets got the warning that the long-awaited suicide blitz was imminent. Sixteen radar pickets were stationed around Okinawa. Destroyers and smaller escort frigates circled, usually in pairs, at distances ranging from 15 to 100 miles from Cape Misaki, the chosen projection point not far from the center of the island. Scattered among the pickets, covering the landing force, were the antisubmarine destroyer screens. While one group searched the skies for attacking aircraft, the other, with its pinging sonar, kept watch for subs.

According to the latest scuttlebutt those little yellow bastards had developed a Kamikaze torpedo. It was launched underwater from a fleet submarine with some lunatic driving it on target. The Japs had tried it out some weeks before at Ulithi Lagoon, the main assembly area for the Okinawa invasion, and had sunk a tugboat. Well, there were plenty of buckets here for them to aim at. The gobs agreed the jockeys who piloted these things must be doped or drunk or both . . .

The Japanese firmly believed the Americans were terrified of the Kamikaze. The cooing tones of Tokyo Rose warned nightly of the horrors yet to come. "You'll be sorry, boys," she told her grim-faced listeners. "You just don't know what you're in for. Just as well you said goodbye to mom. You won't be seeing her again." The Japanese misread American reaction just as they had at Pearl Harbor. The Americans were not so much terrified as perplexed. What sort of people were they up against? Surely they weren't human? Anyone who fought that fanatically would obviously never surrender. They must be killed without mercy . . . A perfect argument, back in Washington, for using atomic bombs.

Winston Churchill had begun lobbying in 1944 for a British

naval presence in the Pacific. He pressed his case so eloquently at the Octagon Conference in Quebec that Roosevelt overruled the protests of such vocal Anglophobes as Douglas MacArthur and the U.S. Navy chief, Admiral Ernest J. King, who indignantly kept insisting that this was *their* war. The Americans had fought the Pacific war almost single-handed through three bitter years. British efforts against the Japanese were dismissed as incompetent or inadequate. The Limeys had no right to come prancing in at this stage to claim a share of the American victory. Anti-British feeling still ran high among the U.S. military. The arrogance of these Britishers, the highfalutin accents of their aristocratic commanders, and their devious imperial designs were anathema to men who found themselves suddenly and unexpectedly on the threshold of world power. It would be years before they could tone down to an attitude of patronizing contempt for the British and their fading empire.

Opposition was publicly couched, of course, in diplomatic language. Admiral King professed a shortage of supply ships. The British produced their own. The European war had given them no opportunity to develop the techniques of long-range ocean operations perfected by the Americans. But they had centuries of seamanship behind them. MacArthur tried to divert the intruders to southeast Asia in preparation for the recapture of Singapore. The British were adamant. They were anxious for action—the main action. With U.S. carrier strength drained by the damaging Kamikaze, Nimitz and Spruance could scarcely refuse reinforcements.

Admiral Spruance was particularly aware of the lesser menace from Taiwan, or Formosa, as it was usually called then. The Japanese First Air Fleet there mustered about 300 naval Kamikaze aircraft. Its Nitaka unit first attacked U.S. carriers off the island in January 1945. The flying distance from the northernmost airfields was about the same as from Kyushu and there were emergency landing strips in the Sakishima Islands, the southwestern tail of the Okinawan island chain. The Royal Navy could usefully block any attacks from this direction.

The British contribution was modest enough by American standards. Although designated a task force, for political as well as administrative reasons, Task Force 57 was no bigger than one of Mitscher's task groups. But it was a well-found force of 4 carriers, 2 battleships, 5 of the latest cruisers, and 15 destroyers.

Critical Americans complained that the British ships carried insufficient antiaircraft armament. This was especially true of the carriers. The Royal Navy, operating wherever possible under land-based air cover, had never completely accepted the potential of the seaborne airplane. Pioneering British naval aviation had once led the world. The lead was lost in interservice squabbles between the two world wars, squabbles which gave birth to the Royal Air Force but stunted the fleet air arm. While the Hurricane and the more successful Spitfire were being developed as RAF fighters, the Royal Navy was fobbed off with archaic biplanes. The venerable Swordfish torpedo bomber inflicted a crippling blow upon the Italian fleet at Taranto in 1940—an attack which inspired the Japanese raid on Pearl Harbor—but the British were unable to match the carrier-borne fighters and dive bombers developed by the two protagonists in the Pacific. British carriers off Okinawa mostly flew American aircraft.

The carriers themselves were superior. They were built to take fewer planes but a lot more punishment. Kamikaze bounced off their flight decks. And as it turned out, they played a valuable subsidiary role in the Okinawan campaign by blocking the air approach routes from Taiwan. The Americans were thankful, though ungrateful. When U.S. carriers destroyed the few remaining Japanese warships holed up in Kure three months later, the Royal Navy was politely excluded from the operation. Its presence was not vindicated until the end of the war. Ignoring the orders of Americans who secretly sought the liberation of Hong Kong by their trusted Chinese ally Chiang Kai-shek, the Pacific Fleet commander, Sir Bruce Fraser, sent ships from the task force into the captured colony to rehoist the Union Jack.

PART

III

APRIL 6, 1945

OKINAWA, WITH YAMATO'S PROJECTED ATTACK ROUTE

IHEYA — RETTO

IZENA — SHIMA

II — SHIMA

OKINAWA

YONTAN AIRFIELD

KADENA AIRFIELD

CAPE MISAKI

LANDING BEACHES

NAHA

BOMBARDMENT FORCE

KEISE—SHIMA

TROOP SHIPS

KERAMA—RETTO

BM'S

SUPPLY SHIPS

AGUNI — SHIMA

SUBMARINE I—58'S PROJECTED ATTACK ROUTE

YAMATO'S PROJECTED ATTACK ROUTE

EAST CHINA SEA

PACIFIC OCEAN

✛ INSHORE RADAR PICKETS

• JAPANESE OBSERVATION POSTS

✗ APPROXIMATE POSITION OF LT. MATSUOKA'S LOOKOUT

Navy Chief of Staff's Office, Tokyo

APRIL 6

EVERYTHING SEEMED TO BE happening at once. Small wonder Admiral Koshiro Oikawa was flustered. Prime Minister Koiso, the militarists' last, lame-duck hope, was out of office. Admiral Kantaro Suzuki, the 80-year-old figurehead of the peace faction, was in. Or so it seemed. The senile war hero kept changing his mind. Early on the morning of April 6, after maddening hesitations, he began trying to form a new cabinet. It was not easy. The military were closing ranks. As former foreign minister Prince Fumimaro Konoye said in a secret memorial to the emperor, "Although they know they cannot win the war, I believe they will fight to the death in order to save face."

Oikawa did not put it that bluntly when sounded out by the emperor's key adviser, the lord privy seal Marquis Koichi Kido, but confined himself to a gloomy review of the situation. The navy chief of staff was in a quandary. He was out of his depth in the tides of Byzantine intrigue swirling around the throne. Privately he agreed with Yonai that all was lost. But it was easier to draw the sword than sheathe it. Publicly he was saddled with preparing plans for a suicidal, last-ditch defense of Japan.

"A hundred million die together" was the awesome slogan.

135

And a million Yankees were supposed to go with them. Pentagon proponents of the atomic bomb would have needed no further argument than the findings of the joint army-navy conference which had been meeting between March 24 and April 5 at Ichigaya Heights, in western Tokyo, where army headquarters had taken refuge after the March fire raid. But naval general staff secret directive 31 did not come to light until after the war:

> ... efforts will be made to build defense positions around Japan from which the advancing enemy can be destroyed, thus ensuring ultimate victory. The latter half of the year 1945 will be devoted to strengthening these fortifications so that the offensive can be resumed at the earliest opportunity. These war preparations will be carried out as follows:
> 1. All war preparations will be carried out in the spirit of suicide attacks and the total national manpower will be united into a fighting force that can furnish the necessary manpower for the coordinated war plans of the army and navy.
> 2. The main combat strength will be composed of air forces (including air special attack forces) and underwater and surface special attack forces. The greatest emphasis will be placed on the maximum development of their combat capabilities.

It was a charter for doomsday. Despite his preoccupation with the political crisis—and the ominous news that the Soviets were allowing their neutrality pact with Japan to lapse—the overburdened Oikawa was saddled with the task of approving the final text.

It was due for circulation the next day, April 7, about the time *Yamato* would be heading for Okinawa.

The battleship's fate was far from his thoughts. Conventional surface warships did not enter into the plans; even the regular armed forces and civilian population were expected merely to throw away their lives in hopeless struggle. Horrified GIs had watched them do it in Saipan. This time it would be on a massive scale. The imperial homeland would become an empty wilderness. The Japanese were doomed to extinction. This gristly vision was beginning to haunt Emperor Hirohito, prodding him toward active support of the peacemakers.

The joint conference, discussing every aspect of the national defense effort, had made it clear to the participants that Japan was at the end of its tether. It uncovered an additional problem besides the crucial shortages of fuel and raw materials. Dispersal of production plants to escape the air raids was seriously reducing the output of aircraft. The number of Zero fighters built this year was only 665, a drop of 20 percent. It was the same story with other, newer types of planes. Dispersal seemed to be damaging the war effort almost as much as the raids themselves.

Engines were in particularly short supply. All of the available mechanics, including members of skilled design teams, were drafted into repairing the hundreds of planes standing idle for lack of maintenance. There was little they could do, however, about the poorly machined parts and ersatz components being produced these days.

The target was to have 5000 conventional aircraft ready for suicide attacks when Operation Ketsu-go ("Homeland Decisive Battle") came into force on July 15, 1945. It would mean converting the unlikeliest planes for Kamikaze duties. Training aircraft were to be armed with 250-kilogram bombs and sacrificed along with the rest.

A ghoulish mathematical exercise produced a satisfactory if optimistic equation. Over 500 enemy ships would have to be sunk if the invasion were to be stopped in its tracks. Working on the questionable averages established for Okinawa, nine Kamikaze would be needed to knock out one carrier and six to destroy a troop transport. Answer: 3350 aircraft. But bearing in mind the state of many of the planes and the ineptitude of their pilots, the defense command would require a further reserve of 1650.

These would be supplemented by a variety of piloted flying bombs, still untested in March 1945—and never actually produced. Mostly they were sophisticated versions of the Ohka (Cherry Blossom) II, a piloted, jet-assisted glide bomb dropped from a bomber. The newer Ohka 22 was equipped with a jet engine to operate independently of a parent plane. The turbojet versions were Ohka 33 and 44. Other variants included the exotically named Baika ("Plum Blossom") driven to destruction by a pulse jet; another turbo model called Kikka ("Orange Blossom"); and the Shinryu ("Divine Dragon") glider, which used solid fuel rockets at takeoff. All carried warheads of about 2600 pounds of explosive, a fearsome advance on the single 500-pound bombs carried by most conventional Kamikaze aircraft.

This aerial suicide fleet was meant to be supplemented by an

assortment of midget Kairyu submarines, human Kaiten torpedoes, and explosive-filled Shinyo motorboats stationed at 98
secret bases in southern Japan. The 70 regular mainland airfields and 24 seaplane bases would be strengthened by construction of bombproof revetments, underground workshops, and
munition stores. Some 200 emergency strips, code-named "pas-
turelands," would be prepared throughout the country in the
next three months, with houses and trees left in position until
the last moment to disguise their presence. Obstructions could
be quickly cleared when the time came. It was unfortunate, the
conference agreed, that fuel shortages made "restriction on the
aggressive use of interceptor fighters inevitable." All the more
reason to build adequate ground protection.

Admiral Oikawa grimly set his seal on the document. He dispatched an advance copy to the Palace. *That* would give them
something to think about! As he argued later, it was just what
the war faction demanded. Chief among the hard-liners was
Admiral Toyoda, commander in chief of Combined Fleet, now
aroused to such bitter hatred of the Americans by the recent
fire raids that he was siding with the army in its campaign to
prolong the war. Perhaps if he studied the directive more carefully the militant admiral would be sobered by its implications.
Read with any objectivity, the findings strengthened the arguments of those who wanted peace. Someone must quickly put
a copy before the emperor, Oikawa mused; the militarists had
pleaded, until now, that unpleasant news should not disturb the
August Mind. Well, here was the peace faction's golden
opportunity.

Kamikaze Headquarters, Kanoya Air Base

APRIL 6

IT WAS A LOVELY day to die. Someone said so ruefully, almost reverently, when the drummers reported for duty. Two men from the Kanoya navy band took their posts exactly at 1300 in the sun-dappled shade of the cherry trees. Blossoms settled gently on their shoulders as orderlies arranged the long tables, rows of empty sake cups, and plates of rice wafers. Ugaki and Kusaka arrived in crisply starched combat uniforms with swords, medal ribbons, and snow-white cotton gloves. The admirals looked tired and tense . . . for them, too, it had been a long, sleepless night.

The pilots destined to die looked fresh and confident by comparison, though all of them had been up since dawn helping the mechanics check out their hidden machines. Engines were tuned and bombs loaded aboard; nothing now remained but to bid farewell.

Each man wore a white Hachimaki (sweatband) over his leather flying helmet. It was an incongruous anachronism. The samurai the pilots were supposed to be emulating wore sweatbands in battle, centuries ago, to avoid pausing to wipe their brows as they hacked away at each other with razor-edged swords. They wore neck scarfs and perfumed themselves and so did these pilots. Many carried sacred charms like the warriors of old, or belts with 10,000 stitches contributed by mothers and sisters who stood at the street corners back home begging passersby to sew a prayer for the future hero. Not a prayer for good luck or a happy homecoming, but an appeal to the gods to help the young man to strike a successful blow for the emperor.

There would be no medals. Japan had not awarded a single decoration to a living serviceman since the war began. The best a Kamikaze could expect was posthumous promotion one rank higher and an honored place among the spirits of the glorious dead who haunted the great Shinto shrine at Yasukuni in Tokyo. Even the emperor would bow to them there.

First takeoff was scheduled for 1320. It was up to their commander, Vice Admiral Matome Ugaki, to give the word. He spoke in such a soft monotone that his listeners leaned forward politely to catch the words. He reminded the pilots of the importance of their mission. They were the vanguard of the ten-stage attack plan which would cripple American naval strength and raise the siege of Okinawa. The attacks beginning this morning would continue tomorrow, April 7, the flag officer said, and at intervals over the next two months until the Americans were annihilated. Two thousand aircraft were being assembled for the task, three-fourths of them for Kamikaze attack, the remainder as escorts. There should have been more, he explained apologetically, but recent U.S. carrier raids had destroyed many planes on the ground.

"Remember those carriers," said Ugaki. "They are your prime target. Do not be misled by your enthusiasm. Do not attack the first ship you see. The enemy has many ships, large and small. Pilots from other airfields will attack battleships, transports, and radar pickets. You men from Kanoya have the honor of destroying the greatest danger to the survival of the Japanese empire. I invoke the blessings of the gods in your sacred task."

The senior staff officer of Fifth Air Fleet, Captain Takashi Miyazaki, walked down the table as the vice admiral was speaking, filling the sake cups with water. Wine was unsuited to such a solemn occasion. Ugaki, Kusaka, and the staff took up their cups, facing the pilots.

"I will follow you," Ugaki said. "We shall meet at Minatogawa."

They drank in unison, saluted, and bowed. The drummers under the cherry trees began a long low tattoo. Ugaki gave the final order:

"Pilots, to your planes!"

The drums rolled louder. The pilots yelled three hearty banzais and scattered to the revetments, accompanied by friends who were not flying this particular mission. The pilots ducked under the camouflage nets in their bulky leather flying suits, shook hands with the ground crews, and climbed aboard. Motors spluttered and roared; the onlookers cheered. Some were sobbing with emotion. One after another, 56 Zeros broke cover and hustled out onto the bumpy runway in the prescribed manner. The radar indicated there were no fliers within 100 miles, but it was best to stick to the drill; no radar was infallible.

Promptly at 1330 the first aircraft lumbered into the air. The bright afternoon sunshine glinted on its silver wings and Perspex cockpit cover and the big armor-piercing bomb slung beneath. An escort of ten fighters, all that could be spared, scrambled up from a distant corner of the field. Their job was to observe the attack. They would protect the Kamikaze during the long flight to Okinawa but not to the point of sacrifice. Experienced escort pilots were too valuable to waste at this stage. And it was common knowledge that the once unbeatable Zero was no match for the dreaded U.S. Grummans.

The young Christian Ensign Ichizu Hayashi joined the disconsolate group watching the departure. Soon the Zeros were specks in the cloudless sky. He walked sadly back to the bomb-damaged schoolhouse where one of the Ohka pilots, Lieutenant (jg.) Saburo Dohi, was busy sweeping floors. Like Hayashi, the lieutenant was not due to fly until April 12. He had protested about this because the men trained to handle the flying bombs—nicknamed *baka* (stupid) by the Americans—strongly felt they should be given a chance to strike the first blow of the Kikusui assault. They were refused.

Ugaki was still haunted by the costly failure of the first Ohka raid. On March 21 the admiral turned this new weapon on U.S. Task Force 58 while its carriers savaged Kyushu. Eighteen lumbering Mitsubishi-1 land bombers (code-named Betty by the

Americans) were ordered to attack carriers 123 miles southwest of Kanoya. Each of 16 carried a stubby-winged, piloted glide bomb in its belly. At the last moment it was discovered that the fighter group had been so hard hit it could muster only 55 planes—far too few. The Betty bomber was slow and unmaneuverable at the best of times; it lacked armor and self-sealing gas tanks, and American pilots called it the Flying Lighter. Encumbered by the 4718-pound Ohka bombs, the bombers stood no chance at all unless a large, lively escort could keep the Americans at bay.

Staff officers pleaded with Ugaki at the last moment to cancel the mission. The admiral was adamant. "If the Ohka cannot be used in the present situation," he declared, "there will never be a better chance for using it."

The squadron commander, Captain Motoharu Okamura, a veteran navy flier and Kamikaze enthusiast, shrugged his shoulders in bitter resignation. "We are ready to attack, sir," he announced and went off to lead the flight himself. He was dissuaded from doing so and watched with tear-filled eyes as the force took off. Only 30 fighters eventually joined them in the air. There was the predicted massacre. All the bombers and most of the fighters were shot down miles from the target. Six months of intensive training was snuffed out in as many minutes.

The Ohka unit's pennant still flew over Ugaki's command post in memory of the disaster. The vice admiral now argued that a repeat performance was unthinkable until enough carriers had been knocked out to reduce the effectiveness of Task Force 58's combat air patrol. He was confident this would be done. A total of 230 navy and 125 army Kamikaze planes were to be sent in on April 6 and 7. It would be the largest suicide assault ever staged against the American fleet.

Lieutenant Dohi accepted Ugaki's decision philosophically. It was not his job to question orders, especially the orders of anyone as popular and trusted as Ugaki. His pilots sensed the man's inner pain at sending so many of them to their death. He constantly promised to join them and they (rightly) believed him. So the lieutenant was singing cheerfully to himself as he worked away at improving the billet. Several multi-tiered bunks had been found, at his instigation; they were too narrow, but it was better than sleeping on the floor. The bedding belonging to the men who had just taken off was put out for airing in the sunshine. Their replacements would need it tonight . . .

Vice Admiral Ugaki took up his customary seat in the command post. The dugout was damp and chilly. Instruments glowed unnaturally bright in the subterranean gloom. Sour cigarette smoke clouded the concrete ceiling. Ugaki sat stiffly, silently in his ops-room chair, hands folded in his lap, staring fixedly ahead. To Kusaka he seemed to imagine himself in an airplane cockpit. The hours ticked past, radios jabbered, and disjointed snatches of muted conversation came from officers manning the telephones. Signals piled up on Ugaki's desk, but he ignored them. Suddenly he came to life. He sighed and looked at his watch. It was 1630. Five minutes to target.

U.S. Fifth Fleet, Off Okinawa

APRIL 6

IT LOOKED AS THOUGH the Japanese would never come. Since dawn the Americans had waited anxiously at their guns, eyes scanning the cloudy skies for the Kamikaze they'd been warned to expect. An entire armada hovered on tenterhooks, a nervous crescent of assorted shipping surrounding Okinawa. From the northernmost radar pickets through the battleships and transports off Hagushi beachhead to the supply vessels sheltering in Kerama-retto and, way off to the northwest, the vast scattering of carriers and escorts that was Task Force 58, crews manned their guns and cursed the balky enemy.

The weather was getting worse. A cold wind from the northeast whipped up the sullen swell. Destroyers pitched heavily through the white-capped waves. The watery sunlight was beginning to wane when crackling headsets warned that something was happening at last. The combat air patrol was locked in deadly combat somewhere beyond the northernmost tip of Okinawa. Gun crews braced themselves for action as the radar twirled ceaselessly overhead and lookouts with powerful binoculars scanned the approaches.

The two most exposed ships of the U.S. Fifth Fleet, the

144

destroyer *Bush* at number one radar picket station and her sister ship *Colhoun,* 10 miles to the west at station number two, lay directly in the path of the Kikusui raiders from Kyushu. Their crews had no illusions about the dangers; since the start of the Okinawa invasion they had been kept busy day and night by isolated intruders. The first of Vice Admiral Ugaki's 24-group attack force now bore down on them, heading for the vulnerable shipping off the landing beaches and inside the Kerama-retto supply sanctuary. Those were certainly their preselected targets. But instead of pressing on southward, 40 or 50 of the first wave began circling *Bush.* The pilots seemed determined to expend themselves on this one small ship in flagrant disregard of Ugaki's instructions. Perhaps they mistook the destroyer for something much bigger. Altitude, excitement, and waning light can play havoc with the imagination.

The Aichi (Val) dive bombers, black-nosed with fixed wheels sheathed in matching "spats," led the attack from a height of 8000 feet. The two-seater planes usually carried an air gunner; now there was only a pilot. But antiaircraft defenses had markedly improved since these Stukalike bombers had terrorized the Indian Ocean. One plane burst into vivid flame and exploded well clear of the destroyer. The other splashed after a direct hit on its starboard wing. It was a Tenzan (Jill) torpedo bomber, one of the key executioners at Pearl Harbor, which pierced the curtain of American gunfire.

Without carriers to fly from or elite crews to pilot them, the last of these planes were being expended on *Tokko* operations. Instead of making the usual approach run to drop his "fish" before sheering off in a sharp climb, the pilot kept on coming. He weaved skillfully at wave height through a storm of flak to crash between the destroyer's twin smokestacks. The high explosive bomb slung from the torpedo lugs killed every man in the forward engine room. *Bush* listed to port as the sea poured in.

Colhoun raced to help the stricken ship, calling for cover from the heavily engaged combat air patrol overhead. Carrier fighters were downing attackers in all directions before they themselves ran out of gas and ammunition. *Bush* was still fighting topside fires, her 5-inch turrets jammed, as her sister ship appeared, guns blazing, downing three Zeros on the way. Too late the

Colhoun's gunners caught a fourth Zero diving toward the port bow. The flaming fighter plunged through the destroyer's deck, destroying the after fire room and everyone inside. Speed dropped to 15 knots. The main turrets lost power and had to be trained by hand. The gunners blasted another wave, the fifth in 15 minutes. An Aichi hit the water 200 yards to port. Yet another was downed by *Bush* and a nearby landing ship. But at 1717 a Zero slammed into *Colhoun's* side, destroying both boilers, cutting a massive gash below the waterline, and breaking the keel. The destroyer drifted dead in the water.

The Japanese pilots could well have broken off at this stage in search of other targets. But they seemed determined to finish the two cripples. They resumed the attack at 1725. *Colhoun's* gunners splashed a Zero. Fire from the 40-mms hit an Aichi dive-bomber which seemed set for a near-miss until one wing clipped the after stack. The attacker bounced overboard, dousing the deck with burning gasoline and exploding alongside. Water deluged the topside fires and washed the after damage party overboard.

Another Aichi made for *Bush* and struck her a mortal blow. The dive-bomber smashed into the already gutted amidships section between the stacks, cutting the destroyer virtually in half. There was a pause while crewmen brought the fires under control. Then at 1745 another Zero spun into the destroyer's port side, killing the overflow of wounded undergoing emergency treatment in the wardroom and rekindling fires no pumps could quench. *Bush* began to go down by the bow. At 1830, her spine broken, she jackknifed and sank in the heavy swell.

By that time *Colhoun* had again been hit. She was abandoned and sunk by gunfire from an attendant destroyer. Many men, frightfully burned, were lost without trace in the darkness. Rescue ships searched the sea without lights for fear of attracting further attacks. A total of 129 officers and men, most of them from *Bush*, were killed or missing.

Leutze and *Newcomb* maintained radar vigil closer to the bombardment force. The two twin-stack *Fletcher*-class destroyers provided early warning for the battleships and transports off the main west coast landing beaches. They circled in the lee of Ii-shima, an as yet unoccupied island capped by an extinct volcano where two weeks later America's most popular war correspondent, Ernie Pyle, was to meet his death. The battleships were preparing to take up night cruising dispositions. Admiral Spruance aboard *New Mexico* watched with grim satisfaction as task force fighters splashed four Kamikaze over the tiny island. Nine other battleships circled offshore waiting for *New Mexico* and her sister ship *Idaho* to join them. They offered a target no enemy pilot should have been able to resist.

But the next wave of Kamikaze again ignored their basic instructions. A dozen planes made straight for the two destroyers. Most of these fliers were army men. Ship recognition was probably not their strong point. Ten army O-1 (Oscar) fighters, similar in looks (but not in performance) to the navy Zero, roared in at deck level beneath the radar. Behind them trundled two Nakajima (Kate) torpedo bombers with bombs instead of torpedoes slung from the fuselage. Lookouts spotted them first. Men gawked momentarily at this unexpected mass attack— "Why us, for Christ's sake?"—before both destroyers let fly with their 5-inch guns, splattering the evening sky with blobs of black smoke. The quadruple 40-mm Bofors, the twin 20-mm Oerlikons added their patterns of tracer, spitting rapidly from the blazing barrels and arcing more lazily toward their target. The barrage threw up fountains of spray in front of the fast-closing aircraft. The Japanese kept grimly on course. Nothing was going to stop them.

The next three dreadful minutes saw *Newcomb* reduced to a wreck. One O-1 hit her after stack, another splashed nearby, and almost immediately afterward one of the torpedo bombers plowed through the amidships upperworks causing a tremendous explosion which wrecked the engine and boiler rooms. The lights went out. Guns froze as the power died. A fourth plane diving from port crashed the forward stack, "spraying the entire amidships section of *Newcomb*, which was a raging conflagration, with a fresh supply of gasoline," as her commander later reported. It looked like nothing could save her.

Lieutenant Leon Grabowsky, commander of *Leutze*, pulled alongside to help fight the inferno. Minutes later, at 1815, yet another O-1 charged through the flak straight at *Newcomb*'s bridge. A 5-inch shell burst hit the approaching cockpit and with the pilot probably dead at the controls the plane spun into *Leutze*'s fantail. The explosion set off a fire in the after ammunition handling room. Bulkheads blew out, the sea rushed in, and the would-be rescuer was in urgent need of rescue. She slid away into open water jettisoning torpedoes, depth charges, and top hamper in an effort to negate the flooding.

Tugs brought the two shattered ships to overnight shelter in Kerama-retto; *Leutze* with the remains of the Kamikaze plane still sticking out of her after deck, *Newcombe* scorched and buckled and down by the stern. Total casualties were 47 men killed and 58 wounded. But despite the damage both destroyers were eventually repaired—a further tribute to the durability of American construction and design.

The first attack wave to break through the defending fighter screen reached the Hagushi beachhead at 1710. The five planes which dived on the troop transports were survivors of an attack group originally some 20 strong. Three were Kawasaki Ki-45 (Nick) twin-engined army fighters with red propeller spinners and speckled silver camouflage. The other two were more Aichis drawn from the Japanese navy's obsolescent reserves.

Antiaircraft fire erupted from the transports. Much of the shooting was wildly undisciplined, with flak frequently hitting nearby ships, but four of the attackers were quickly sent crashing into the sea. The fifth plane turned away through the clouds of bursting shells and disappeared. Gunners went on blazing away for another half hour, mostly at nothing, occasionally at friendly planes, before the firing could be brought under control. Kamikaze attack made men understandably jumpy. Still, there was cause for self-congratulation around the beachhead once the first flush of searing excitement died down. Gun crews boasted unnaturally loudly, smoked a mite more feverishly while keeping a wary eye cocked toward the darkening sky.

The Kikusui raiders continued to press their attacks in spite of grave losses at the hands of the combat air patrol. And they continued to waste their efforts against secondary targets. Two destroyers of the antisubmarine screen, *Witter* and *Morris*, were damaged, many of their crewmen sustaining terrible burns. A Kamikaze hit the destroyer *Hyman* in the torpedo tubes causing an enormous explosion which flooded her forward engine room. *Howarth* stopped one in the main battery director while rushing to her aid. Other attackers searching the east coast of Okinawa for Task Force 58 set the destroyer *Mullany* on fire but failed to sink her.

A minesweeping force was caught working the channel between Iheya-retto and Okinawa. Two minesweeper-destroyer escorts, *Rodman* and *Emmons,* became the target of concentrated attacks. One plane destroyed most of *Rodman's* superstructure. And although Marine Corsair pilots from Task Force 58 managed to down some 20 enemy aircraft, *Emmons* was hit by five planes. Two hit her fantail, blowing off the rudder. One blew a hole in the bow. A fourth hit the bridge, killing everyone in the combat information center; and the fifth plunged into the blazing superstructure. The burning hulk was sunk at midnight to avoid drifting onto an enemy-occupied beach.

The Japanese were so preoccupied with the escorts that they overlooked the tempting targets at Kerama-retto. Or perhaps many tried but failed to make it. Few Kamikaze appeared that day over the tankers, ammunition ships, and supply ships packed into the sheltered anchorage. None of these ships had the defensive armament of the destroyers. Some were manned by merchant crews who were less sanguine about Kamikaze attack than their brethren in the navy. Most cargoes were highly volatile. A few hits here could cause heavier loss to the invading force than the destruction of a dozen escort vessels. The first Zero to reach the area at 1627 picked on the smallest target in sight: a landing ship loaded with fuel oil. The ship burned like a torch for 24 hours before going to the bottom. Other attackers crashed two Victory ships loaded with ammunition. Both drifted afire, showering the anchorage with flames and sparks from exploding shells before they were sunk by gunfire. But it was a mere taste of what might have happened had the assault been better directed.

Task Force 58 came in for curiously little attention. Carriers escaped the successive death dives expended on isolated destroyers, possibly because most of the Japanese pilots failed to locate Mitscher far out in the Pacific. Those who did were fumbling amateurs. Four carriers, two cruisers, and two destroyers were near-missed. *Cabot* had the closest shave. A Zero came in low on the port beam, skimmed the crowded flight deck where members of the harassed combat air patrol were refueling, hit the radar antenna, and exploded alongside. Shrapnel from neighboring ships damaged four torpedo bombers on the open deck. During the day about 30 attackers were splashed around the force.

Darkness did not halt the suicide attacks, although the Divine Wind was dying to a zephyr. Kikusui One had shot its bolt. Ugaki's best men and machines were gone. Some 230 army and navy Kamikaze with 175 escorts and conventional bombers had taken off from Kyushu in the morning. Forty-one escorts, 17 conventional bombers, and a handful of frustrated Kamikaze returned that night. Losses included a number which crashed at sea through engine trouble or faulty navigation. From now on the quality and size of the suicide squadrons would deteriorate. Even tomorrow, Saturday, April 7, when the follow-up attack was scheduled, there would be fewer planes. Soon the Japanese would be fitting bombs to training aircraft.

Radio Tokyo hailed the costly failure as "a blow from which the enemy will never recover." Two American battleships and three cruisers had been sunk, an ecstatic announcer declared, together with 57 smaller vessels. Another 61, among them 5 carriers, were badly damaged. The Japanese celebrated this break in the growing gloom. The tide of war must be turning at last! Only the higher-ups remained skeptical. Even they would have been horrified to learn that Japan's costliest-ever air assault sank no more than three destroyers, two ammunition ships, and a small landing ship. Ten other ships were damaged, eight of them destroyer-types. Over 200 American crewmen were wounded and 286 killed. But the Kamikaze corps failed to hit a single major target—proof enough that improved fighter direction and gunnery were blunting this fearsome weapon. The carriers escaped unscathed, eager for their final settlement with Yamato.

The attacks increased Mitscher's determination to get his task force away from Okinawa. His carriers were too much at risk near this wretched island. Bodies of seamen were already washing ashore there as a reminder to the marines and soldiers of the price the navy was paying for their protection. Over 4900 sailors were killed or missing and 4824 wounded by the end of the campaign. Task Force 58 lost 763 aircraft. The final toll was 31 warships and auxiliary craft sunk and 368 vessels damaged.

U.S. Fighting 30 Air Group, With Task Force 58, Off Okinawa

APRIL 6

THE MEN WHO REALLY broke the greatest-ever Kamikaze assault of the Pacific war were the American pilots. But by the time darkness brought flying to a halt, the pilots and their devoted deck crews were exhausted. No airfields were yet operational in Okinawa, so the entire burden of aerial support and protection fell on the carrier-borne planes of Task Force 58. Gone were the agonizing early days when a handful of regulars flew until they cracked up—or died. The training programs were churning out so many able fliers that a Pacific combat tour was restricted to six months. In that time, however, as Lieutenant Roy Gillespie recalls it, "The brass were absolutely merciless, the way they worked us. They just flew our tails off."

Roy was executive officer of Fighting 30, the air group aboard the carrier *Belleau Wood*. The 6-foot Alaskan was already feeling the strain. He lost 65 pounds by the time he got home. He was so tense that "if anyone dropped a spoon, I'd jump over the table." When his Hellcat pilots were not escorting bombers over enemy targets—a hateful job if they faced heavy antiaircraft fire—they were making ground strafing attacks with machine guns, bombs, and rockets on Japanese positions ashore;

151

or they were circling high over the battle zone on combat air patrol.

That could be the most boring job of all. Way above the fleet at 27,000 feet, wearing oxygen masks in unpressurized cockpits, pilots kept slipping off their heavy leather flying gloves to examine their fingernails. If the nails were turning blue around the cuticles it was time to come down. Oxygen deficiency caused unconsciousness, quickly and without warning; the pilot would slump over his controls and plunge down into the sea. Staff officers might fume about the amount of unnecessary radio chatter between the men of the fighter screen, but mostly they were keeping in touch with one another out of self-protection. It was their ironclad rule to help a buddy whenever he seemed in trouble.

The day began like any other. That meant well before dawn. On the bigger carriers pilots traditionally ate steak for breakfast before an important mission. The more nervous ones were liable to leave the table halfway through and throw up; then fly all day without demur. *Belleau Wood* did not enjoy such culinary luxuries. She was one of the small *Independence* class, built on cruiser hulls, with little room for sophisticated provisioning. Breakfast consisted of reconstituted dried eggs, fruit juice, and coffee—except on Thursdays, when the cooks served beans. These caused endless trouble to pilots assigned to combat air patrol: the stomach gases expanded at high altitude producing agonizing cramps and nausea . . . but the beans were a welcome change—even at four o'clock in the morning. Rations were a major gripe. A lot of miscellaneous frustrations were vented on the wretched cooks. It was all "ham, Spam, and jam," as Gillespie put it, washed down with coffee that grew thicker as the day progressed. "By dinnertime you could stand a spoon in it."

Belleau Wood carried 24 assorted planes and 36 pilots. Sixteen of the planes were Hellcats. There were plenty more replacements, men and machines, waiting just across the horizon in a supply fleet of minuscule *Kaiser* carriers. Concern was mounting among Mitscher's staff about the prevailing attrition rate, especially the increasing loss of aircraft, and Nimitz was urgently requested to divert supplies to the task force from less crucial Pacific battle fronts. These anxieties did not percolate down to the men of Fighting 30. They were positively cocky. Enemy air power was no longer a menace.

"They were sending kids out of Japan who probably didn't have 50 hours in an airplane," Lieutenant Gillespie recalls. "They were brave enough, but half-trained. It did not demand great skill on our part. The Japs were sitting ducks. It was just that there were so many swarming over us ...

"At that time we still thought we would have to conquer Japan. Someone would have to wade ashore there. I don't think we really knew how close it was to the end. We didn't realize that the Japanese were as badly off as they really were. We knew their fleet was taking a beating but we also knew they were very fanatical. They proved this in their Kamikaze raids."

Pilots might despise the suicide fliers' ability but they did not underestimate the damage potential in this unprecedented form of warfare. According to the scuttlebutt a massive Kamikaze attack was imminent. There were a few apprehensive faces among the men who manned the ready room the regulation one hour before takeoff. The young veterans smoked and chattered in folding chairs while the operations officer scrawled information on a blackboard. It came in from Mitscher's staff through *Belleau Wood's* own combat information center: weather forecasts and navigational and target data. Messboys circulated an endless supply of coffee. Cigarette smoke curled up to the deck head.

The flight deck lay directly above: it was necessarily close, for speedy access. There were no elevators or escalators in these ships. Pilots had to scamper up the steel ladders and across to the aircraft park burdened with gloves, helmet, oxygen mask, parachute, and navigational plotting board whenever the squawk box ordered them to their planes. On the boards they scrawled their point option data immediately before takeoff. This gave them their carrier's projected course and speed. Despite their electronic navigational equipment, they might still have to find their way back to the ship by traditional calculations.

The first flush of dawn was tinting the eastern sky when *Belleau Wood* launched her initial sortie. Fourteen oil-streaked Hellcats thundered down the flight deck. (Two were delayed by mechanical troubles.) The carrier was small, but the pilots were used to it. They kept to the left half of the deck when landing occasionally on *Yorktown* or any of the other big fleet carriers. The big-ship pilots watched in amazement. The three flights climbed up to begin their endless circling at 27,000 feet. Once more they had drawn the top of the stack. Below them at 17,000 feet was a flight from *Hornet* and a *Yorktown* flight at a mere 10,000 feet. Fighters from yet another carrier patrolled 5000 feet lower. No matter what the altitude the Kamikaze chose for their approach, there would be U.S. fighters waiting to pounce.

It was a typical Pacific day: big, fluffy, fleecy white clouds stippled a bright blue sky. Roy Gillespie led his flight toward their patrol zone 40 miles northeast of the task force. The twinkling sea was carpeted with ships stretching out toward the horizon. The sky seemed full of fighters. Flying with Roy were Ensigns Dave Philips, Ken Dhams, and Michele Mazzocco. The time was just past 0500.

The boys from *Belleau Wood* might be cocky, but they were not blasé. They were expecting trouble. Intelligence officers confirmed that it looked as though the Japanese were preparing massed Kamikaze raids on the fleet—something different from the heckling of recent days by single intruders based on nearby islands. This could be the big one, mounted from the main Kamikaze bases in Kyushu. The enemy airfields seemed to have miraculously survived weeks of nonstop bombing. So much for the vaunted B-29s! Every man scanned the indigo skies for the first trace of approaching aircraft.

Nothing happened. Stiff and slightly heady from the hissing oxygen, the pilots turned back after a fruitless two hours of patrolling to find their carrier. *Belleau Wood* was steaming east with her cluster of escorts and there was the usual breathless pause while the pilots fired recognition signals and prayed some jumpy gunner would not mistake them for the enemy. One by one they bumped down on the deck, jerking to a bone-shaking halt as the arrester hook connected with the safety wires. Deck crews wheeled each plane away to the refueling area while the pilot went below for a glass of powdered milk, a bologna sandwich, and a brief rest. It was going to be a long, long day . . .

Michele Mazzocco, a 21-year-old ensign from Peekskill, New York, already felt dog tired. Aviators got no rest off Okinawa. He seemed to be up all night and all day too. Daylight lasted 12 hours in these latitudes. Some days they spent as much as eight hours in the air. Feeling sure that his flight would soon be needed again he stayed on in the cockpit munching an apple while the mechanics toiled around him.

At 0730 they were off again, circling 5 miles above the fleet, their radios crackling with warnings of approaching enemy planes. Bogies were already appearing on the fleet radar heading in from the northeast at a range of about 50 miles. Ken Dhams spotted the first. A converted bomber was trying to dodge in and out of the clouds, apparently on a reconnaissance mission. Gillespie tallyhoed the flight toward the intruder and Ken flamed him with his first burst. The Hellcats' six 0.5-inch wing guns were adjusted for aerial combat to converge at a range of 1000 feet. Every fifth round was an incendiary which ate into the bomber's unprotected fuel tanks and produced a blast of orange flame. The dying Japanese plane spun over, shedding one wing and engine, and plunged toward the sea.

Next came the Zeros. They were camouflaged brown and yellow but looked silver in the glaring sunlight. Mazzocco saw the big red "meatballs" on their wings. These were no Kamikaze. Their pilots were veterans, probably sent ahead of the attack waves to clear the air of protecting fighters. There must have been at least 30 of them, and they were looking for a fight.

The young ensign never remembered exactly what happened next. It was all so quick—and confusing. Fragmentary snapshots lingered years later in his memory. Dodging, dancing airplanes like dragonflies above a pond. Streams of flowing tracer creeping closer and closer. The sudden shocking glimpse in his rearview mirror of a Zero lining him up for the kill. A cloud of smoke and exploding wreckage tumbling leisurely through the air where seconds before there had been an enemy plane.

He had always considered himself a good shot. Now he got his chance, swirling his way through the melee. At this altitude neither side was noticeably agile, although the Zero could out-turn the heavier Hellcat. The Zero, on the other hand, was more fragile—a single burst from Mazzocco's guns could tear one to pieces—and its dive-speed limit, the dreaded "redline," was only 400 knots. Anything faster tore the wings off. The Hellcat, by contrast, could hit 435 knots in a dive before endangering the airframe.

The American fighters carried a 30 seconds' supply of ammunition. It was easy to fire it all off unthinkingly. Michele husbanded his shells until he had a target square in the electronic bullsight. Then a short burst sufficed, maximum three seconds duration, from the trigger on his control stick. A wildly turning

Zero flashed through his sights hot on the tail of another Hellcat. The ensign pressed the trigger, accurately and economically; the enemy plane staggered, rolled over, and went down trailing fire and smoke. He got briefly behind another, which exploded in a great gout of flame. More Japanese planes got the same treatment until he had counted seven kills.

An eighth Zero was already smoking badly from a burst in the engine when it spun round and dived directly at its attacker. Mazzocco's Hellcat shuddered as he emptied his guns into the approaching foe. But it was like trying to stop a charging elephant with a pea shooter. No doubt about it: the Japanese pilot was determined to ram. The ensign cursed his luck. He had been warned often enough of this ultimate maneuver. There was no escape. Whichever way he turned now, the Zero would be on him. He held course until the last minute, then yanked back the stick and gunned the engine into a shuddering climb. The G-force pinned him back in his seat. He watched disbelievingly as the Zero scraped beneath him, shearing off his belly fuel tank. For the briefest moment he saw the man who was trying to kill him staring up glassily from his cockpit. Then the Hellcat's propeller sawed off one of the Zero's wings. It spun away into oblivion.

The sky was suddenly empty. Mazzocco wiped the sweat from his eyes. It was cold sweat and he was trembling. Was it fear or excitement? Maybe a bit of both. His engine was running ragged, streaming smoke. He raised Ken Dhams on the radio and asked him to check him over. More than 50 bullets had pitted the Hellcat's wings and fuselage, but Ken reckoned Michele could make it back to the carrier. He landed safely, only to find the fighter damaged beyond repair. Deck crews pushed it over the side.

Roy Gillespie was in worse shape. A gun had exploded in his wing. He crept back, escorted by Dhams, and let down cautiously. The arrestor hook broke and he plowed through the crash barrier and flipped over into some of the parked planes.

"On our ship we had a very devout Catholic chaplain," Roy recalled. "He was a very quiet and conservative priest, about as fit for that job as I would be in a maternity ward. I happen to be a Catholic. Our flight surgeon was Jewish, the nicest guy that ever lived. They were both dear friends of mine. They pretty near pulled me apart getting me out of that plane.

"I was hanging there upside down. I'd banged my head. It would have been pretty bad except that I'd stuck my plastic goggles on my forehead. I knocked off the rearview mirror, shearing off two ¼-inch ribbons of glass with my goggles and helmet. The plane did not catch fire, although gas was dripping down. The chaplain came up from one side and the flight surgeon from the other. They were there even before the asbestos-clad men could reach me. I figured I was in pretty good hands."

Pilots from *Belleau Wood* were credited with 47 kills on this first day of Kikusui One. The task force claimed to have destroyed a total of 249 attackers. *Essex* led the pack by splashing 65. Michele Mazzocco was awarded four confirmed kills, recorded both by his camera gun and fellow flight members. He was ready now to settle scores with *Yamato*. But Gillespie was temporarily out of action. There was no flying for him the next day.

Japanese Army Observation Post, Okinawa

APRIL 6

LIEUTENANT GORO MATSUOKA missed most of the air battles. His well-concealed observation post in the southwestern corner of Okinawa looked out on the ocean—not up to the sky. The few planes he saw spiraling down in flames must be American. Those Yankee pilots might put up a brave show strafing undefended island targets, but he felt sure they cut a very different figure facing ace Japanese airmen, victors of a thousand battles from Pearl Harbor to the Phillppines. The Americans were cowards—well-equipped ones, true enough—but cowards when it came to the crunch. Matsuoka was quite confident of this. No amount of equipment could compensate for their lack of fighting spirit, of sheer spiritual power with which all Japanese warriors were traditionally imbued. The patriotic lieutenant was quite convinced this same spirit would drive the Americans back into the sea at the given signal.

It was the typical Japanese army view of the Pacific war. The bulk of the defending forces on Okinawa had spent their war years fighting in China. For men like Matsuoka that was a walkover war, since the Chinese were both disorganized and demoralized. He had been conditioned to believe Americans were the same. Against such enemies, the Japanese were invincible.

The Japanese army's counterattack should have been launched on April 6 to coincide with the first phase of Kikusui One. It had been postponed until April 12, rumor had it, because of disagreements among the high command. A pity, Matsuoka thought, because the air attacks were an ideal diversion. Better still to counterattack tomorrow, when the navy was due to sortie into Okinawan waters. Headquarters said the ships would be run aground nearby on the coast. The crews would leap ashore and join in the defense. He chuckled disbelievingly at that part of the story. Just as well someone could crack a joke nowadays.

The Americans must be regretting the day they ever set eyes on Okinawa. From his new lookout in the hills above Naha, Lieutenant Matsuoka commanded a bird's-eye view of the Kamikaze havoc in the East China Sea from the anchorage at Kerama-retto, across the huddle of intervening islets, northward beyond the Hagushi beaches to Cape Misaki. Columns of black smoke were still rising there beyond the bombardment force. It must be burning battleships, because that was where they headed every night.

"At least one battleship on fire," he reported to headquarters. If pressed, he would admit he couldn't see it. But with so many prime targets in view, you could hardly expect a self-sacrificing pilot to go for anything else.

More smoke billowed from Kerama-retto, where a fleet of tankers and ammunition ships seemed well ablaze. Flames and sparks belched from behind the shielding mass of Tokashiki Jima as if one of the island's dead volcanoes had sprung to life. His trusty radio operator Tanaka, grubbier and more unshaven than ever, thought he had spotted fires on the opposite coast, where the rollers pounded in from the Pacific, but other watchers were better placed to make an accurate assessment.

The weather was unseasonably cold. Both men wrapped themselves, shivering, in their thin army blankets as the sun burst from the overcast and plumeted toward the twinkling horizon. A few weeks more and this place would be a sweatbox. Provided they were still there . . . the Americans were probing so slowly forward that it would probably be a couple of days before they ran into the hedge of bayonets impatiently awaiting them on Kakazu Ridge.

Matsuoka checked his maps and notes while the light lasted. He longed to climb outside onto the blasted hilltop and stretch his legs. But that would be asking for trouble. He scrambled to the pit in a corner of the lookout and urinated. How the place stank! Or was it them? Neither had bathed since the invasion began. He brushed vainly at his soiled uniform and vowed that next morning Tanaka would be made to shave. He glanced enviously at the radio operator, who had settled back, oblivious to the future, over a bottle of sake and a freshly opened can of salmon. Unless the Kamikaze, the navy, and the ground defense troops defeated the Americans, the two of them would eventually find themselves joining some last-ditch charge. Officer and enlisted man had vowed to die together. The lieutenant dismissed all unpleasant thoughts, unbuckled his sword, and reached for his sake ration.

Three battered Zeros attempted the dangerous night landing at Kanoya. Their green and red recognition flares reassured the gunners who watched anxiously from the sandbagged gun pits as the fighters thumped onto the scarred runway in the deceptive light of the declining moon. One plane flipped over and caught fire, but the pilot scrambled clear. Reports coming in from other fields advised that four other survivors from this morning's ten-Zero escort group had made it back from Okinawa. Only three lost? Remarkable! But then these were veterans with orders to observe instead of fight. The exhausted arrivals were hurried into the command post where Vice Admiral Ugaki received them at his desk. He was relaxed and smoking now as he welcomed them cheerfully home. Staff officers added noisy congratulations.

The senior pilot, a lieutenant commander, was burned about the face and hands and in need of medical treatment. He politely brushed aside the medics in order to complete his report. There was no doubt in his mind that Operation Kikusui had gotten off to a magnificent start. An hour after takeoff the Kanoya attack squadron found itself mixed up with some of the army fliers and those Aichi dive-bombers from the nearby base at Kokuga. Before they even sighted Okinawa a frightful air battle developed with the American fighters. There must have been hundreds of them, Grumman Hellcats and Wildcats and gull-winged Vought Corsairs. He himself had downed at least six in the melee. His wingman hit three before catching a cannon burst in the engine. The air was full of flaming planes—he shook his head to clear the vision—but the bulk of the Kanoya force had headed for the carriers. Before breaking off the action he saw two battleships under Kamikaze attack, one of them on fire. The other two pilots were telling much the same story when Ugaki cut them short. The lieutenant commander was swaying on his feet. Ugaki ordered him off to the hospital.

Reports still coming in were carefully collated. The unsleeping Ugaki stayed obstinately at his desk, snatching a hasty bowl of boiled rice, soup, and pickles, piecing together his impressive jigsaw. Two main points emerged: first, the day's attacks had caused widespread damage. The escort pilots' hazy accounts were bolstered by the eyewitness evidence of coast watchers on Okinawa. But, second, it was evident that their chief enemy, Task Force 58, had escaped the full force of the attack. Phase two next morning would need to head further eastward into the Pacific, provided, of course, that the weather held. The meteorological officers were getting worried. The flag officer yawned and stretched. He had been nearly 18 hours at this wretched desk. There was little time to snatch a nap. Gratefully he gulped a cupful of Scotch taken from a waiting steward.

The chief of staff, Vice Admiral Kusaka, still played the role of Observer. He stepped out for a breath of fresh air. Word had just gone round that Vice Admiral Ito's son would lead tomorrow's token fighter escort over *Yamato*. The chief of staff watched the moon set behind the cherry blossoms, wondering whether this would inspire his deathbed haiku. The stanzas refused to form. He was too busy thinking of the heroic young men who had gone today, never to return. The next batch now slept innocently in the battered old schoolhouse among the empty bedding and the farewell letters and little bundles of personal possessions awaiting dispatch to the bereaved families. When he walked back into the command post a communications officer produced a delayed "eyes only" cable. Kurita knew the contents before he read it: *Yamato* had sailed on schedule.

Japanese Fleet,
Tokuyama Oil Depot,
Inland Sea of Japan

MORNING, APRIL 6

THE TELEPHONE ROUSED the drowsy duty officer at Tokuyama. It was two o'clock in the morning. Supply Department, Kure, was on the line. The men in charge of Tokuyama, the largest navy oil depot in the empire, were advised that *Yamato*, *Yahagi*, and the rest of the Special Attack Force would be arriving soon after dawn. A confirmatory signal was on the way. Instructions from Combined Fleet, now being forwarded, insisted that all ships be given only enough fuel to get them to Okinawa.

From the sound of his voice, the man in Kure didn't like it. He had already said as much in an angry exchange with Hiyoshi. The staff at Tokuyama didn't like it either. The acres of huge oil tanks, capacity 3 million tons, which filled this desolate and closely guarded anchorage on the Inland Sea were almost empty. The depot's logs recorded a residue of some 15,000 tons. That was just over a third of all the heavy-duty oil left in Japan. The American invasion fleet off Okinawa consumed more than that every 24 hours. But the Japanese, unlike the Americans, had scant hope of replenishment except for minuscule shipments of Manchurian soybean oil that nobody wanted. Very soon nothing would be left to fuel the submarines, maintain the escort screens for Korean and Manchurian convoys, and continue what was left of the war at sea.

Kure explained this to Combined Fleet, only to be told it was all for the glory of the Imperial Navy. "Glory, my ass," spluttered the chief supply officer. "Fools! Idiots!" He slammed the phone down. The staff in Tokuyama agreed. While they husbanded their resources for this battle of Japan everyone talked about, those desk-bound admirals ("Fools, the whole lot of them!") wasted precious oil and ships on an ill-considered, no-hope operation to relieve Okinawa. The island was as good as lost anyway.

Very well, if the top brass were going to be this stupid, Tokuyama would see that the ships were given a fighting chance. At a predawn conference the unshaven, bleary-eyed staff officers perfected their plan. They would tap the secret reserve. The big steel oil tanks stood on concave concrete foundations. Even the empty ones each held a residue of about 200 tons beyond the reach of regulation pumps. Men could climb down inside—breathing apparatus might be necessary because of the fumes—and then it should be possible to extract the last drop of oil with hand pumps. It would be hard work, but it might produce enough to evade Combined Fleet's suicidal instructions and give the ships a chance to return. Gangs in overalls and rubber boots were sweating away at the task long before the attack force hove in sight from Mitajiri.

Tokuyama lies in a shallow bay formed by four hilly islands. Today it houses one of the biggest petrochemical complexes in Japan. In April 1945 there was little more than a long steel jetty protruding from the nest of camouflaged oil tanks and administrative buildings, a handful of tugs and oil barges moored close inshore, and a battery of antiaircraft guns pointing patiently at the sky. Since there was insufficient water in the inner anchorage for anything bigger than a destroyer, *Yamato* and *Yahagi* moored well outside. The destroyers took turns topping up alongside the jetty while the tugs towed out oil barges to the cruiser and the battleship.

Yamato's total fuel capacity was 6300 tons. A full load would give her 7200 miles at the designed cruising speed of 16 knots. She was carrying less than 600 tons. The other ships' tanks were equally low. The Combined Fleet directive permitted Tokuyama to supply a total of only 2000 tons to the entire force. This allowed a margin for high-speed combat maneuvers, which always guzzle oil. There would not be enough fuel, however, if they tried to return home.

The supply officers defiantly provided nearly 8000 tons. Their private records later revealed that *Yamato* sailed with 4000 tons in her tanks, *Yahagi* with 1250 tons, and the escorts with from 900 to 500 tons. It was a kindly, futile gesture that few of the ships' crews ever knew about.

Yamato's executive officer, Captain Nomura, was in on the secret. It wouldn't do a bit of good, he felt; they were all doomed. But he willingly signed a false requisition return to keep the bureaucrats happy in Tokyo. He interrupted his paperwork to make a quick round of inspection. The weather deck was crowded with noisy cheerful sailors off-loading combustibles and unwanted stores. If any of them had a hangover, they did not show it. Noisiest of all were the cadets, tripping over themselves in their efforts to be helpful. Some tried to help with the oiling. Others pestered the gunners. The rest helped bundle bedding, spare lumber, paint pots, and furniture into a waiting lighter. Further aft, four of the ship's six spotter planes were already in the water. They would fly back to a naval seaplane base to end up, probably, as Kamikaze. The remaining two, together with two more aboard *Yahagi*, would fly back tomorrow after an early morning search for submarines. No sense in holding on to them any longer than that; floatplanes were easy meat for Grummans. On board they were simply a fire hazard.

The executive officer's secretary kept glancing at his watch. The mail boat was leaving at 1000. So soon? Before dashing off a farewell letter to his wife, Nomura broadcast the word throughout the ship.

Ensign Mitsuru Yoshida had almost forgotten. Sadly he scribbled a note to his parents: "Please dispose of all my things. Take good care of yourselves and give the best in whatever you do to the last. That and that only I pray of you."

The letter severed his last tie with home . . . It was the beginning, he thought, of the end of everything.

Captain Hara on *Yahagi* found time to write:

> The Combined Fleet has shrunk unbelievably in the past two years. I am about to sortie as skipper of the only cruiser remain-

ing in this fleet—8,500-ton *Yahagi*. With my good friend Rear
Admiral Keizo Komura on board, we are going on a surface
Tokko mission. It is a great opportunity as well as a great honor
to be skipper of a ship in this sortie to Okinawa. Know that I am
happy and proud of this opportunity. Be proud of me.
    Farewell.

He just managed to catch the mail boat. The letter gone, he
no longer felt worried or upset. The fleet would fight to the
death—and he with it. A mixture of resignation and resolution
steeled his nerves. A great calm settled on his soul. He too
savored the calm of one who is already dead.

The air-raid alarm sent the ships' companies scurrying to general quarters as two destroyers came alongside to pass extra oil
to *Yamato*. It was an awkward moment. All ships were at emergency moorings, their cables temporarily uncoupled and
snagged down on the forecastles. One blow of a bosun's hammer
would release them instantly at risk of losing the anchor and all
attached cable. The stand-down soon sounded. The enemy was
identified as a solitary B-29 flying miles above them, almost
invisible to the naked eye. No danger there: just another
snooper.

Captain Frank W. Scheible of the Third Photo Reconnaissance 21st Bomber Command, headed his camera-equipped B-
29 eastward from Kure. So far, so bad. Weather conditions over
the naval base were disappointing. "Kure socked in," he
reported. It looked like it would be a frustrating trip. Oil leaks
had developed in three engines during the monotonous mara-
thon flight from Tinian. The radio lacked a suitable antenna.
Iwo Jima homing beacon was jammed by some untraceable signal. And the rations were lousy.

Flying parallel with the Honshu coast at a height of 30,500
feet, mission 3PR5M 121 sought clearer weather. Just past Etajima (across the harbor from Kure) they glimpsed a moored aircraft carrier. It was probably *Amagi* trying vainly to hide from
further air attacks. Technical Sergeant Zitek began methodically taking pictures. No naval vessels seemed to be lurking in
Hiroshima Bay. This part of the Inland Sea was devoid of shipping. Japan was under such close scrutiny that the Americans
detected defense moves almost the moment they were made.

What their cameras could not unveil, nor their intelligence experts divine, was the desperate state of the Japanese economy, the growing hunger, exhaustion, and terror of the civil populace, and the desire for some kind of peace settlement among an important if still inarticulate segment of the hierarchy.

Cruising over Tokuyama at a ground speed of 195 mph, Frank Scheible's mission paid off. Just beyond the oil depot he spotted the *Yamato* attack force. The clustered ships were refueling. Sergeant Zitek's cameras picked up an escort force of one *Agano*-class light cruiser (*Yahagi*) and six destroyers. The other two destroyers were probably inside Tokuyama Bay.

"Excellent coverage," the squadron commander later reported.

The B-29 flew on toward the wreck-strewn Shimonoseki Strait, noting the minutiae of every anchorage, air base, and factory in its path. Many installations were already allotted target numbers. Kure had been subdivided into separate bombing zones. Smaller targets like the seaplane base at Najima, the Hakata rail yards, and the Watanabe aircraft plant became designated targets nos. 1237, 1270, and 662. Thousands of targets were similarly pinpointed for destruction in every corner of the imperial homeland. The avenging eagle was preparing to pounce. The floating chrysanthemum was destined to be torn apart, petal by petal . . .

Ariga sent for Nomura. The skipper must have been talking to Vice Admiral Ito, because he gave the order to disembark the cadets and anyone unfit for duty. A ship's commanding officer, no matter what his seniority, had no authority to make a decision like that on the eve of battle. The executive officer thought of the excited youngsters romping ineffectually up on deck.

"They'll be disappointed," he said.

"They'll be useless to us," said Ariga. "They haven't even had time to find their way around the ship. Besides, we've got to think of the future."

The future? Nomura wondered what that would be. The Japanese navy had very little future once this attack was spent. He hoped something could also be done about the 40-year men, veterans like Chief Quartermaster Koyama, who had served as a boy seaman in the war against the Russians. Quite a number of these veterans still served afloat. They should have been given shore billets years ago. Ariga shook his head. They were short of experienced men. Some of the best gunners had already been taken off to man antiaircraft batteries on the mainland.

"I've advised *Yahagi*," Ariga said. "Order the cadets to assemble in the senior wardroom."

The cadets came in with hangdog looks. They suspected the worst. Ariga looked them over in embarrassed silence. Speaking slowly in affectionate fatherly tones, he told them:

"I know you all want to sail with us. I've thought the matter over carefully. But we are going to Okinawa. I am sorry you cannot come. I understand your feelings, leaving just before this sortie, but we want you to stay behind and fight for us. There will be other *Yamatos* awaiting you. Work hard. Help strengthen the war effort. Bless you."

He bowed and left for the bridge. There was another awkward silence. One of the cadets approached Nomura.

"Executive officer," he pleaded. "We're determined to stay. Please intercede with the captain for us."

"Please," others of the 53 cadets echoed.

Nomura was sympathetic.

"I understand your feelings," he said. "I'd feel the same in your place. But after only three days aboard you'd be more hindrance than help. Take it philosophically."

The cadets refused to give up. A spokesman was elected to tackle Ariga on the bridge. The captain was sitting in his chair in battle uniform. He appeared to be expecting his stammering visitor. Forgetting his rehearsed speech, the young man blurted out a plea to go along on the mission.

Rear Admiral Ariga told him a story every Japanese child knew by heart. Before leaving home to fight his last fateful battle at Minatogawa, Masashige Kusunoki refused to allow his ten-year-old son to accompany him. The heroic warrior was defeated by the overwhelming forces of the Ashikaga shogunate. He very properly committed *seppuku*. But his son lived to fight another day.

Other senior officers gathered round the skipper, voicing agreement. The weeping cadet climbed slowly and sadly back down the steel ladder. No more was said. The tearful group joined ten sick and ten inexperienced young sailors from *Yamato* in the waiting launches.

Captain Tameichi Hara felt he had to give everyone a chance

to quit *Yahagi.* "If any of you believe you can be of better service by skipping this sortie," he told the ship's company, "you are to leave the ship along with the cadets, the sick, and others considered unfit for the mission." He waited in his cabin for some reaction. As he said years afterward, "The idea of herding 1000 men to certain death did not appeal to me." He was surprised to find only 37 men were waiting to leave *Yahagi:* 22 cadets and 15 sick sailors.

"Are there none of the crew who wish to leave?"

"No, sir," the exec replied. "Every man is eager to comply with the orders."

The cadets were far from eager to leave. One of them leaped from the ranks, crying: "Please allow me to stay, sir. I may not be much use but I will do any job if you'll let me." Another tearfully offered to clean latrines. Hara groaned inwardly. He must be firm.

"As skippers of the future your lives must not be wasted," he told them sharply. "My orders are to put you ashore."

He saluted, bowed, and walked off to check the weaponry his crew was preparing for the moment they leaped ashore onto the beaches of Okinawa.

Aboard *Yamato,* Vice Admiral Seiichi Ito calmly prepared to die. He ignored the overnight festivities, the clamor and bustle of fueling the following day. Apart from a brief conference with his staff and another, briefer one with his trusted aides, Morishita and Yamamoto, the admiral left the drafting of detailed operational orders to their skilled judgment. Their task was crudely simple—what more could he hope to add? The rest of the time was spent alone in his in-port cabin, spectacles on the end of his nose, penning farewell notes to his friends and his family. It was the same way Kusunoki spent his last hours centuries before, if legend is to be believed, on the eve of his hopeless stand beside the dried-up bed of the Minato River.

The legendary samurai had for three years shored up the shaky restoration of fickle Emperor Go-Daigo. With the overpowering forces of the Ashikaga clan bearing down upon the luckless monarch, Kusunoki urged the emperor to flee for shelter to the fortified monasteries on Mount Hiei, temporarily abandoning his capital at Kyoto. But Go-Daigo, influenced by whining courtiers, ordered his trusty general to sortie against the rebels as they swept up the Inland Sea.

It was a hopeless task. The loyalist forces were too weak for anything but the kind of guerrilla struggle they had conducted successfully in the past. Kusunoki obeyed, regardless of the grim consequences.

On a blazing July day in 1336 he faced the enemy at the river estuary. A strong Ashikaga force was advancing up the coastal plain, reinforced by a huge fleet of warships and transports. All night before the fatal clash the loyalist general sat committing his last thoughts to posterity. Next morning he strapped on his lacquered armor, unfurled his floating chrysanthemum banner, and fought until all around were dead. Exhausted, bleeding from 11 wounds, he dragged himself to a nearby farmhouse with his brother Masasue. Nothing was left but to take his own life.

Had Masasue one last wish, the hero asked? "I should like to be reborn seven times," his brother replied, "to go on destroying the emperor's enemies." They then disemboweled themselves.

Now it was Ito's turn to meet his end with the same dignified resignation. He was doomed to obey impossible orders. He felt bitter about the thoughtless haste in which those orders were conceived, and hinted as much to his colleagues, but the objective was undeniably noble. The fleet could not stand idly by while the Americans overran Okinawa. The fact that without air support on a scale Japan could no longer muster the naval sortie had no hope of success was immaterial; the very hopelessness of the effort gave it added luster. It might even invoke the sympathy of the gods; love of a well-lost fight is another of those traits the Japanese share with the British. Gallant failures like the charge of the Light Brigade are still more highly prized in Britain than brilliant victories. The one foreign flag officer who earned ungrudging admiration in the Japanese navy during the Pacific war was neither Nimitz nor Mitscher. He was not even American. He was Karel Doorman, Dutch commanding officer of the mixed Allied fleet in the Java Sea, sunk with colors flying in useless defiance of vastly superior Japanese forces.

One glance at the battle chart showed Ito how heavily the odds were stacked against him. Dawn tomorrow, April 7, would find his ships south of Kyushu heading west-northwest into the

East China Sea. They would need to hold this course for about four more hours before turning south toward Okinawa. The northwesterly track might fool the Americans into thinking they were bound for Sasebo as originally planned. It would usefully kill enough time to synchronize *Yamato's* arrival in the midst of the American fleet with the early hours of April 8. The kind of night battle the Japanese excelled at would help reduce the enemy's numerical advantage.

The difficulty was getting into this attractive tactical situation. As Ito had reminded Kusaka, the approach run exposed them to a possible ten hours of daylight air attacks. There would be less than that if the Americans failed to find them soon after first light, but six hours would be bad enough. It had only taken that long to mortally wound *Musashi*. Their slim hopes rested on the weather and on the success of today's Kamikaze strikes against the carriers. Ito trusted neither. He reached for his writing brush . . .

The mail boat was long gone, but Seiichi Ito still had time. The ship's boats were among the combustibles being sent ashore. His own launch waited for final dispatches. Brief notes to old colleagues were piled up on his desk. Now for the farewell to his wife, who was 43. Ito was 54. They had been married 23 years. Neither of them had any say in the matter; this union of proud samurai families was arranged above their heads. Yet they made an exceptionally good match. Even the strict formalities of the day could not conceal his feelings:

To my wife Chitose,

I am proud and highly honored to have received an order to do battle. I will fight with my entire soul trying to give thanks to the emperor for this opportunity, even though it may amount only to one ten-thousandth of the love he has given Japan.

I must take this opportunity to say that the life we have shared was full of happiness. But the time has now come for me, as a naval officer, to prepare to meet my end. I have no doubts at all about asking you, whom I believe in and love, to take over everything after I go. I am truly happy that I can ask this of you.

I know that you will have difficult and lonely times but to make it easier for you, understand that I believe in what I am doing and that in my last moments I shall be happy.

From the deepest part of my heart I am praying for your happiness. My dearest Chitose.

Seiichi

The flag officer predated the letter April 5, the day the operational order was received. He wrote another letter to his two younger daughters, aged 15 and 13, trying to avoid ominous or brooding feelings:

> At this time I am thinking of my two lovely girls and hoping you know your father is going to perform an honorable task for our country. Maybe I won't be able to write you any more letters. My last request is that you will become ladies like your mother. Please take care of yourselves.

An older daughter was married in Tokyo. The only son, a 21-year-old navy lieutenant based in Kyushu, would briefly lead the air escort over *Yamato* next morning. Before Ito could rush off an additional note to the boy, Yamamoto knocked on the door. It was 1508.

The vice admiral stamped his letters with a red-inked ivory seal and gummed down the envelopes. With a little help from his chief of operations he buckled on the family sword, flicked a duster across his gleaming knee boots, pulled on his cap and his white cotton gloves, and marched out into the companionway, taking a last, quick glance at the cabin he did not expect to see again.

Ariga sat humming to himself in his aerie atop the tower. The fuel barges were gone. A solitary launch swung at the lower boom abeam the after ladder. As the skipper watched, an officer hurried over the side with a sealed bag of dispatches. He handed them to one of the Tokuyama men waiting in the launch. A crewman slipped the line and the launch headed for shore. Ariga looked impatiently at his watch. They were running late. It was 1518. The force had been scheduled to sail at 1500.

The voice-pipe shrilled. It was the executive officer. Vice Admiral Ito was on his way to number one bridge. Ariga hauled himself off his high chair and tramped down the communications ladder. He saluted the fleet commander and reported all ready for sea.

"Carry on, rear admiral," replied Ito.

Ariga saluted again.

"Weigh anchor," Ariga ordered.

"Weigh anchor," shouted the signals officer.

"Weigh anchor," echoed the signalmen on the portside platform projecting from the bridge. No need to rummage in the
lockers for the requisite bunting: they'd had the "Able Charlie"
flags bent onto the halyards for the past half hour. As the signal
whipped to the yard, acknowledging pennants shot up around
the fleet.

The anchor party in the battleship's bow stood squinting up
at the tower. They had already recoupled the cable and taken
in a few spare meters of chain. When the signal hoist shot down,
the bosun in charge clanked the cable in, link after massive link.
Hoses siphoned off the mud before the chain vanished into its
locker. A signalman stood by with semaphore flags ready to
report each incoming meter and finally, "STRAIGHT UP AND
DOWN," the moment the anchor was ready to leave the seabed.
The same drill was being enacted, on a smaller scale, throughout the fleet.

The shank of the 12-ton bower anchor broke surface. The signalman flagged "FREE AND CLEAR." A word from Ariga on the
tower, the engine room telegraphs clanged "SLOW AHEAD ALL
ENGINES" and the great ship gathered way, spray sluicing over
the still rising anchor flukes. It was 1524. Another hoist of multicolored signal flags brought the force swiftly into formation,
Yahagi in the lead, the destroyers disposed in columns on either
beam of the battleship. Ahead of them cruised a guardian escort
of only four minesweepers, all that the fuel shortage would
allow. But out on the port beam came an unexpected send-off
from three destroyers, which accompanied them a few miles
before turning off to Kure. Their fuel tanks were almost empty.

More bunting: "COURSE 175°" to take them past Hime Island
and the bulbous Kunisaki peninsula which forms the northwestern corner of Kyushu. The extinct cone of Mount Futago
was splashed pink, on the lower slopes, with blooming cherry.
Clusters of trees flaunted their blossoms in the depths of Beppu
Bay, famous for its hot springs. Beyond that was Mount Yufu,
often called Bungo-Fuji because of its resemblance to the sacred
mountain. The Saganoseki peninsula reached out without quite
touching the fingerlike projection of fur-capped rocky hills from
nearby Shikoku Island. Between them the Hoyo Strait led into
the wider, deeper Bungo Strait and the open sea.

The hands crowded the rails for a last glimpse of their homeland. Most of them were Honshu men, recruited from Hiroshima, Kure, and as far up the coast as Kobe, but this wild southern region was still home. The young gunner Masanobu Kobayashi was a stranger among them, coming as he did from close to Tokyo. The navy preferred to pick its crews from selected districts. The army did the same when it formed local regiments. But volunteers, especially those who enlisted in such out-of-the-way places as Manchuria, were apt to be posted anywhere around the fleet.

The entire crew seemed to find some excuse to crowd on deck; even the engineers, deserting their great throbbing engine rooms, took turns staring wistfully at the passing landscape, grabbing a quick smoke, wiping their oily hands on bundles of cotton waste. Idle sightseeing was not ordinarily allowed, but this was no ordinary occasion.

The ship's company mustered forward as the task force entered the Bungo Strait. The sun was plunging toward the Kyushu mountains. It went down, a glowing symbolic orb of fire, burning a peephole through the gathering overcast. High winds far above shredded the pink-tinged clouds into mare's tails. Any sailor knew this heralded a change of weather. Perhaps the gods would blanket their advance beneath a stormy curtain.

Nomura deputized for Ariga on top of A turret. A light wind clutched at his cap as the ships crept forward at 12 knots behind the screening sweepers. The exec fastened the leather strap under his chin and read a brief order of the day from Vice Admiral Ito: "This operation will be the turning point of the war. The future of the empire rests on our efforts. Every man will do his utmost for the glory of the Imperial Navy and of Japan."

It was reminiscent of the great Admiral Heihachiro Togo's signal, raised at 1345 on May 27, 1905, as he closed the Russians in Tsushima Strait. This was based, in turn, on Nelson's signal before the equally historic battle of Trafalgar.

The forecastle became a sea of fluttering caps as the crew roared the ritual banzais. The sun died away behind bars of broken cloud. Kyushu turned misty mauve, then black, a serrated cutout on a golden sea. A waning moon took temporary command of the darkening night sky.

Captain Hara felt the need to add a few words of clarification to *Yahagi's* crew. Their mission might be suicidal, but suicide was not the objective. The objective was victory.

"Do not hesitate to come back alive," he said. "Once this ship is crippled or sunk, do not hesitate to save yourselves for the next fight. There will be other battles. You are not to commit suicide. You are to beat the enemy!"

There was a puzzled silence. The captain was contradicting basic naval doctrine. Lieutenant Kenji Hatta, his smartest young officer, respectfully said so. It had been dinned into him throughout his years at the academy that an officer should die with his ship. The captain explained that times had changed. There was a crucial lack of skilled manpower. Ships could be replaced, but it took five years to train a naval officer. The casualty rate among Etajima graduates which had averaged 5 percent since the academy was founded 85 years before, was now running at 95 percent. Too many had already died through a misplaced belief that this was expected conduct under the Bushido code. Hatta appeared satisifed and joined in three cheers for the emperor.

Ensign Mitsuru Yoshida stood behind Vice Admiral Ito on *Yamato's* darkening bridge. The chief of staff of the task force, Rear Admiral Nubii Morishita, leaned out of a starboard window, smoking a cigarette behind cupped hands. The instruments glowed dim red; just bright enough to read but not enough to impair a man's night vision. Yoshida's job, when he was not in the radar room, was to relay lookouts' reports. His fellow ensign Mitsuo Watanabe manned the talk-between-ships (TBS) on the port side of the bridge beside the chart table. The place seemed large enough when empty, but now it was crowded with staff officers, signalmen, and messengers. The radar room was crowded, too, with some 20 men on watch. Aircraft were registering on the tubes, but they were friendly. Floatplanes from the Saeki Air Station further down the Kyushu coast were combing the channel for enemy submarines.

Ito ordered the escorts into a brief round of simulated attacks upon *Yamato;* it was the only chance the torpedo crews would have of lining up a target before they met the Americans. *Yahagi* surged off first at her full 35 knots, swinging in a wide arc that glistened in the twilight. She raced toward the battleship, turning onto a parallel course at 8000 yards before pretending to launch torpedoes into *Yamato*. The battleship's main turrets kept the attacker in their sights. One broadside at this range and the cruiser would be blown to bits. The destroyers took their turns in a fine flurry of spray before Ito ordered Watanabe to secure the intership VHF radio. It might be monitored by the submarines already reported in the vicinity. An emergency signal from escorts 100 miles farther south warned they were depth-charging a contact.

The floatplanes still growled overhead. So far they had sighted nothing. Enemy submarines were lurking there in force—the pilots felt sure of it—but the floatplanes' radar equipment was not powerful enough to detect one on the surface. The target was too small. The Japanese were way behind the Allies in the development of airborne centimetric sub-spotting radar. Each plane carried a 120-kilogram (264-pound) bomb slung under the starboard wing—more than enough, given a precise hit, to blow a submarine apart. There was little chance of spotting one, however, in the dying light. At about 1940 a hydrophone operator in one of the destroyers thought he heard a submarine cruising on the surface. A coded message passed furtively round the force by night signaling lamp. It ordered number one cruising formation, speed 22 knots, "I" zigzag, a simultaneous course change of 20° at five-minute intervals. *Yamato* took up station in the rear, *Yahagi* on her port bow with the destroyers in arrowhead around them.

Now it was pitch dark. Lookouts were understandably jumpy. Periscopes and torpedo tracks were sighted in all directions. *Asashimo* was sent off to investigate. But at this speed the task force would be difficult to hit and impossible to follow. Vice Admiral Ito climbed down one deck from the bridge to his small sea cabin for a quick supper. Ariga stretched out in a deck chair in its lonely command post on top of the tower, munching rice crackers, critically watching his newly appointed navigating officer handle the high-speed dash close to the Kyushu coast. Tricky waters round here, he warned, with all navigation beacons doused. The navigator nodded nervously. Ten days in the ship and here he was zigzagging in fast formation three miles off a treacherous combination of islands, cliffs, and submerged reefs. He couldn't wait to finish his watch.

The phone shrilled at Ariga's elbow shortly after 2030. Coded signal transmissions were being picked up somewhere in the vicinity. They could only come from a submarine. The Americans had spotted them. Bugles sounded general quarters. Escorts closed in around *Yamato* to fend off torpedo attack.

U.S. Submarines,
Bungo Strait

EVENING, APRIL 6

THEY'D BEEN SUBMERGED since dawn. Their position, according to the chart, was 10 miles south of Fukashima, a tiny island at the mouth of the Bungo Strait. But the crew of the U.S. submarine *Threadfin* took a more dramatic view of their location. They were poised on the threshold of the hall of fame. Here off the most desolate stretch of the east Kyushu coast an Ultra (secret) signal from Hawaii had warned them to expect a sortie by *Yamato* and the surviving remnants of the Japanese fleet.

There was only one snag, as far as the submarine was concerned. All boats in the area were under strict orders to delay attacking until they got direct permission from "Uncle Charlie" Lockwood, the Pacific submarine commander, now aboard his tender *Holland* in Guam. The brass feared a premature attack might lead to the submarine being sunk before a sighting report could be coded, dispatched, and above all, received. It was not always easy to break through the mass of radio traffic converging on Pearl. The precaution was understandable: two U.S. subs had been lost in these waters in the past month.

Today there were encouraging signs of unusual activity. The most *Threadfin* had seen so far, after 23 days at sea, was a

177

swamped sampan wallowing off the Japanese coast with a dead fisherman lashed to the mast. Now there were aircraft scouring the entrance to the channel. Nakajima A 6M2-N (Rufe) float-planes, lumbering adaptations of the ubiquitous Zero, were cruising low over the sunlit Pacific swell as it rolled in to explode on the sheer Kyushu cliffs and cluttered, myriad islets. One plane appeared suddenly overhead, forcing the skipper, Commander John J. Foote, to ease down to 100 feet—but not before he had spotted two vessels 6 miles off in the mouth of the channel, bearing directly down on him.

They appeared to be 940-ton escorts of the *Ukuru* class, hast-ily constructed ships of the most basic design, ordered in 1944 when the Japanese realized, too late, that the American sub-marine campaign was strangling their war effort. Eyes glued to the scope, John Foote ordered the forward torpedo doors opened. A sudden change of course took the targets closer into the coast, their sonar pinging, lookouts scanning the listless sea.

The arrival of that wretched Rufe and then seven more of them, flying a tight search formation 100 feet above the channel mouth, was excuse enough to postpone an attack. Tension noticeably relaxed inside the crowded tube of welded steel where men worked, ate, and slept cheek by jowl for weeks on end, encased in pipes and dials and the frail, dripping shell of the pressure hull which even the inefficient Japanese depth charges could buckle and puncture in a few seconds. All hands agreed: the appearance of these two sub hunters meant only one thing: the target of a lifetime was approaching.

Threadfin was not alone. The brand-new *Hackleback*, on her first war patrol, covered the eastern approaches to the Bungo Strait 20 miles farther south. Fifteen other boats lurked nearby. Some were "lifeguards" posted to pick up the crews of ditched B-29s. Most were watching for *Yamato*. There was little else worthy of their attention. Supply ships no longer ventured into these waters. Escorts were too short of fuel to convoy them; nor were there ever enough to ward off the huge American subma-rine fleet, which by the spring of 1945 had swept the high seas almost clean of Japanese shipping.

The Imperial Navy gave surprisingly little thought to the pro-tection of sea-lanes when drawing up its otherwise detailed plans for war. This was partly the influence of British naval thinking, which chose to ignore, for equally inexplicable reasons, the lessons of 1916–17. The development of asdic, the original British name for sonar, lulled the lords of admiralty into believing an effective antidote to the submarine had at last been found. Besides, Britain's limited resources could no longer support the full panoply of naval power, including an adequate escort force.

The Japanese were similarly strapped. With their doctrinal emphasis on attack they preferred to invest in battleships, carriers, cruisers, and just enough destroyers to screen them. Working on the premise of a short, sharp sea war, settled in one "decisive" battle, they were unprepared for a lengthy attritional campaign directed not only against their battle fleet but at the vulnerable supply line to their newly captured empire in southeast Asia.

The Americans, for their part, were slow to slash at this inviting jugular. They too failed to grasp the real potential of undersea warfare. American pioneers like Bushnell, Fulton, and Holland once led the world in submarine theory and development. But blinded by big-ship ambitions, ignoring the impact of the Kaiser's U-boat campaign, U.S. admirals in the interwar years assigned their neglected submarine force to a supporting role. Just as the aircraft carrier was only the scouting eyes of the main battle fleet, the submarine was expected to hunt for enemy capital ships, especially when the fleets met for their destined showdown.

The Pearl Harbor attack deprived the U.S. submarine force of its battle fleet. It also provided a convenient excuse to revoke Washington's many pious interwar promises never to engage in unrestricted submarine warfare. American revulsion at the sinking of the Lusitania had helped propel the United States into World War I. But now, overnight, the Japanese became fair game.

Unfortunately the U.S. Navy had only the vaguest idea of how to conduct a ruthless, sink-'em-all submarine campaign. Standard naval doctrine habitually exaggerated the submarine's vulnerability. The appearance of aircraft within a hundred miles sent skippers crash-diving to the depths. Aging regulars staged timid, unimaginative patrols. The bolder, younger submariners were plagued by persistent failure of the Mark XIV torpedo—undoubtedly one of the major scandals of World War II—and it was not until the Pacific campaign was half over that the faults were rectified.

It took almost as long to weed out the deadwood and reshape tactical doctrine to concentrate on busy choke points like the Luzon Strait and around the imperial homeland. Only then was the U.S. submarine force able to cut the flow of fuel and raw materials and throttle the now wheezing Japanese war machine.

The struggle was unnecessarily prolonged. Properly directed from the start, U.S. submarines could have brought Japan to her present plight almost a year earlier. Without food and fuel the island empire was doomed. The costly invasions of Iwo Jima and Okinawa, the atomic bombing of Hiroshima and Nagasaki might never have been necessary . . . As it was, the Americans lost a total of 52 submarines in this little-publicized war. Twenty-two percent of the force lost their lives: the highest casualty rate of any U.S. service branch. The subs sank 1314 Japanese naval and merchant ships totaling 5.3 million tons, or 55 percent of all enemy losses. Of the 122,000 men in the Japanese merchant marine at the start of the war, 27,000 were killed and 89,000 injured . . .

Threadfin kept a wary eye on the floatplanes. Skippers no longer panicked when they spotted an aircraft—they were growing positively cocky these days—but these pilots meant business. U.S. submarines were around, this much the Japanese knew; so far they had failed to spot one. The two escorts were serenely steaming 8 miles down the coast, unaware of their watching quarry.

At 1647 two more ships were sighted: tiny auxiliary minesweepers, some 215 tons apiece, built in trawler yards under the emergency program. They began sweeping a stretch of inshore waters, well inside the 100-fathom line, between the rocky extrusion marked on the charts as Sen Seki and a point 2 miles clear of Fukashima. It was a logical exit for any task force planning to clear the Bungo Strait without straying too far from the shoreline. It was not only a difficult spot for a submarine intercept, but also for surface craft, whose room for maneuver was limited. John Foote worked to within 5000 yards of the busy sweepers to await developments.

A little over an hour later the sub hunters down the coast

began depth-charging. They dropped more than 50 charges at regular intervals during the next 90 minutes until sunset repainted the pastel spring seascape in tones of somber mauve and purple. Who could they be attacking? Surely not *Hackleback*, unless she had strayed way out of her designated area.

The men aboard *Hackleback* were asking themselves the same question. The explosions sounded muffled and distant to them, lying way off in the depths at the eastern edge of the Bungo Strait. The ocean floor fell away sharply here: a hull-crushing 900 fathoms lay beneath their keel. Perhaps *Threadfin* had run into trouble? It seemed unlikely if John Foote was sticking to his orders. He should be farther north, 20 miles away on their port beam.

Lieutenant Commander Frederick E. Janney of Winnetka, Illinois, was on his 11th war patrol, his first as commanding officer. Few envied him this boat. *Hackleback* was a product of the Cramp Shipbuilding Company in Philadelphia, a yard plagued by labor troubles and inefficient management. With four operational slipways, Cramp produced only seven submarines throughout the war. Four more on order had to be finished elsewhere. *Hackleback* took 22 months to build, commission, and shakedown. Still there were complaints about the workmanship.

The Cramp case was unusual. Most U.S. yards adapted superbly to the production line methods which first enriched Henry Ford. They were lucky in that most of the prototypes, like the *Essex*-class carriers, had already been perfected before the United States went to war. The standard fleet submarine, so suited to action in the wide Pacific, the *Balao* class, was sired by the earlier *Gatos* out of the prewar *Tambors*. Displacing 1526 tons, with a 5-inch gun and ten 21-inch torpedo tubes, these all-welded boats could hit 19 knots on the surface and 8 knots submerged. They were equipped with air conditioning and an increasing profusion of gadgetry, including a primitive torpedo data computer (TDC) designed to plot a target's course from all available visual, sonar, and radar information.

After the war the Americans were surprised to find the Germans equipped with superior submarines, which were faster underwater and used a snorkel breathing tube that did away with the need to surface at night to charge batteries. And there was no disputing that the Japanese led in torpedoes. The U.S. Bureau of Ordnance was too occupied with the pork-barrel hassle surrounding the bug-ridden Mark XIV torpedo to develop anything as lethal as the Japanese Long Lance.

Fred Janney passed up his first target, a shallow-draft patrol boat. It looked to him like a landing craft. He was right: the Japanese were using 80-ton type L transporters with bow ramps as auxiliary patrol ships. But now they carried passive sonar, depth charges, and type 22 radar. Scarcely worth a torpedo. At 1815 another of these strangely shaped boats hove in sight, followed swiftly by a third. *Hackleback's* sonar picked up no sound of enemy echo ranging, the underwater pulse sent out to bounce off and betray their submerged sub. The Japanese must be listening on their hydrophones for telltale engine sounds. With all extraneous noise damped down, including the air conditioning, Janney worked his way southwest around the patrol. So much antisubmarine activity must mean something was coming out of the Bungo Strait tonight. He wanted to be in position to surface as soon as possible.

Hackleback and *Threadfin* were not part of a wolf pack. The latter had been assigned to one, tentatively named Hydeman's Hellcats after the commanding officer of *Sea Dog*, but the idea was abandoned when the veteran *Trigger* failed to join them at the end of March. *Trigger* was now assumed lost. *Silversides* was ordered to backstop the two guardians at the mouth of the channel. Farther south lurked three more boats, including *Lionfish*, commanded by Admiral Spruance's son Edward. He might yet be able to beat his father to the punch.

By 1930 it was almost dark. *Threadfish* picked up the sound of high-speed propellers to the north. The radar-equipped night periscope gave a range of 6¼ miles. Possibly it was minesweepers. The submarine surfaced and John Foote thankfully left the cramped quarters of the conning tower, where he seemed to have spent most of his waking hours, to shiver in the cool night air blowing northeasterly across his open bridge. A calm sea gurgled along the gray steel hull. Three watchmen shared his exposed perch, alert for approaching planes and ships. Everyone below toiled at his well-drilled task, tense, silent, expectant in the knowledge that after weeks of routine boredom, this could be the night they'd waited for.

Fukashima lay curtained off by darkness, 8 miles away; but it was visible on the pale green scope of the plan position indicator (PPI), which provided a moving radar map for miles around. The island showed up as a glowing green dot, dying and then reviving as the radar beam maintained its remorseless sweep. But there seemed to be something else ... the skipper was hardly settled at his post, eyes accustomed to the enshrouding gloom, when four pips broke free of the land clutter. The nearest two were 5.3 miles away, moving at 25 knots. Two minutes later they became two large ships and at least four small ones.

Threadfin switched on all main engines. The four new nine-cylinder Fairbanks Morse diesels roared into life. The submarine thrust forward, clouds of exhaust smoke billowing from the hull vents. John Foote hugged the target bearing transmitter, a pair of night binoculars which automatically provided a bearing, chanting "Stand by, stand by, mark!" to the plotting parties crouched beneath him in the conning tower. The dimly lit computer kept track of the countless variables, the boat's own erratic course, the zigzagging target, bearing, speed, range: every component of the constantly fluctuating equation which must be solved before a torpedo can be fired in time to run several miles and still hit home.

The setup looked perfect. Excitement mounted as the nearest ship closed to just under 4 miles. It was a destroyer plowing ahead of two larger targets inside the screen. They were there for the taking! The forward torpedo tubes were cleared for action, the doubled plotting crew called off range and bearing. A few minutes more and it would be too late.

John Foote cursed his orders. The contact report must be cleared first. A scribbled course, speed, and target description was rushed down the two flights of ladders into the radio room for coding and transmission. It seemed to take forever. Meanwhile they must maintain their position. Desperately the skipper screamed to the control room: "Give her a five-minute blow! Blow safety! Blow negative!" The low-pressure pump began expelling the last residues from the ballast tanks in order to lighten the boat.

Another agonized yell from the bridge: "Speed. Give me more speed."

The electrician's mates cautiously advanced the rheostats

beyond the safety limit. A few more amperes reached the rack-eting engines. The propellers picked up an additional four or five revs but the pitometer log read only 19½ knots. And the enemy was hitting 25!

Every man and his dog seemed to be calling Pearl. The air waves were cluttered with signal traffic. The blaspheming *Threadfin* operator tapped out NPN . . . IIIJ: "RADIO PEARL, VERY URGENT. . ."

The enemy force steamed directly toward them. If they stayed here on the surface much longer Foote expected a blast of radar-controlled gunfire. He overestimated Japanese technology. But the leading destroyer, probably *Isokaze*, was getting dangerously close. He altered course to run parallel with his onrushing targets. The engines strained to keep pace. Every man jack of the crew held his breath, hoping for the best. "The best never occurred," Foote wrote ruefully in his patrol report. "The contact report was not cleared until 2000, by which time *Threadfin's* chance for the hall of fame [had] passed."

He watched helplessly from the bridge as the Japanese destroyers formed an antisubmarine screen around the two big ships. He reckoned there must be eight of them in all. His frustration was compounded by the obvious fact that the enemy destroyers were blissfully unaware of the submarine's presence. At 1956 the nearest destroyer (still *Isokaze*) was abeam at the ideal range of 5000 yards. A milk-white bow wave leaped halfway up her gracefully sheered forecastle. Her twin smokestacks cleft the night sky above the murky backdrop of Kyushu. The two ships she was screening remained invisible to the human eye. One of them left such a big blip on the radar it could be a carrier.

The formation began zigzagging at 2011, so radically that the range to *Threadfin* rapidly widened. The bigger ships were already beyond the range of low-power torpedo runs. The Japanese reduced speed slightly to 22 knots, but that did not help. The outpaced submarine was falling gradually away on their port quarter. It was scant consolation to learn at 2020 that the contact report had finally been received at Pearl. But the game was not quite over. A radical zig to port brought the force directly across *Threadfin's* bow. A yell from Foote sent fresh shivers through the crew.

"This is a shooting observation. Are the torpedoes ready?"

"Shooting observation. All tubes ready, sir," came the voice from the TDC. "Depth setting 15 feet. Range five oh double oh. Angle on the bow, starboard eight oh. All ready to shoot, sir!"

A destroyer was passing 5000 yards ahead. The large ships were a further 4000 yards away. TDC reconfirmed the course, the skipper prepared to fire ... just as the targets zigzagged away again out of torpedo range. The chase was over. Their last remaining hope was that a hit from *Hackleback* or *Silversides* would slow the enemy enough for *Threadfin* to catch up for the kill.

It was just about this time, close to 2030, that Fred Janney made contact. The first radar pip, over 17 miles away, was so weak it could be an aircraft. Closing rapidly, it was soon recognizable as a large warship. A contact report flashed off to the alerted operators at Pearl. By now they were all ears. Repeats were already heading toward Nimitz in his Guam quonset, Charlie Lockwood lingering over coffee on *Holland*, Spruance unwinding with Dvorak aboard *New Mexico*, and Mitscher, stretched out with his usual pulp detective saga.

Search aircraft resumed combing the Bungo Strait. They did not seem to have radar, though the Americans couldn't be certain. One plane circled at a distance of 4 miles without spotting the surfaced submarine. *Hackleback* surged ahead at flank speed on all engines. Spray flew high over the bridge. Waves crashed across the forward deck.

Six pips were now appearing on the radar, one considerably larger than the others. Range just over 11 miles and coming on fast. Four minutes later, with the presumed task force 8 miles away, the scope revealed a seventh contact. No doubt about it: this was what they had been waiting for! The small, skilled team crouched over the TDC set up a torpedo attack on the closest pip, one of the outside destroyer screen. The target was almost certainly *Hatsushimo*. A second, more detailed report of seven contacts heading south at 20 knots had scarcely been tapped out in the radio shack when lookouts on the bridge saw signal lights blinking between the enemy ships. One of the escorting destroyers turned toward *Hackleback*.

"Immediately the destroyer commenced closing us at high

speed," Janney wrote in his report. "We put our stern to him, thus losing bearing on the task force, but when the range closed to 10,000 yards the destroyer turned off and opened to 13,500 yards."

Hackleback struggled to catch up again. The hull vibrated, the engines howled, and waves broke over the bridge. The skipper puzzled over the radar pips. The big one in the center seemed too big for a battleship. Like his colleague in *Threadfin*, he reckoned it could only be a carrier, and a big one at that. Yet they had been warned to expect *Yamato*.

The enemy zigzagged 25° and increased speed to 22 knots. Again the TDC team drew a bead on the nearest destroyer (probably *Asashimo*); again signaling sent the potential target racing toward the submarine. The destroyer swung away without pressing the attack. The third time this happened, around 2130, Janney felt sure the destroyer meant business. The enemy ship headed toward them at 30 knots. Her bow wave flared up at them from the darkness. This time, surely, they'd been detected. Expecting a broadside of radar-controlled gunfire, the skipper was preparing to dive when at 9000 yards the enemy sheered off again. The hunter was being harassed, if not exactly hunted.

Evasive action lost *Hackleback* more precious mileage. A lot more speed would be needed than these engines could muster if they were to catch up. The task force was over 11 miles away and gaining. A course change to south-southwest at 2155 put the enemy stern-on to the disappointed submariners. Twelve minutes later, contact was lost. Other boats, *Silversides* among them, monitored the contact reports but saw nothing.

The crowning blow came at 2300. A dispatch deciphered in *Threadfin* revoked the order to submit reports before attacking. "The less said about our feelings at this stage of our careers the better," John Foote noted. He cruised sourly back to the patrol area, cussing his missed chances in the hall of fame.

PART
IV

APRIL 6-7, 1945
Night

Japanese Submarine, Approaching Okinawa

NIGHT, APRIL 6

THEY JUST WEREN'T going to make it. The sea was rough, the batteries were down, enemy aircraft were everywhere. The closer they crept to Okinawa, the worse it became. The suicide mission would have to be postponed. Lieutenant Commander Mochitsura Hashimoto reached his decision after hours of careful deliberation. He knew his job. He knew his enemy. That way he had survived three years of submarine warfare. He eased *I-58* cautiously toward the surface.

Crouched in the conning tower, the veteran skipper checked out his surroundings with the night scope. Outside it was black as the devil's armpit. Wind-tossed waves kept frothing across the periscope lens. He ordered up the radar antenna. The submarine was newly equipped with the improved type 22 set which picked up patrol planes 70 miles away. The glowing emerald scope was empty.

Pumps whined as ballast tanks were blown: the bow bit through the stormy waters until the low black silhouette of the conning tower was up and clear. The steel hull was treated with pebbly, asphalt preparation to reduce radar reflection; thus far this had proved notoriously ineffective. Ever since leaving the

Bungo Strait two days before, on April 4, they had been ceaselessly harassed from the air. The boat was seldom able to stay
on the surface longer than ten minutes. Four hours were
needed, cruising surfaced at night, for a minimal battery
recharge. Very soon they would be in trouble.

Hashimoto dashed up to the dripping bridge, followed by his
seven handpicked lookouts. He had learned not to rely solely on
radar. American patrol planes carried equipment which could
pick up *I-58*'s slight protrusions 30 miles away. At any moment
a searchlight could snap on from the sky or an aerial depth
charge could crash down from nowhere. The lieutenant commander headed the submarine into the swell—anything to stop
this sickening rolling—turned on a quick, invigorating blast of
diesel power, and took hasty stock of the situation.

It was pretty much what he feared. A gusty northeasterly
breeze whipped foam off the wave caps. Spray lashed the
bridge, leaving everyone soaked and chattering with cold. A
man on a lifeline groped his way down to the foredeck to check
the four large, cigar-shaped cylinders. He did not dawdle. The
boat might be forced to dive at any moment. Anyone caught
out there would be left to drown. As it was, the *Kaiten* suicide
torpedoes were still secure in their lashings. But they were quite
unusable in this weather.

Storm clouds scudded across the sky, obscuring the stars and
destroying all chance of grabbing a quick star sight. The underemployed sextant remained in its waterproof box. They had
been navigating for two days now by dead reckoning and had
only the vaguest idea of their position. The track kept by the
executive officer, Lieutenant Shigeyoshi Miwa, put them some
50 miles east of Amami-O-shima, the last big island in the Ryukyu chain before Okinawa. If that was correct (and it wasn't),
they could be 60 miles from the Hagushi invasion beaches. All
around lay small islands and reefs waiting to trap anyone foolish
enough to go groping blind through these tricky waters. The
strong current overtaxed their engines and bore them slowly
toward shore. Soon they would skirt the western edge of the
main Japanese minefield stretching across the East China Sea
all the way from Shanghai.

Lieutenant Commander Hashimoto, 59th class of Etajima, 35-
year-old commander of His Imperial Majesty's submarine *I-58*,

had learned one hard lesson from the war: the art of patience. Much of his professional life had been devoted to submarines since his graduation in 1931. He was probably the most competent submarine officer in Japan. He was also a considerable authority on technical innovation and design. Just before this commission he had been conducting sound transmission experiments aboard the obsolete *I-158* in the Bungo Strait. Early in 1944 he sent an underwater message 330 miles to Nagoya from off the hot-spring resort of Beppu, close to the spot *Yamato* had passed this very afternoon.

The lieutenant commander knew all the tricks for staying alive. The never-ending watch for aircraft. The stealthy game of hide-and-seek at extreme depth, the hull groaning under the water pressure, the sub edging away at snail's pace from the alerted enemy. Nerve-searing hours when perspiration poured down men's faces as they tiptoed about their tasks and the air grew foul, instruments misted up, and the walls, pipes, and bulkheads of their submerged steel coffin ran with condensed moisture.

Those were the testing times when discipline and training paid off; a minor mistake by any of them—the gray-faced men controlling the hydroplanes, the sonar operators, the skipper himself—would bring swift oblivion. So far he had been lucky. He had survived when so many friends and colleagues failed to return. Sometimes the enemy announced a kill which might pinpoint a particular boat. All too often there was silence. And more names went down on the lengthening roll of honor.

It was getting to the point where submarine skippers were hesitating to report their positions. The enemy had some secret means of fixing their location by monitoring the boats' VHF radio transmissions. Yet those hidebound bureaucrats back in Kure still insisted on regular reports. Pleas to allow individual skippers more personal initiative went persistently ignored. Hashimoto's last instruction on leaving Kure was to signal at 12 hourly intervals. *I-58*'s last report was long overdue. Yet how could he risk 100 men's lives and the survival of his boat by breaking radio silence on the enemy's doorstep? There were good reasons for suspecting that the Americans were somehow breaking the Japanese codes.

He decided to postpone the mission. He would work his way

back toward the China coast, surface, recharge, report, hastily change position, and resume the attack. By that time *Yamato* should be in the area. The submarine had been radioed full details of the sortie. Better if he tagged along with the battleship; in any big surface action there were always plenty of pickings for a submarine . . .

A sudden warning came from the radar operator just below them in the conning tower. Enemy aircraft were approaching from the southwest. Hashimoto pressed the alarm bell, yelling "Dive!" into his telephone. The Imperial Navy used more complicated diving orders in peacetime. Procedures were simplified after a few inexperienced officers froze with fright and failed to get the rulebook orders out in time. One word was enough to set the lookouts slithering down the slippery steel ladder, followed by their bulky skipper. He had scarcely slammed and locked the conning-tower hatch before the hydroplane operators were guiding them down. Key men, these operators. Every man's life hung on their nimble judgments. A wrong twist of the big steel wheels could shoot the sub up to the surface again, where depth charges would swiftly finish them off, or drop the sub to depths that cracked its pressure hull like an eggshell. Hashimoto picked his operators himself, much to the annoyance of the personnel officers back at base who swore he was poaching on their prerogatives . . .

Japan had entered the Pacific war with over 60 submarines. They were sturdy boats, ideal for long-range operations across this interminable ocean, manned by experienced crews and armed with effective torpedoes. Like the Americans, the Japanese failed to appreciate the potency of their undersea weapons; unlike the more adaptable enemy, they persisted in their tactical fallacies. Throughout the Pacific war, Combined Fleet insisted on treating the submarine as a fleet weapon, an adjunct to the main strike force, useful for scouting out or attacking enemy warships. Early successes like the sinking of the carriers *Wasp* and *Yorktown* and damaging the battleship *North Carolina* appeared to vindicate these tactics. But the myopic big-ship mentality which pervaded all Japanese naval planning soon assigned submarines a secondary role. No sooner had growing American air superiority prevented freighters from getting through to outlying island garrisons than submarines were diverted to the task. Scarce resources were consumed building a special class of boat capable of transporting fuel ammunition and foodstuffs.

Nothing better illustrated Japan's inability to fight a prolonged war than this anarchic submarine building program, which paralleled the failure to produce a new generation of combat planes. Designers frittered away their time turning out the smallest, the largest, the slowest, and the fastest submarines in the world without concentrating on mass-produced boats capable of spreading the undersea war the length and breadth of the Pacific. That was not part of the master plan. Combined Fleet had geared itself to a swift campaign of conquest followed by a negotiated peace. Once it became obvious that the enemy stubbornly refused to admit defeat, the strategists in Hiyoshi ran out of ideas. Instead of concentrating on an all-out submarine war against the vast and vulnerable American supply lines crisscrossing the Pacific, they searched vainly for more dramatic solutions.

On September 9, 1942, a former farm boy, Warrant Officer Nobu Fujita, flew a tiny 300 Lp seaplane off the 3000-ton submarine *I-25* and dropped a small load of high explosive and incendiary bombs into the coastal forests of Oregon. The attack passed unnoticed, except at Hiyoshi. Staff planners became obsessed with hopes of carrying the war to the United States. Work began on Type STo, a 6000-ton submarine with a range of 37,500 miles and a crew of 144. It was the biggest boat built by any combatant during the war, or for years afterward; so big, in fact, that when surfaced the submarine erected a dummy smokestack abaft the conning tower to camouflage itself as a freighter. Three seaplanes were stowed in a deck compartment. Their prime target was the Panama Canal.

The idea, of course, was absurd. The seaplanes could not be carried ready assembled. Even these monster subs were not big enough for that. Each machine had to be taken out, piece by piece, from the big, bulbous deck hangar and put together while the submarine cruised on the surface; a dangerously time-consuming business in waters close to any major target. Nor were the planes capable of carrying a damaging bomb load. The idea of bombing the canal, however, still fired the imagination of Japanese admirals long after the bulk of U.S. and Allied naval reinforcements were streaming out to the Pacific through the Mediterranean or going around South Africa.

Another questionable scheme launched shortly after Pearl Harbor might have enabled Japan to make token long-distance strategic bombing raids. The 4000-ton type SH boats (only one of which was finally completed) were designed to carry aircrew, fuel, and weaponry for flying boats. *I-351* was designed to rendezvous with aircraft at remote Pacific lagoons and refuel them for raids on the U.S. West Coast. The plan came to nothing.

Type ST (*sen taka*, "submarine, high speed") was developed from German designs toward the end of the war. Its streamlined hull could cut through the water at the unprecedented submerged speed of 19 knots. By then it was too late. Production of conventional craft was coming to a standstill. Only three of these remarkable boats were completed. Properly employed, they could have preyed heavily on enemy supply traffic.

Small coastal craft weighing less than 400 tons also diverted the designers. These type STS boats were highly maneuverable, capable of diving to 350 feet, hitting 13 knots submerged. None saw action, although they might have proved menacing had the Allies been forced to proceed with the invasion of Japan.

The Americans meanwhile brought sub hunting to a fine art. Many skippers were veterans of the battle of the Atlantic. Their myriad escorts employed the latest radar, sonar, telltale sonobuoys, and the deadly "hedgehog" rocket which rained patterns of impact explosives around a suspected contact. Unlike depth charges, the rockets made no sound unless they hit. It was little use telling green submariners: "If that happens, you won't need to care anyway." The suspense was electric as propellers stopped threshing overhead and the escorts vectored in on their hidden prey. Better to endure the crash of underwater charges that bruised the pressure hull, smashed crockery, warped doors, and started leaks in the bilges . . . better that than hours of eerie silence, wondering what the enemy was up to. Some skippers stayed down until their air and batteries were almost exhausted, then shot up to fight it out. Most of them met a blast of gunfire that sent them promptly to the bottom. A few found the sea empty. It was very much a matter of luck.

By April 1945 hesitation, experimentation, and decimation had reduced the once proud Japanese submarine fleet to about eight active attack boats. The rest were reserved for training or transportation, while fuel supplies lasted. There was no prospect of serious reinforcement. Conventional building plans were scrapped. Half-built fleet subs were being abandoned to rust on the ways or broken up and replaced by suicide craft.

The Imperial Japanese Navy began experimenting with midget submarines in the mid-thirties. Five two-man boats were off-loaded from fleet subs to attack Pearl Harbor. All five were lost. Their mission was so hazardous that Americans believed they were suicide craft. They were in fact manned by deliberately assigned, hand-picked regulars, who were expected to make their way back to the mother submarines after torpedoing their assigned targets inside the U.S. naval anchorage. It was the kind of dangerous gamble Japanese sailors were expected to tackle unflinchingly, ever since the days of the Russian war. But there was no question of the crewmen committing suicide.

Changed fortunes, changed views. Suicide attack won respectability in the desperate latter stages of the war, when it appeared to offer some hope of stopping the unstoppable Americans. A new type of midget submarine, the Kairyu ("Sea Dragon"), was tentatively designed in 1943. The crew would sacrifice themselves ramming enemy ships with an aerial torpedo slung on either beam of the sub. When torpedoes grew scarce, the submarine's nose was stuffed with TNT. The problem was getting these comparatively large but short-ranged boats safely within range of a target. No Kairyu was ever used in action, despite vast amounts of time and material wasted building them.

Two young naval lieutenants, Hiroshi Kuroki and Sekio Nishina, came up shortly afterward with a slightly more practical idea. They produced a man-guided version of the famous Long Lance, the type 93 oxygen-propelled shipborne torpedo. Their designs received reluctant approval early in 1944 once it became apparent even to conservative admirals that some desperate new gimmick was urgently needed.

The human torpedo was dubbed the Kaiten because it would "roll back heaven." The pilot occupied a small cockpit equipped with a crude periscope, sandwiched between a hydrogen peroxide engine developing 40 knots and a 1½-ton warhead. The original blueprints included an escape hatch which allowed the pilot to swim to safety moments before impact, but the concept was discarded before work on the first model began.

A Kaiten training base was opened in Midsummer 1944 on Otsujima, the hilly, wooded island oddly resembling a miniature Okinawa which shields the western approaches to the Tokuyama Oil Depot. It was here on September 6 that Lieutenant Kuroki lost his life in a test dive. His ashes were handed to Nishina, who vowed to carry them into battle. Volunteers from two naval air bases in north Japan worked in great secrecy to perfect the weapon.

Regular submariners knew nothing about it. The first Hashimoto heard of the human torpedo was a reference to *Maru Roku Kanemono*, "Circle 6 Metal Fitting." It was a code name, not a spare part. He was astounded to learn that four of these new "fittings" would be strapped to the deck of his latest command, *I-58*, just completed in Yokosuka navy yard. There was no question of seeking the cooperation, let alone the expert advice of an experienced seagoing skipper, Hashimoto constantly complained. The opinions of lowly lieutenant commanders received scant attention in the hidebound Japanese naval hierarchy. Besides, he had to admit, it was useless to argue. *Tokko* operations were now official policy.

The human torpedoes were first fired on November 20, 1944, into the U.S. fleet anchorage in Ulithi Lagoon. The pioneering Lieutenant Nishina was the first to go, carrying the box containing his coinventor's ashes inside the cockpit. He had joined Lieutenant Commander Zenji Orita's *I-47*, one of the two submarines first equipped to carry Kaiten. They spent two weeks at the Otsujima base learning to release the Kaiten. It was harder than it looked. *I-47* hurriedly surfaced: the pilots boarded their suicide craft: the submarine submerged; and, at a word from the departing heroes over the telephone link, deck shackles were cast off and the torpedo motors started.

One hour before sunrise just outside Ulithi reef, Orita surveyed the mouth-watering mass of targets through his periscope. Three miles away lay a cruiser, beyond that battleships, aircraft carriers, and more carriers. "We should have begun launching Kaiten years ago!" exclaimed Nishina as he swished away to his death. His three fellow officers soon followed. The submariners heard a distant explosion. A column of flames burst among the anchored ships. More explosions, more fires. The crew stopped cheering only when approaching destroyers forced them into an emergency dive.

Radio Tokyo trumpeted another victory. Sixth Fleet glowed with self-congratulation. At least two battleships had gone down. Carriers, cruisers, and transports were damaged. But as so often happened with *Tokko* operations, the claims outstripped reality. The U.S. fleet oiler *Mississinewa* blew up with 400,000 gallons of aviation gasoline. The other three human torpedoes missed their targets. An accompanying submarine managed to fire only two of its Kaiten (the others were stuck with mechanical trouble); they too hit nothing.

Experts like Hashimoto greeted the Kaiten with considerable reservations. From the technical point of view the human torpedo was what would today be called a standoff weapon. It was best suited to "shooting round corners"; seeking out its own victims when a straight, more conventional attack was impossible. But it did not work that perfectly in practice. The pilot attacked blind. Water sprayed up over his cockpit at the ideal attack speed of 40 knots. Anything slower offered too easy a target. Some kind of breakwater was needed in front of the pilot to keep his vision clear. Hashimoto recommended a suitable modification after conducting his own tests, but by that time the war was nearly over.

Lieutenant Commander Hashimoto harbored no objections to suicide operations on ethical grounds. All Japanese were destined to die in this war, he reckoned: the Kaiten pilots and their like would only die a little sooner than the rest. He suffered none of the agonies of older officers at sending men deliberately to their death. He admired the young men's dedication and patriotism.

But apart from the operational inadequacies of the Kaiten, there were serious tactical grounds for questioning its use. Since the human torpedo was most effective against moored targets, attacks were naturally aimed at busy American anchorages. These were always the most closely guarded. In order to deliver their suicide missiles, submarine crews were forced to stick their heads inside the lion's mouth. To men like Hashimoto this proved that more than three years of war had failed to teach the Japanese naval command the proper use of submarines. They persisted in selecting heavily guarded targets when hundreds of helpless freighters were there for the taking—farther out in the undefended Pacific. Surely it must by now be obvious to head-quarters staff, who used bicycles to save fuel, that the destruction of a few tankers and ammunition ships would do more to hobble the enemy than sinking the odd carrier or battleship? But no . . . U.S. naval strength must be whittled down in preparation for that elusive "decisive" battle.

Combined Headquarters was in no mood to argue. The top brass were sold on Kaiten. They pronounced the initial raid on Ulithi "a triumph." A spectacular follow-up was quickly planned. Operation Kongo would strike a hammerblow, aiming six Kaiten-carrying submarines on January 11, 1945, against widely scattered Pacific straits and anchorages in a single, synchronized attack. The code name for this operation had a strong religious significance. Kongo literally means "steel," but among Buddhists it symbolizes great strength. The planners seemed to be pleading for divine muscle.

I-58 was ordered to attack Guam. The reoccupied American island, largest of the Marianas chain, lay well south of Japan. It was already an important submarine base, in addition to being Nimitz's new Pacific Fleet headquarters: a challenging target for Kaiten operations. Hashimoto took two tortuous days working into position. Several big supply vessels went by unchallenged as he did his best to slip undetected inside the Luminao Reef. His task was made doubly dangerous because the human torpedoes could not be boarded beneath the surface. I-58 was forced to surface 17 miles from Apra Harbor and wait and watch for enemy air patrols as the heroes scrambled aboard, before diving again to periscope depth. After that, there was little time to lose. The pilots' air supply in their tiny compartments could last half an hour at most. The deck shackles slipped: the pilots sped off round the bend in the reef and out of sight.

First to go was Lieutenant Seizo Ishikawa, another of the Kaiten pioneers. There was no question of fear for these men. Wearing a white Hachimaki sweatband and short ceremonial sword, the lieutenant let out a last exultant "Banzai!" before the telephone connection parted. After him went an ensign and two 20-year-old petty officers. Hashimoto watched their phosphorescent wakes trailing away into the darkness. He was, frankly, worried. The pilots had rehearsed their attack countless times upon the chart table. The real thing was very different. The young men had only a rough idea of which direction they were heading. They would have trouble finding the harbor entrance. And he had an uneasy feeling the Americans were operating an efficient antisubmarine net. But it was impossible to get any closer; the attack was already two hours behind schedule.

The dull thud of an explosion was clearly heard. Columns of smoke rose over the harbor. *I-58* turned sharply north and headed home. It was impossible to assess what had happened. The answer, in truth, was nothing. Apart from the first lucky kill at Ulithi, Kaiten human torpedoes sank only one other ship, a freighter, and damaged one destroyer. But one of the Japanese mother subs was lost after a fruitless repeat raid on Ulithi and others gradually fell victim to the alerted Americans as the persistent imbeciles at fleet headquarters flung their force against ever-thickening anti-submarine defenses.

Hashimoto was glad to abort this latest mission to Okinawa. He ordered an alteration of course which would take them west toward the China coast, where it would be safe to recharge batteries and radio his position to submarine headquarters in Kure. Then he walked stiffly aft to advise his latest batch of suicide pilots that their deaths must be postponed.

Some boats offered the pilots little in the way of accommodation, but *I-58* was built with an extra cabin to bring back marooned aviators and other specialists from bypassed Japanese bases in the south Pacific. The senior Kaiten lieutenant was sitting at a table playing go with one of his three subordinates. He took the news calmly. One more day to live . . . what did it matter? He was already as good as dead.

"Tomorrow we'll be in glorious company," the lieutenant murmured. "Imagine dying along with *Yamato*."

Hashimoto was feeling the strain. He had been on his feet for 14 hours. One more check on their course: he strolled along the lower deck dispensing cheerful remarks to ease the tension, visited the bathroom, sipped half a cup of warm black tea, and paused before the shrine. The 10-by-16-inch box of white paulownia wood was suspended from the bulkhead near his cabin. It contained good-luck charms and mementos from the great imperial shrine at Ise. During their last voyage the Americans had gutted Tokyo; the lieutenant commander muttered a short prayer for the thousands who perished in the fire. He could yet avenge the dead, if only the gods would smile upon this mission.

Aboard Yamato,
Off the Japanese Coast

NIGHT, APRIL 6

ENSIGN SAKEI KATONO was still struggling with *War and Peace*. It looked like he would never finish it. He was only two-thirds of the way through Tolstoy's masterpiece. Tomorrow he would be dead. No way was he going to escape from his dreaded tomb above the inner starboard propeller. But the novel was so enthralling that he was determined to read on. He slung his hammock in the main companionway. Sleeping space was severely limited with all these extra staff officers and technicians aboard. He was still leafing through the pages when someone bumped into him. His book went spinning to the deck.

An apologetic flag officer stood looking up at his embarrassed junior officer. Vice Admiral Seiichi Ito was making an unobtrusive trip to the ship's shrine. A third submarine alert had just sent *Hatsushimo* dashing after a nonexistent contact; now they were heading away from the coast, still at high speed, hopefully clear of the enemy submarine screen.

The vice admiral retrieved the ensign's book and glanced at the title.

"Interesting," he said. "A strange thing to read, though, when you're just about to die."

"It helps compose my mind," stammered Katono. He was overawed by Ito. Senior officers were godlike figures in the Imperial Japanese Navy.

Ito nodded. "What's your battle station?" he asked.

"Number eight starboard damage control, sir."

Ito nodded again. He seemed to be working out where that was. "Good luck," he said with a fatherly smile, "and good night."

Unsure whether to bow or salute, the flustered ensign almost fell out of his hammock.

Many men found it difficult to sleep that night. Young Masanobu Kobayashi lay in his bunk wondering how he would acquit himself on the morrow. He felt confident that *Yamato* would succeed and survive. He would shoot down his first enemy plane. Perhaps several. He drowsed off to the high-speed throbbing of the engines.

The young officers lolling around the junior wardroom were as cynical as ever. Ensign Mitsuru Yoshida caught snatches of their morbid conversation: "There are three great follies known to man: the pyramids, the Great Wall of China, and *Yamato!*" . . . "How do you think we will make out against the enemy surface fleet?" . . . "Without air cover we'll never see an American ship. Only planes. You should worry about them" . . . "Remember the Grummans at Leyte? There'll be plenty of them tomorrow" . . . "What about those big Beehive shells we've got for the main battery? Surely those will shake them" . . . "Are you kidding? Wait and see!"

The ensign buckled on his sword, donned a light blue raincoat, and made his way to the upper deck. He paused to readjust his vision. At first he felt completely blind. Objects grew slowly visible: the long undulating deck, upper works piled high above him like children's bricks, the white waves curling away from the bow. Out on the beam were the dim shapes and wakes of the escorting destroyers. The hull shuddered, the sea hissed past, a cold wind sang through halyards and antennas.

He clambered up to the radar cabin. The watch sat huddled round the inadequate 8-inch scanning tubes. The air was thick with cigarette smoke. After a quick word with the petty officer in charge he headed for lookout duty on number one bridge. The time was 2345. He was due there at midnight.

"I started up the ladder to the bridge," he wrote years later. "Like a piece of paper, my body was pressed by the wind against the iron rungs. I was alone. No telling when another such opportunity might arise. From our course I estimated the direction and faced toward my home. Grasping the iron rail tightly, I lowered my head in a brief prayer. This done, I was soon up the ladder.

"On the darkened bridge not a soul was moving. The vague silhouettes of some 20 men silently engrossed in their work came into my sight. To distinguish one from the other in the dark, the highest-ranking officers wore fluorescent initials on the back of their caps. The sight of these caps glowing eerily in the blackness was encouraging."

They were halfway down the Kyushu coast, standing 30 miles out to sea. Speed was maintained at 22 knots. The five-minute zigzag continued. Ariga was settling down for a quick nap in his deck chair beside the binnacle when the first drops of rain began to fall. It was the lightest of squalls, but encouraging. The rear admiral reported the news delightedly to number one bridge. The fleet navigating officer there confirmed that the barometer was falling. Low cloud and rain might provide ideal concealment in the morning.

A signal arrived for Ito, hours late as usual, announcing that the emperor's brother, Prince Takamatsu, himself an Etajima graduate, had left earlier in the day aboard a special train for the grand shrine at Ise to pray for the success of the Special Attack mission.

"And to pray for our departed souls," thought Yoshida with quiet resignation. He tried to imagine the scene at Tokyo station as the prince paraded the red-carpeted concourse. Everyone in top hats or gaudy dress uniforms. Cocked hats, plumes, gold braid, and tinkling decorations. The prime minister-designate, old Suzuki, bowed over his walking cane. Meticulous Yonai, fussing with his watch, checking the train's departure to the very second ... these trips had been made before every major attack since Pearl Harbor. Occasionally the emperor went himself. The imperial prayers had lately gone unheeded, but there was still time for the divine ancestors to come to their aid.

Another course alteration brought *Yamato* and her escorts back close to the Kyushu coast, ready for the run through the

Osumi Strait, shown on Western charts as the Van Diemen Strait. More submarines could be lurking there. They were not, in fact, but the Japanese were taking no chances. The task force took shelter below the high black bluffs which ended in Cape Sata and its towering lighthouse. The light, along with everything else ashore, was thoroughly blacked out. At 0300, the channel negotiated, another course change was ordered, almost due west across the mouth of the long fjord of Kagoshima Bay.

It was here—in a region where men had to be tough to survive, the homeland of Japan's bravest samurai, the Shimazu clan—that the Imperial Japanese Navy was born in the 1860s. Many top officers still hailed from Kagoshima. It was also here, in the deep bay dominated by the dormant triple cones of Ontake, that pilots practiced their torpedo runs in preparation for Pearl Harbor. The dropping range against "battleship row" was short and shallow: tactics and torpedoes had been modified here with painstaking attention to detail.

The rain had stopped when Captain Jiro Nomura came out on deck. He couldn't sleep. He had been passing the time in damage control, at the base of the bridge tower, checking and rechecking the switches, pumps, and circuits. Everything seemed in order. A cot awaited him in a corner of the heavily armored room away from the banks of dials and warning lights. He preferred a walk in the fresh air. Shapeless forms in oilskins stirred in the gun positions, a lookout leaped to attention from time to time, but there was no other sign of life. The steel colossus might have been a windup toy, virtually untouched by man. Two pilots were smoking sullenly in the after hangar with their maintenance crew. They were due to fly off in the morning and make a brief antisubmarine search before heading for Kagoshima. The pilots did not want to go. One of them began pleading with Nomura to let them stay. The executive officer shook him off impatiently. He had more important things to worry about. The emergency casualty stations, for example. He went down to check the junior wardroom.

Ensign Yoshida came off watch before dawn and crawled gratefully into his bunk. Young Kobayashi relieved a fellow member of his crew in their after gun tub. Moisture was dripping off the canvas gun covers; it was damp and cold. Ensign Mitsuo Watanabe took over the silent TBS on number one bridge. The ships were still maintaining radio silence, but he checked out the circuits with the radio room deep in the hull. Ensign Sakei Katono mustered his damage control party in their violently vibrating compartment. The judder from the crews set their teeth on edge. They would have to bear with it an hour or two until breakfast time. He sat smoking, hands in pockets, on a coil of rope, wishing he could get on with *War and Peace*. But it would not be a good example for an officer to be seen reading a book on duty. A foreign book, at that.

The task force chief of staff, Rear Admiral Nobii Morishita, started a fresh pack of cigarettes as he checked the ship's track in the after chartroom. His chief of operations, Yuji Yamamoto, projected an unvarying westward course, 280° at 0345, which would take them to a point some 150 miles west of Kyushu. It was there, at about 1000, that they should start their southeast run parallel to the islands. Eight hours of that and they would be ready to turn in for the dash toward Okinawa.

Morishita leaned into the cone of light above the chart. He peered at his old friend through a cloud of smoke.

"Is there any change?" he asked.

Another rain squall beat briefly on the windows.

Yamamoto shrugged.

"I think you ought to sleep," he said. "It's going to be a busy day."

A lookout aroused Ariga as the first streaks of watery dawn combed the cloud banks behind Kyushu. The weathermen were right: the sky was blanketed by low-lying layers of grimy gray rain clouds. The sea slid by in a long oily swell. The commanding officer's steward brought tea, a mug of hot water, razor, soap, and a navy issue hand towel. Ariga completed his toilet, humming absently, pulled on a clean pair of white gloves, and stretched himself stiffly. He gazed aft past the sodden battle ensign and the staggered bulk of the smokestack to the misty mountains of Japan.

It was barely light before the deck sprang to life. Gun crews stood to. After "firing practice" had been hoisted to warn the escorts, a few rounds were loosed off at sea gulls. The birds scattered, unhurt. Junior engineers began exercising on top of the after hangar, to the annoyance of the aircrews preparing the catapults for takeoff. "One, two, three . . . one, two, three . . ." The youngsters, stripped to the waist, flung their arms about before descending to their noisy engine rooms.

"Take a good look back there," a voice shrieked. "Japan. Look at it. You'll never see it again."

It was old Koyama, the chief quartermaster. He stood pointing and cackling at the vanishing Kyushu coastline.

"Drop dead, you old fool," the engineers jeered irreverently. "No one's going to sink *Yamato!*"

The wizened veteran watched them, mumbling. He'd been a boy sailor at that battle with the Russians. Sometimes if he had drunk enough whiskey he would tell the youngsters about it: the great ships with slim cigarettelike funnels belching flame and smoke and capsizing in the Tsushima waters. They didn't fight wars like that anymore. Pity *Yamato* wasn't around in those days ... they'd have finished those Russians in half the time.

The ship's loudspeakers crackled to life. It was the executive officer. A delayed signal from Combined Fleet advised that yesterday's Kamikaze attacks had gravely damaged the American fleet. At least four carriers were knocked out. The attack force could expect considerably less air opposition.

The engineers cheered. They jeered louder at the glowering quartermaster. Old Koyama shook his head in disbelief. A flight of five Zeros appeared, right on cue, from the threatening overcast. They banked three times round the fleet, dipped their wings, and headed for home. Vice Admiral Ito came out to wave at them from the starboard signal platform. As far as he knew, his son was up there. The engineers cheered again. All this talk about sinking! They were getting air support! A bugle call and a rain shower drove them below deck for breakfast. There was time for a light meal of rice and pickles before the bugler was back at the intercom sounding general quarters. Enemy aircraft were circling beneath the rain clouds.

U.S. Fifth Fleet, Off Okinawa

NIGHT, APRIL 6–7

No one could accuse Raymond Spruance of being a romantic. There wasn't an admiral in the U.S. Navy who could match his remorseless logic. But when the submarine report finally arrived confirming *Yamato's* sortie he made an oddly illogical decision. He ordered Rear Admiral Morton L. Deyo, commander of Task Force 54, a collection of superannuated battleships, to deal with the Japanese attack force. He should form his two battleship divisions, two cruiser divisions, and 20 destroyers into line of battle and head north next day to engage the enemy.

The order went out well after midnight. At about the same time Spruance told Mitscher and his aviators to forget *Yamato*. Task Force 58 should concentrate its "offensive effort ... in combat air patrols to meet enemy air attacks." Spruance did not know it, but the carriers of the task force were already speeding north to attack position.

The black-shoe admiral's strange decision is still the subject of occasional speculation. He may have doubted whether Task Force 58 could get close enough to the approaching Japanese force and still maintain its commitment to the Okinawa invasion. It is equally valid to wonder whether the traditional sailor in Spruance sensed the opportunity to stage the last big-ship encounter in history.

Battleships had seldom squared off against each other in the classic manner during the Pacific war. Air power had been the clincher, and after Guadalcanal big guns were seldom fired by either side at anything other than land targets. *Yamato's* mighty turrets had only been turned once on surface ships and then only for a few disappointing minutes. Here now was the once-and-for-all chance to put decades of traditional theory to the glorious, gun-blasting test. The very idea of battlewagons slugging it out in the style that dated back to the day in 1588 when Drake's men challenged the Spanish Armada must have been very appealing to Spruance, especially the possibility of ending this phase of naval history in such an unlikely oriental encounter.

Marc Mitscher nursed his own dreams. Task Force 58 was the obvious instrument for fulfilling the Japanese death wish. But there were other reasons for his aching desire to get at the giant battleship. His pilots had trained against an imaginary *Yamato* on the Great Lakes. Two converted paddle steamers, *Wolverine* and *Sable*, provided the practice flight decks from which trainees took off and landed in preparation for this very battle.

And there was something more basic. The aging Pensacola pioneer was determined to prove what he had been saying throughout his navy career: that air power outclassed the battleship. The sinking of *Yamato's* sister ship *Musashi* was not conclusive, in Mitscher's opinion; there was still a strong feeling in the upper echelons of the U.S. Navy that she had been finished off by submarine torpedoes. This time there would be no room for argument.

The island superstructure rising above the starboard side of *Bunker Hill's* flight deck usually fell quiet after the evening alert. The task force controller down in the combat information center kept tabs on approaching enemy bogies, friendly night fighters, and the widely scattered units of the task force. Otherwise, the routine bedlam was over. It was time for a game of cards, relaxing gossip, or a movie. Some films had been in circulation two or three weeks, but sex-starved men who had begun to forget what a woman looked like gladly sat through the same show three or four times to catch another glimpse of Alice Faye's bosom or Betty Grable's luscious thighs.

Tonight it was strictly business. In their untidy cubbyhole, intelligence officers struggled through a rash of evaluations and secret signals. Detailed information about *Yamato* was limited and inaccurate. The battleship's equipment supposedly included two midget submarines! Extra hands were being summoned to the combat information center. Frenzied activity gripped flag plot as Mitscher and his chief of staff, Arleigh Burke, prepared a defiant Nelsonian showdown. To hell with the battleships; this was a job for the carriers.

First of all, what have we got available? Answer: three of the four task groups. Ted Sherman's task Group 58.3 and "Jocko" Clark's 58.1 were in position 70 miles east of Okinawa. Arthur Radford's 58.4, fueling during the day, was due to rejoin them overnight. Only 58.2 (Rear Admiral Davison), now setting off to top up tanks at the safe refueling area 100 miles to the southeast, would be unavailable for the action. That still left 12 carriers and 986 planes, quite sufficient to blitz the Japanese attack force without reducing combat air patrol over Okinawa. Local air defense would be further reinforced by the British Task Force 57 and by the support group of those wonderfully versatile little *Kaiser* carriers commanded by Rear Admiral Durgin.

Arleigh Burke tells what happened next:

> The flag plot controlled the operation. We usually conferred before a battle to determine what we should do. The admiral and I never left that bridge at sea. We slept there. We had cots. After conferring on what we might do, we would put people onto "What might happen?" "What can we do if things go wrong?" "What data do we need to make quick decisions?" These decisions are usually made after a long, earlier study.
>
> In this case we got information from intelligence reports and from a submarine that reported the *Yamato* was standing out to sea. So we put our intelligence people onto it. The Japanese knew we had the [Bungo Strait] covered. They knew they would probably be sighted and reported. Obviously they had something pretty drastic in mind. So we asked the intelligence people: "Where will this go? What might she do? What is she coming out for?"

Mitscher was in no mood for procrastination. He wanted

answers—and quickly. Fifteen minutes and he would be fuming. The intelligence men left and went into a huddle. They sized up every possible course of action, taking account of the weather, potential targets, timing of their attack—even whether the Japanese were really planning an attack. Back breathlessly in flag plot, they presented the vice admiral with half a dozen options, all roughly plotted out.

Yes, it looked like the Japanese were planning to attack. The enemy would do their best to keep well clear of Task Force 58's avenging angels. That ruled out the chances of a quick run down the eastward side of the island chain.

"*Yamato* will probably go to the west of the string of islands," the senior intelligence officer reported. "She will probably try to make her final run in the dark in order to hit Okinawa about dawn. It's an old Japanese trick—and a good one.

"From where she is now, *Yamato* will most likely vary her speed and try to get through our submarine screen as fast as she can. She will probably make a feint to the east just before dawn, so that our scout planes will see her."

Vice Admiral Seiichi Ito couldn't have summed up his plans better himself. The Americans pored over their charts. The enemy would work south as far as possible while trying to convince the U.S. fleet they were heading someplace else. Sasebo perhaps? Then a high-speed run toward the Hagushi beachhead. Repeat signals were coming in from Spruance to Deyo in preparation for a surface action. Mitscher threw them aside contemptuously. He leaned over the chart table, looked his staff in the eye, and growled: "What the hell can we do?"

Task Force 58 was too far off to launch air strikes. Its major task, supporting the Okinawa operation, precluded moving any great distance from the island. The problem demanding urgent solution was how to head northward within range of the approaching Japanese without abandoning the troops ashore. They must work out a compromise plan to achieve both missions simultaneously.

It was going to be a gamble. The task force would have to speed as far north as it dared, altering course and turning into the wind whenever it was launching planes. A series of colossal zigzags appeared on the charts as the flat tops edged their way into strike position northwest of Okinawa. There was no margin for error. Planes would still be operating at extreme range and pilots were warned to spend the minimum time over the target. Fifteen to 20 minutes would be about all they'd have to spare; otherwise they'd never make it back.

Communication posed problems. Aircraft radio signals petered out after about 100 miles. Four newly arrived marine pilots were given the boring task of circling at 60-mile intervals along the attack route to pick up, amplify, and on-pass messages from carrier squadrons back to flag plot in *Bunker Hill*. This would help warn Mitscher if anything was going wrong. If the Japanese headed farther east than expected, for instance, or changed their minds and headed home . . . Mitscher shook his head thoughtfully.

"They'll fight," he said. "And we will get 'em."

A stream of signals to the task force warned of the busy day to come. There would be little sleep for maintainance crews. Orders were to tune every aircraft to full pitch, ready for some very hard flying. Squadron leaders prepared small charts for each pilot's clipboard, detailing navigation points to and from the expected target area. Some Avengers would fly without gunners so that torpedoes could be replaced by maximum bomb loads.

One thing seemed certain: there would be little or no air opposition over the Japanese fleet. That would make things a lot easier. But they would know for sure when the search planes, due to take off at dawn, sent back their first sighting reports.

Spruance was left blissfully ignorant of their plans. It could ethically be argued that nothing was firm yet; at this stage Task Force 58 was prudently preparing for contingencies. Plenty of time yet to signal commander in chief, Fifth Fleet. Old Deyo, the battleship rear admiral, was not even going to start planning his surface battle until the morning . . . and a great deal could happen in the next few hours.

Sometime past 0200 Mitscher managed to climb onto his cot. The lights were still on in flag plot. Staff officers clumped around his cot. Chatter never ceased into the bulkhead telephones. Mitscher picked up his detective story and tried to read. He found it hard to sleep.

PART
V

APRIL 7, 1945
Morning

Kamikaze Headquarters, Kanoya Air Base

BEFORE DAWN, APRIL 7

THE RAIN AWOKE Kusaka. It was beating a tinny tattoo on the roof of the dilapidated shack that served as the VIP guesthouse at Kanoya. The sound seemed a mockery of the drumroll the previous day which sped the Kamikaze pilots to their waiting planes. The chief of staff peered at his watch. Nearly 0430. The field should soon be swinging into action. The follow-up phase of Kikusui One was due to begin shortly after dawn. He groped around the blacked-out hut for the oil lamp, lit it, and shaved and dressed in the spluttering yellow light. He pulled on a raincoat before venturing out into the storm.

Great rain sheets were gusting across the empty airfield. The trees dripped groaning in the blustery wind. The place was already a quagmire. No one appeared to be moving. A Zero stood unattended beneath camouflage netting. Water streamed off its oil-streaked cowling. A heavy bomb awaited installation on a rubber-wheeled trolley. There was no sign of movement from the pilots' billet. The former schoolhouse would soon be coming to life as selected occupants prepared for the last day of their lives.

Vice Admiral Ryunosuke Kusaka strode beneath the flower-

213

ing cherry trees, treading the carpet of fallen blossoms into the mud. The chief of staff, Combined Fleet, found the command post unusually empty. Ugaki had not yet turned up, nor had the bulk of his operations staff. The duty officer confirmed what Kusaka feared: all flying was canceled.

But where did this leave the *Yamato* attack force? The last active surface unit in the Imperial Navy might be resigned to clawing its way south without air cover. The least it could expect, however, was a continuation of yesterday's Kamikaze attacks to impede interdiction attempts by U.S. carriers.

If the pilots' claims were anything to go by (and who could be that confident?), the Americans would have difficulty mustering an all-out strike while simultaneously mounting combat air patrol over Okinawa. Another attack wave now would throw them further off-balance.

Kusaka checked the overnight signal file. No word from *Yamato*, naturally enough; the force was maintaining radio silence. Coded reports from American submarines had been picked up off the Bungo Strait. That meant the enemy was alerted. Prince Takamatsu was making a special pilgrimage to Ise. The commander in chief, Combined Fleet, Admiral Soemu Toyoda, was flying down to Kanoya to supervise the sortie. Arrival time would be advised later, dependent on the weather.

It was dawn before Vice Admiral Matome Ugaki reached the command post with two or three aides. He looked desperately tired. He noted Kusaka's obvious concern for the attack force, but insisted that no one was to take off in this weather. His inexperienced pilots had difficulty enough making their way south on the clearest day, with the island chain visible to guide them.

"Some kind of diversionary raid is essential," Kusaka insisted. "Otherwise *Yamato* hasn't a chance."

Vice Admiral Ugaki was frankly indifferent. He had enough problems of his own. The Kikusui assault had been evolved long before Combined Fleet decided to throw in a surface element. His responsibility as commander of the Fifth Naval Air Fleet was to ensure the success of the month-long suicide campaign. He was in no mood now to risk valuable aircraft to shore up a dubious last-minute operation. The Japanese had spent most of the war trying to persuade land-based naval air groups and the battle fleet to work together; the operational paralysis at Hiyoshi finally dashed all hope of coordination.

"The weather should help the attack force," Ugaki said.

"Not as much as another raid on the American carriers," Kusaka countered.

The two men sat scowling at each other across the operations desk. There was no love lost between them. Each had good reason to feel resentful. Ugaki objected to being asked to pull the navy's chestnuts out of the fire. Kusaka thought only of the 6000 sailors going bravely to their deaths. Didn't they deserve all the support they could get?

Ugaki mustered his operations staff. He checked meteorological and status reports. The storm centered over Kyushu was moving slowly down into the China Sea. Closer to Okinawa, the weather was clearer. A few sorties could be mounted by 0800, using his better pilots, but half of the planes still available would have to be held back until the next major attack on April 12. That was when he planned to have another go with the Ohka piloted bombs.

"See how the weather looks in another hour," he said. "We will do our best. Izumi Air Base will send a flight of fighters over the ships. Only for a short time. It's all we can spare."

Kusaka nodded glumly as Ugaki issued his orders. He hoped no one sensed his own mounting feeling of despair.

U.S. Task Force 58,
Off Okinawa

MITSCHER DID NOT sleep long. He was off his cot and onto the walkway long before dawn, freshening up in the keen breeze sweeping the flight deck as *Bunker Hill* circled north at 32 knots. The three available task groups of Task Force 58 spread out around him in the darkness. Some 75 ships of all shapes and sizes were somewhere out there, scattered across 150 square miles of ocean. Twelve of them were carriers.

The vice admiral ran below to shower, shave, and change. He emerged from his sea cabin half an hour later in starch-crisp suntans, the twin shirt pockets bulging with odds and ends: wallet, cigarettes, matches, and sunglasses.

No decorations; his vice admiral's collar stars and aviator's wings, nothing more. Some flag officers put up a chestful of medals on occasions like this, whenever there was the slightest chance of impressing the war correspondents. That wasn't Mitscher's way. Even ashore he seldom wore his regulation cap with gold braid across the peak.

This promised to be a heavy day. Mitscher came prepared with an extra pack of cigarettes. From now on he would be smoking ceaselessly. He could light a cigarette in the strongest

216

wind, match cupped in both hands, a trick that impressed visiting landsmen. He settled down with Arleigh Burke in Flag Plot to decide the opening gambit.

First, find the enemy. Three divisions of Hellcats with extra fuel tanks took off at dawn to search a fan-shaped quadrant stretching halfway up Kyushu and far out on either side into the Pacific and the China Sea. The area ranged from 336° to 56°, reaching a maximum range of 325 miles from the task force. With them went the vital communications links, four ill-fated Marine Corsairs. Their inexperienced pilots miscalculated the wind strength, circling endlessly for hours at 20,000 feet to on-pass radio messages between attack planes and their distant mother ships. The fighters eventually ran out of fuel on the way back to the carrier. Three of the four pilots were rescued by submarines. Second Lieutenant John Garlock was never seen again.

The searchers pressed on through rain and heavy cloud. At 0754 there was a false alarm. One pilot spotted what looked like a merchantman and two escorts heading northward, possibly to Sasebo, "but this was not the target everyone was waiting to hear about." Twenty-one minutes later the division commanded by Lieutenant (jg.) William Estes, "flying a cross leg of their search at 3500 feet, sighted 5 miles dead ahead of them the pride of the Japanese navy, the battleship *Yamato,* accompanied by one light cruiser and seven or eight destroyers."

The first sighting report was misleading. The fliers caught the attack force on a northerly zigzag. Course was reported as 300°. Surely they were heading for Sasebo? A tense hum filled the crowded flag plot aboard *Bunker Hill.* Ensign Jack Lyons of *Essex* made a much-needed correction at 0823. Course 240°. No doubt about it now. Destination Okinawa. Staff officers received the news with sighs of relief.

More information: weather conditions over the target area were broken to overcast with intermediate clouds at 10,000 to 14,000 feet. Lower broken cumulus clouds, ceiling 3000 feet. Visibility 5 to 8 miles. Surface wind light southeasterly. Flying conditions average.

"Doesn't sound average to me," one aviator remarked. "Sounds like one son of a bitch."

"But plenty of cover," replied another. "Good attacking weather."

"Hell, if it rains, those bastards could dodge in and out of squalls all day," grumbled a third.

Another piece of vital information: no enemy fighters were sighted over target. The enemy ships were without air cover. Mitscher nodded grimly. It was exactly what he expected. The Japanese were not planning to waste their air strength protecting this forlorn foray. He ordered 16 more Hellcats to relieve the circling search planes. Then back to the charts. The time had come to take the biggest gamble of his career.

Yamato was still too far off for comfort. It would be an hour and a half before Task Force 58 closed the range sufficiently to launch attacks. Otherwise he risked losing a lot of planes on the way back. Mitscher had already experienced one such costly disaster—overreaching himself in the Marianas nearly two years before with 104 planes down in the drink. He could not afford a repeat performance. But Mitscher could be leaping to the dangerous assumption that the enemy would do exactly what he predicted. There was a good chance that contact could be lost in the next two crucial hours. The Japanese could confound them all by turning back, eventually, to seek haven in northeast Kyushu. There would be a lot of red faces around—and none redder than Mitscher's if the carrier strike struck out.

The vice admiral mulled it over momentarily. Then he turned to Burke. "Order a full strike for 1000," he said. "Target 344°, range 238 miles." His cold blue eyes gleamed with excitement, but the wizened, walnut face was otherwise devoid of emotion. He might have been ordering a fresh cup of coffee.

A foreign observer watched the proceedings with astonishment. The Royal Navy's liaison officer, Commander "Taffy" Owen, considered himself acclimatized to the Yankees' odd antics. He had long been cured of any lingering British contempt for this comic opera outfit which had never fought a major modern war. Some of Uncle Sam's naval customs were bloody weird. All that ice cream and no liquor. Orders like "Away gasoline gig" were guaranteed to send a British sailor into convulsions. There was a familiarity between officers and men unthinkable among class-conscious Britons—yet it was marred at times by bursts of punitive discipline. An offense which might earn a British sailor a sharp rebuke could land an American in the brig.

The commander was convinced by now, however, that he was dealing with a thoroughgoing bunch of professionals. The British might still excel at seamanship—the Yanks themselves admitted that—but technically the U.S. Navy was second to none. This amphibious operation against Okinawa was a triumph of organization. The Americans had the resources, and they knew how to use them, especially aboard their carriers. But this morning seemed an exception; Owen could hardly believe his ears.

"My God," he burst out. "You're launching before you can be certain where the Japs are heading?"

Arleigh Burke confidently tapped a point on the chart less than 100 miles southeast of the tip of Kyushu.

"Of course we are taking a chance," he admitted. "We are launching against the spot where we would be if we were *Yamato*."

"You'd better be right," replied Owen. No one would argue with that!

Controlled chaos exploded across the carrier decks. It was 0945. Clouds of blue-gray smoke gushed from spluttering engines. Splashes of color darted in and out of the camouflaged aircraft—plane directors in yellow shirts and helmets, plane handlers in blue, chockmen in purple, hookmen in green. The fire fighters with their portable extinguishers wore red. Two apparitions could be seen in cumbersome asbestos suits. Pilots in the ready rooms watched the ticker tapes for up-to-date information. Briefing officers at the blackboards handed out their last scraps of advice.

"Everyone remember his target recognition? This is an *Agano*-class light cruiser. There may be two of them."

"It's going to be a long haul. No lingering over the target. Observe fuel conservation to maximum on the flight back."

"Dumbos are available at the following coordinates..." Heartening to know that anyone who ditched safely stood a better-than-average chance of rescue. The marine flying boats making rescue and reconnaissance patrols out of Kerama-Retto were nicknamed appropriately after Disney's airborne elephant.

Aircrews had downed a sustaining breakfast. It would be hours before they ate again. Rations were still good at this stage of the Okinawa campaign: cereal, powdered egg omelet, bacon, and toast. Plenty of orange juice and coffee. There was as much as anyone could eat and drink. In another month there would be less variety—and less chow.

Carrier skippers began pronouncing their valedictories over the ships' intercom. "Our air group today takes off for a major strike against the remaining elements of the Jap fleet ..."

Finally the order: "Pilots, man your planes." A stream of men in the new blue nylon flying suits rushed onto the upper deck.

A Lutheran chaplain stood watching on one flight deck. He murmured the text for his next sermon, plucked appropriately from Isaiah: "But they that wait upon those who revere the Lord shall renew their strength; they shall mount up with wings as eagles ..."

The deck rocked and thundered as the first aircraft hurtled into the sky. Fighters, dive-bombers, and torpedo bombers: more planes than the Japanese used at Pearl Harbor would soon be winging toward the enemy, and still there were hundreds of fighters left to protect the Okinawa operation ...

" ... they shall run, and not be weary; and they shall walk, and not faint."

Mitscher was a Freemason. He kept clear of organized religion. But at this moment he needed all the prayers he could get. He sat hunched in his walkway chair, peering aft, as Task Groups 58.1 and 58.3 got their planes smartly airborne. Planes from *San Jacinto*, *Bennington*, *Hornet* and *Belleau Wood* of 58.1 were swiftly followed by 58.3's *Essex*, *Bataan*, *Bunker Hill*, *Cabot*, and finally *Hancock*. Two hundred and eighty aircraft headed northeast: 132 fighters, 50 bombers, and 98 torpedo bombers. *Hancock's* 53 planes took off 15 minutes late and promptly lost their way. One hundred and six planes from *Intrepid*, *Langley*, and *Yorktown* of Task Group 58.4 followed at 1045.

When the last of his eagles were airborne, Mitscher gave the obligatory order to Arleigh Burke: "Inform Admiral Spruance that I propose to strike the *Yamato* sortie group at 1200 unless otherwise directed." He could conceal his intentions no longer. "Ask him, 'Will you take them or shall I?'"

Now was the worst time—the silent, waiting time. Something was going badly wrong with the communications. Nothing had been heard recently from the tracking planes. The weather could be interfering with their signals. Or the enemy could be: radio jamming was a fast-developing art.

Mitscher would have liked to relax over a whodunit. But as he told Burke, it would set a bad example sitting around reading pulp novels where everyone could see him. He made a halfhearted attempt to clear the endless paperwork. Fan mail, for instance. All sorts of people he had never heard of were writing to him these days. An Indian gentleman from Poona addressed him as Most Noble Admiral M. A. Mitscher. "We drink to the health of you, most noble Mr. Mitscher," the letter read, and to "His Excellency, Mr. Roosevelt, and His Majesty." The old eagle rubbed his bald head in bewilderment.

The stream of reports and assessments from his carrier skippers and their assorted specialists was designed to keep him appraised of the state of morale, expertise, and readiness within the task force, and to suggest improvements in training tactics and equipment. Unintentionally, the reports added up to a long whine of complaints. They made depressing reading.

Prolonged combat was taking its toll. Pilots and gun crews suffered most. They weren't getting enough sleep, reported *Intrepid.* There were outbreaks of mysterious throat infections. Irreplaceable teams in the combat information centers needed a break after 90 days of continuous duty. Equipment was wearing out: *Yorktown's* catapults were faulty. Pilots were babbling too freely over the radio, *Hornet* grumbled, giving away vital information uncoded, in plain language. The Japanese were effectively jamming the carriers' radar by dropping bundles of tinfoil, known as "window"—according to *Bunker Hill*, whose commanding officer also insisted that one day off in every five for refueling was not enough to rest his weary crew. *Bataan* felt that better tactics should be evolved to defeat the Kamikaze. More reliance should be put upon the combat air patrol and less on antiaircraft fire; it had been noticed that suicide pilots often dived unscathed through the defending barrage.

A reply flashed in soon enough from Spruance. Three simple words, the shortest operational order in naval history, brought cackling laughter from Mitscher. He threw the reply triumphantly across to Burke:

YOU TAKE THEM.

Given a little luck, he would do just that.

U.S. Task Force 54, Off Okinawa

MORNING, APRIL 7

HE HAD BEEN LOOKING forward to a fight. He had attached his flagship *New Mexico* to Rear Admiral Deyo's battle line in order not to miss it. But Raymond Spruance did not hesitate when Mitscher signaled his readiness to attack. Old Baldy wouldn't act so cocky unless he was pretty darn sure of himself. Spruance gave him the go-ahead immediately, albeit with a faint pang of regret. There was still the outside chance, he argued, that Japanese luck or American miscalculation could carry the approaching attack force through their aerial ambush. His massive backstop of elderly battlewagons might yet be needed to bar the approaches to the invasion beaches. They must be allowed to press ahead with their preparations.

No one was keener than the battleship flag officer, Morton L. Deyo—or more anxious. He was confident that Task Force 54's combined firepower would be enough to blow the Japanese out of the water. His only qualms were whether the bombardment force was in sufficient shape to fight a classic night action. Constant slugging away at land targets while steaming a monotonous course parallel to the west coast of Okinawa was poor preparation for a complicated battle of maneuver, where so

222

much depended on skilled station keeping, prompt execution of simultaneous turns, and all the textbook exercises his officers had seldom had the opportunity to practice since peacetime.

As his flagship *Tennessee* hurried from Kerama-retto for a preparatory staff conference, the 57-year-old Admiral Deyo drew up his battle plan. Task Force 54 would go off in the afternoon to a point northwest of Okinawa for much-needed exercises. *Idaho* would lead battleship division three, followed by Spruance's *New Mexico* and his own *Tennessee*. Battleship division four was next in line, comprising *West Virginia*, *Maryland* and *Colorado*. The cruisers *Birmingham*, *Mobile*, and *Biloxi* guarded their right flank with 11 destroyers. On the left were cruisers *San Francisco*, *Minneapolis*, *Tuscaloosa*, *Portland*, and 10 destroyers.

Deyo was signaling Turner, "We hope to land some fish for breakfast," when Mitscher's announced intention to launch air strikes came in. Deyo quickly added, " . . . unless the pelicans get them first." He cursed his luck. The glamour boys on the carriers were horning in on his act. He complained to Spruance but received no reply beyond a routine "Carry on." There was plenty of smoldering resentment among the battleship sailors at the airmen who had superseded them as the most potent force in the navy.

Other anxieties surfaced at Deyo's staff conference. Little was known about *Yamato*; but the latest intelligence report suggested that earlier estimates of her armament were incorrect. The big ship appeared to carry nine 17.7-inch guns, which would outrange anything the Americans could muster. Gunnery officers pored over range tables which predicted that the Japanese would be able to open fire long before the bombardment force was able to hit back. It was cold comfort to note that the report concluded with the words: "It should be borne in mind that all of this information is tentative and subject to further confirmation or denial."

Task Force 54 got under way at 1530, heading for its northwestern rendezvous. Four formations were to be adopted: normal cruising disposition, antiaircraft, approach, and battle dispositions. At 1607 approach disposition was signaled and battle maneuvers began.

"Far too little opportunity is available for drill in battle exercises," Rear Admiral Deyo afterward reported. At this stage of the war, he at least took the battleship seriously.

Twilight Kamikaze attacks mounted from nearby island airfields heckled the fleet as it swung about the China Sea. One plane crashed into the battleship *Maryland*'s main after turret, killing most of the gun crew and putting the turret out of action. The damage went unreported until the next day. Nobody wanted to miss the fun.

U.S. Sighting
of the Japanese Fleet,
East China Sea

MORNING, APRIL 7

IT WAS FOUR HOURS before the Japanese appeared on the American radar. The enemy task force formed one big blip at a range of 80 miles. As the flying boats crept closer, bucking a path through heavy rain cloud, the blip gradually subdivided. Several small shapes flipped up on the screens. No doubt about it: these were the ships they'd been told to look out for. Approaching to within 5 miles, peeping cautiously through the murk, the Americans identified a battleship, two light cruisers, and possibly eight destroyers. They looked more like little gray models at this height, cutting milk-white scars across a lead-topped table.

A coded contact report shot back to Okinawa, breaking the tension aboard *Bunker Hill*. There'd been no radio messages from the carrier search planes for nearly two hours. It was a relief to know that someone was still on the ball, and that the enemy was still on course.

The big, slow four-engined Martin Mariner flying boats were on their fourth operational mission. They were part of a newly formed patrol squadron, VPB-21, flying off the sheltered waters of the Aka Channel in Kerama-retto. This morning's predawn briefing ordered them on a northward search pattern as far as

225

the Kyushu coast. Their primary task was detection of the *Yamato* sortie. They were also supposed to track and if necessary attack any merchant shipping sighted along the route. Both big planes carried bombs, depth charges, and eight .50 caliber machine guns, but the pilots were advised to be careful. Only two repair ships were anchored yet back at base; if their maintenance barges happened to be occupied there was nowhere else to beach a badly shot-up aircraft, especially one with a hull full of holes. It would have to sink in the landing channel before repairs could be made.

Lieutenant Dick Simms set his plane, *Dog Eight*, circling the zigzagging ships. The flying-boat crew watched breathlessly. They were newcomers to the Pacific war and here below them was a whole fleet of Japanese. The enemy weaved skillfully across the swell, maintaining a wide protective circle around the battleship. One destroyer was falling out of the formation and slipping astern. Copilot William Graves, a navy reserve lieutenant (jg.), kept tabs on the lame duck through binoculars. Lieutenant Jim Young followed them in *Dog Ten*, dodging in and out of the tattered underbelly of the rain cloud. Once they glimpsed three small ships in convoy heading for Japan. At any other time this would have warranted a stream of excited reports; they might even have dived to the attack if it seemed they would meet little serious opposition. Right now the warships were their major preoccupation.

One of Dick Simms's gunners yelled a warning over the intercom. He had spotted a puff of smoke from *Yamato*'s main after turret. A great black blob burst a few seconds later beyond the port wing, jolting the plane but causing no damage. The flying boats dodged back into the clouds while crewmen threw out bundles of tinfoil "window." The Americans always wrongly assumed that Japanese antiaircraft fire was radar-directed. The two planes ducked in and out of the low clouds as fast as their slow speed permitted. All they needed now was to run into escorting Japanese fighter planes. None appeared, however; the firing broke off and the pilots settled down to an impudent game of hide-and-seek. There was no hurry. They had fuel enough to play around here all day . . .

Captain Tameichi Hara of *Yahagi* watched the hills of Kyushu sink out of sight. His heart sank with them. This weather was a disaster. The lowering gray sky shuttered off the sun. An unusually cold wind blew in from the Arctic. The sea heaved past in a sullen sluggish swell. Hardly the kind of day any right-minded strategist would have chosen to run the gauntlet of the avenging eagles . . . The sharp silver light distorted distance; the rain squalls were not heavy enough to conceal a surface force.

Yahagi plowed along in the van, the destroyers crisscrossing astern at every switch of the zigzag. The destroyer captains needed every ounce of their skill to maintain formation. Zigzagging, was a waste of time, Captain Hara felt, because there was no longer any danger from submarines. The enemy threat now came from the air. Better if the ships bunched tighter for mutual support.

An alert lookout spotted the escorting Zeros before they registered on the radar. One of Hara's aides hopefully suggested the convoy must be getting air cover. Rear Admiral Keizo Komura lowered his binoculars and rubbed tired eyes.

"They're not for us," he replied sourly. "We will have no air cover. They are making a routine training flight. Kusaka probably told these young pilots to fly over and bid us farewell."

A signal hoist from the flagship announced the departure of the first of her two remaining aircraft. The floatplane would make a brief sweep in search of submarines before homing on Ibusuki Air Base on the Kyushu coast. *Yahagi* was instructed to follow suit. Hara gave the necessary orders. One of the cruiser's spotter planes was hoisted onto the catapult abaft the smokestack. The pilot stomped up to the bridge to make his final report, an incongruous figure in his leather flying suit among so many officers in crisp number three combat fatigues. He saluted, bowed, and said: "I am proceeding as ordered to Ibusuki. There I shall join a Kamikaze squadron. We will meet at Minatogawa." It was more a protest than a farewell.

The planes had scarcely vanished into the overcast before another signal from *Yamato* ordered the others away. *Yahagi's* last pilot complained loudly. He would rather stay and fight. Unexpectedly he got his wish. Flying preparations were halted when an enemy fighter was spotted circling 5 miles to the east. The floatplanes would be easy meat for Grummans. It would be better if they remained aboard. The bugler sounded general quarters. Men tumbled up on deck, grabbing steel helmets and flak jackets. Young Lieutenant Kenji Hatta doubled across the forecastle to his gun position, holding his family sword, a valuable heirloom, clear of the steel deck. Ensign Shigeo Yamada, the reluctant nisei, donned his headset and began combing the radiowaves for the sound of American voices. Komura, Hara, and their staff climbed into the antiaircraft command post above the bridge. It was a small circular steel box, open to the sky, where they reluctantly donned steel helmets but spurned the flak jackets.

Hara personally checked off the antiaircraft defenses. The double 5.9-inch turrets swung toward the patrolling enemy. Clumps of 25-mm machine guns, similar to those on *Yamato*, spun targetward on their power mounts. The cruiser fairly bristled with firepower, and the snappy answers coming back from the gun captains confirmed that the crew was only too eager to use it. But not yet . . . no sense in wasting ammunition until the enemy came closer.

Something was wrong with *Asashimo*. She was losing station, gouts of olive-green smoke spouting from her stubby smokestacks. Surely they had not topped up her tanks with Manchurian soybean oil? Her turbines were in poor enough shape already; they had never been properly repaired since the Leyte battle. Peering through his binoculars, Hara could see a commotion on her bridge. Old Sugikara must be raging! He signaled his friend to find out what was going on. The destroyer commander, using a hand lamp, signaled back: "RUSHING REPAIRS. HOPE TO REJOIN YOU SOON." *Asashimo* fell slowly astern flying the signal "AM EXPERIENCING ENGINE TROUBLE." It was the last they saw of her.

Hara's uneasiness increased. He had felt safer with that trusted veteran on his port quarter. The destroyer was replaced by *Kasumi*, the second-smallest ship in the force. There were already too few escorts to provide adequate antiaircraft cover. Three small merchantmen passed close by, heading north. Crewmen gathered to gawk and wave at this unusual sight. Japanese ships still sailing the open sea! So they weren't all sunk? This was the Oshima transport group, which ferried supplies down the Ryukyu chain and served, where necessary, as a mobile radar picket. It was, in fact, the last time it would venture so far south. The merchantmen flashed the task force a good-luck message, dipped their flags in salute, and followed *Asashimo* over the horizon.

Optimism was growing aboard *Yamato*. The mood on number one bridge was positively euphoric. Yesterday's Kamikaze air attacks seemed to have crippled the Yankee carriers. Even chain-smoking Nobii Morishita began to talk as if they stood some chance of getting through to Okinawa. The rear admiral had commanded *Yamato* before being promoted to Chief-of-staff, Second Fleet. He had handled her throughout the Leyte battle, bringing the big ship back virtually unscathed. Perhaps their luck would hold.

The arrival of the U.S. flying boats was predictable. The Americans were sending out search planes, naturally enough, but it was doubtful whether they could muster enough air power for a heavy strike. Morishita said so and Vice Admiral Ito nodded. No one could be quite sure whether he agreed. Ito stood rock firm, feet apart, white-gloved hands clutching his valuable German binoculars, seldom vacating his customary place on the starboard side of the bridge.

Ariga phoned down to request permission for a long-range shot at the intruders. It was an ideal opportunity to try out the *San-Shiki*, the Beehive projectiles filled with layers of 20-mm shot. Fired from the 18.1-inch guns and ignited by a time fuse, they were designed to blow entire squadrons of aircraft out of the sky. Ito agreed. The after main turret swung toward the two ghostly shapes flitting through the clouds astern and fired a massive salvo. The shock wave shook the ship. Everything abaft the smokestack briefly vanished in clouds of exploded cordite. The gun crews clustered below the bridge tower cheered when the enemy dodged hurriedly back into the clouds.

"That scared them," Ariga said, chuckling. Assistant fleet gunnery officer Miyamoto made a note in his log: "Fired one salvo *San-Shiki* at 1017." Six U.S. Hellcats were sighted at 1107 tracking the force. Another salvo was fired, apparently without effect. The planes kept them tagged from a respectful distance.

A radio message came through from *Asashimo*. Her engines were almost repaired. She was advised to rejoin the force as soon as possible at top speed. A lone ship was helpless prey in these unfriendly waters.

Ensign Yoshida whiled away the time in the main radar room. He was not due on watch until noon. The sets were temporarily switched off, leaving *Yahagi* to maintain surveillance. Men sat around smoking the emperor's cigarettes specially issued on the eve of battle, and sipping liquor from hip flasks. It was not unusual in the Japanese navy to take a drink before action. Old Koyama was said to down half a bottle of Scotch before taking the wheel in combat. An orderly gleefully told the radar crew that there would be a special treat for dinner. The cooks were preparing *shiruko,* a sweetened red bean soup with rice cakes.

When Yoshida reported to the bridge he found the staff surprisingly relaxed. "Halfway there," someone announced. "It's going well so far," said Vice Admiral Ito, smiling. They all laughed nervously. Rice balls with plenty of hot black tea were served by relays of orderlies. The ensign gulped down cup after cup in the auxiliary radar cabin, back of number one bridge where sets were being switched on as *Yamato* resumed radar watch. The small room was uncommonly crowded, he noted, and relatively unprotected, with the bulletproof windows wound down. But it would not do to seek safety when the gunners below stood completely exposed in their crowded, open tubs.

The main radar picked up approaching aircraft. A messenger arrived with a delayed radio report from a lookout post in the Ryukyus. About 250 enemy aircraft were heading toward the force from the southwest. A small black cloud burst like a swarm of angry bees through the dense overcast and began circling to port. The planes seemed to be in no hurry to attack. Lookouts counted 1, 2, 3, 10, 20, 50 assorted fighters, bombers, and torpedo planes. Ariga's voice boomed over the intercom: "This is the commanding officer speaking. Stand by to repel air attacks. The decisive battle has begun."

U.S. Contact with the Japanese Task Force, East China Sea

MORNING, APRIL 7

U.S. TASK FORCE 58 ran into trouble from the beginning. Nothing seemed to go by the book. Takeoffs were erratic. Some misunderstanding sent the air group scampering so fast off the carrier *Bennington's* flight deck that all but one of her Marine Corsairs were left behind. The other fighters were still below decks, unable to get to the elevators. There was so much delay getting *Hancock's* aircraft airborne that the other carrier planes headed for the Japanese without them. A torpedo bomber from this unlucky group turned back with engine trouble and was forced to circle the task force, burning up fuel, for 1½ hours. This harassed Avenger soon became the favorite target of trigger-happy American ships' gunners.

The three-day-old cold front layered the sky with furry cirrus clouds at an altitude of 8000 feet. The cutting wind switched gradually from north-northeast to an east-southeast zephyr that scarcely ruffled the gentle sea swell. Way out to the east of Okinawa the wind was so light that the carriers had to hit top speed to lift off their overloaded planes. But beyond the Amami group, next in the island chain, the weather rapidly worsened, with clouds and rain closing in until pilots were flying blind through the racing overcast much of the time.

Launching from Task Groups 58.1 and 58.3 began simultaneously. Aircraft gathered in two milling crowds 30 miles from the task force and headed abeam of each other into the stormy northern sky. Distance to target was reckoned at 245 miles. It was comfortably shorter than the initial guesstimates: a total of five hours flying, there and back, including ample time for the attack.

The problem was to get there. Shortly after entering the cloud banks, 100 miles from launch point, a lone Corsair went spinning down into the sea. The pilot, Lieutenant (jg.) Al Bearwa of *Bunker Hill,* failed to bail out. No one ever knew what caused him to crash, although his tail could have been clipped off in the melee by another plane's propeller. Given the weather conditions, it was a miracle there weren't more collisions.

The heavy cloud 3000 feet above the sea gave way to sunshine higher up. A few air-group commanders headed for the clearer weather; the rest held formation as best they could. "We looked like a giant crop of blackbirds hunting for Farmer Ito's granary," Lieutenant Thaddeus Coleman of *Essex* reported. "The hunting got tougher and tougher. Clouds and more clouds. Rain and more rain . . . Eventually it was like swimming through soup, we couldn't see a thing."

The strike force included almost every type of carrier plane that helped win the Pacific war. There was a handful of gull-winged F4U Vought Corsairs, flown mainly by marine pilots . . . one of the great aircraft of World War II. With a top speed of 415 mph, range of over 1000 miles, and a kill ratio of 11 to 1, it was rightly dubbed "the Whistling Death" by the Japanese. The Corsairs now carried an additional 2000-pound bombload like most task force fighters; the conversion doubled their usefulness, despite the strain on pilots who were constantly called to launch bombing attacks in addition to maintaining combat air patrol.

SB2C1 Curtis Helldivers had finally replaced the reliable old Dauntless dive-bombers which won the day at Midway. Some, but not all, carried a 1000-pound armor-piercing (AP) bomb for use against thick steel decks. Others had to be satisfied with semiarmor-piercing (SAP) bombs, combining more explosives with less penetrative power, and designed originally for use against concrete blockhouses. The armorers had not anticipated many tougher targets on Okinawa. Using wing racks, the Helldiver's total bombload could reach 2000 pounds. Each two-man aircraft included a radio operator/gunner with a brace of .30 caliber machine guns.

The three tubby, stub-winged members of the Grumman family were all there: a few remaining F4F Wildcats, first U.S. fighter to challenge the irresistible Zero; plenty of large-tailed F64 Hellcats, the faster, more durable and in every way superior derivative of the pioneering Wildcat and nemesis of the now outdated Japanese Zero; and squadrons of big-bellied TBMF-1 Avengers, replacements quite early on for the old death-trap Devastators. The torpedo bombers usually carried a three-man crew. A few flew one man short on this particular sortie to beef up range and load. Some carried a mix of bombs under the wings and in the torpedo bay. Most were armed with the 1-ton Mark XIII Mod 9 aerial torpedo.

The great torpedo scandal which hobbled the U.S. submarine campaign throughout the first half of the war also undermined confidence in the torpedo bomber. The Mark XIII was a slightly smaller version of the Mark XIV supplied to submarines. Endless time-consuming experiment was required before it could be dropped from anything much higher than sea level without diving to the bottom, shooting off course, or prematurely exploding. Plywood stabilizers, which fractured and dropped away on impact, eventually enabled pilots to make "hot, true runs" from as high as 5000 feet. Drops were more often made from between 1000 and 1500 feet. Torpedoes were preset before takeoff at a depth of 10 feet for destroyers, or 18 to 22 feet to hit below *Yamato's* massive armor belt; given a full, well-trained crew, readjustments could be made in flight, but this meant climbing down into the fuselage and leaning inside the torpedo bay. It was a tricky job that no crewman relished . . .

Another hitch occurred halfway out. The air group commander from *Bennington* developed engine trouble and had to turn back. His place as strike leader of Task Group 58.1 was taken by Commander Edmond G. Konrad of *Hornet.* A prewar career officer serving his second year in the Pacific, he assumed the extra responsibility philosophically. As far as he was concerned, this was just another antishipping strike.

"You fly almost every day, so it becomes old hat," he recalled later. "Remember that most of us were professionals and this was part of our job. Your heart might flutter a little but you didn't go around jumping."

The commander was less worried about the Japanese than about his own strike force. Coordinating the attack presented major difficulties with so many planes in the air and the weather this bad. They might very well make a mess of things. Discipline was bound to suffer. Medals were being handed out these days "like so many crackerjacks." Crews got certain medals for a set number of strikes and then, as Konrad put it, "The brass added it all up and presented some more. The better the bomb hit on the biggest target, the higher the award. Since everyone wanted to return home with a chestful of medals, they all went for the jackpot."

Commander Konrad feared that this would upset his attack plans. The objective was to wipe out the entire Japanese task force. Pilots weren't all going to make a beeline for Yamato—not if he had any say in the matter. Those cruisers and destroyers were going to the bottom too. He and his three wingmen pushed ahead to grab the earliest possible glimpse of the enemy. All were flying Hellcats without bombs. Nimitz wanted his senior fliers to concentrate on directing operations. There were plenty of younger men aching to become heroes.

Lieutenant Coleman heard a pilot say, "I'm over the target location, but where are the Japs?" A high-pitched whine was coming over his headphones. It felt as if a fire siren was fixed to his head. He felt sure the Japanese were jamming their communications. Perhaps it was a malfunction in his radio. The enemy were unable to attempt anything so sophisticated—and few other fliers were complaining.

Lieutenant Commander Hugh Wood of Bennington came through loud and clear. His radar had picked up the Japanese task force 25 miles off their estimated position. The formations wheeled 28° to port. Four minutes later the lead planes glimpsed the enemy through cloud gaps at a range of about 8 miles. They were obviously expected. The warships promptly opened fire. Puffs of jet-black smoke tore through the rain clouds 1000 feet below. Yamato must have been firing those san-shiki Beehives, because the blast threw some planes about like shuttlecocks. Odd phosphorescent bursts followed, spewing out smoky tendrils; other shells smudged the sky with blotches of yellow and orange. It was a heavy barrage, though somewhat ill directed. Bomber and torpedo crewmen began throwing out radar-confusing bundles containing the regulation 350 streamers of window.

The two task group formations pulled up through the cloud cover out of sight of the enemy gunners. Scores on scores of cockpit covers twinkled in the watery sunshine. At 1217 the host of dark blue aircraft began a slow circle counterclockwise around the zigzagging enemy. The sunshine vanished as the planes sank back into a sea of cloud. Gaps revealed a leaden sea scored by the foamy wakes of the Japanese ships . . . somewhere between 8 and 12 of them, no one could be certain. Smoke belched from Japanese guns ranging in on the circling formations.

"Naturally we scattered, which began the most confusing air-sea battle of all time," Coleman said. "The Japanese gunnery officers were handicapped because they didn't have the faintest idea from where the next attack would develop. Nor did we, for that matter."

All eyes were on *Yamato*. The Americans had heard so much about this supership, yet they scarcely knew what she looked like. She seemed less formidable from above, steaming quite slowly. Most estimates put her speed at 12 knots. She was racing ahead, in fact, under full power.

Commander Konrad flipped back the Hellcat's cockpit cover while he sized up the enemy. One of his wingmen leaned out, snapping the first pictures. The Japanese were taking independent evasive action, drawing great S-shaped wakes across the waveless water. The lead cruiser (*Yahagi*) had suddenly, inexplicably shot ahead, away from the battleship. Twelve miles to the north lay a lone destroyer (*Asashimo*), apparently deployed as radar picket. There was nothing to indicate to the circling Americans that she had engine trouble. Four destroyers, probably *Kasumi*, *Suzutsuki*, *Hamakaze*, and *Yukikaze*, danced about the battleship's beam. The three others, *Hatsushimo*, *Isokaze*, and *Fuyutsuki*, chased after the fleeing cruiser. Konrad snapped out orders. The fighters would strafe the destroyers, dousing their antiaircraft fire while Helldivers and Avengers dealt with *Yamato* and *Yahagi*. *San Jacinto's* 14-strong air group was dispatched against the lonely picket. *Hornet's* torpedo bombers circled too wide for an immediate attack. The opening honors would have to go to *Bennington*. Konrad called up her Helldivers.

"Sugar Baker Two Charlies," he said. "Take the big boy."

The time was 1237.

The attack plan had been carefully refined during three years of Pacific warfare. Dive-bombers would swoop on their target, ideally from a height of 10,000 feet, to pound *Yamato* with heavy bombs. While the enemy gunners were fighting off the bombers, the torpedo-carrying Avengers would dive close to sea level and begin their hazardous run. It was essential that they hold course long enough, about 300 feet above the water, to launch their fish at the prescribed range of about 1200 yards. At that distance, making due allowance for the battleship's course and speed, one or more of the fish—but not all—were expected to hit. The idea was to drop a spread which no maneuvering by *Yamato* could possibly evade.

Kamikaze Attack
on U.S. Task Force 58

MORNING, APRIL 7

THE KAMIKAZE HIT Task Force 58 at about the same time the American pilots were preparing to attack *Yamato*. Groups of isolated Kyushu raiders grudgingly dispatched from "Kyushu Air Base" braved the bad weather to begin belated raids on the American carriers before the U.S. strike aircraft were halfway to the approaching Japanese fleet. The Kamikaze were too late to prevent the American mass launching, and they were too few and too unskilled to disrupt operations; most of them were shot down 100 miles to the north without ever glimpsing their target. Again the combat air patrol had a field day.

"They were nothing but the ragtail left, the ragamuffins," in Edmond Konrad's opinion. "We used to shoot them down like fish in a barrel. As time wore on we recognized their lack of ability and took care that none of them approached our ships."

Only a handful of Japanese planes evaded the defending Hellcats. At 1235 one Zero pounced on *Hancock*. This Zero pilot was different. He handled his plane like a veteran. It was thought he might not be a Kamikaze but one of the dwindling band of experienced fliers attempting a conventional bombing attack. Just as the American strike planes were beginning their long downward glide toward *Yamato* and her escorts, the Japanese dove out of the clouds, evaded everything the task force gunners could throw at him, and made the 33,000-ton carrier his funeral pyre.

The American gunners did their best. They began blasting away as soon as the fighter bomber hurtled toward them. General quarters sounded and men were still stumbling through the watertight doors when the firing started. Sentries promptly dogged the doors shut. The plane swung in from the starboard beam enmeshed in glowing tracer, with clouds of 5-inch shells bursting ineffectually astern.

The Japanese pilot ignored the barrage. He swung expertly across the carrier's bow, straight down the flight deck. A 520-pound semiarmor-piercing bomb, dropped from a height of 50 feet, penetrated the port hangar before exploding, severely damaging two quadruple 40-mm guns on its way down. Many men on the open deck jumped overboard.

The blast set the attacking Zero cartwheeling along the deck to crash into a group of parked aircraft. Three burst into flames near the elevator; three more and a lot of assorted fire-fighting equipment caught fire forward. Thirteen aircraft on the after deck began to burn in a sea of blazing, spilled gasoline. *Hancock* was in deadly danger. The Kikusui Kamikaze had claimed their first major victim.

The bridge filled with black smoke. Number one elevator buckled and jammed. Fireroom pressure dropped. Engineers donned gas masks as smoke billowed into the machinery spaces. Hose water poured into the elevator well, fusing electrical gear. The port forward hangar deck curtains, designed to contain the blaze, were blown away. Dozens of dead and dying lay among the stored planes.

Essex threw out life rafts and dropped scrambling nets over the side to save men struggling in the water. Destroyers moved in to help. The stricken *Hancock* swung to starboard, then to port, to clear the smoke from the bridge. Blazing gasoline fountained off the deck and into the sea as she listed with each turn. Surviving gunners opened up on a fighter plane heading, apparently, for *Essex*. Twenty seconds later they realized the plane was friendly.

Damage control crews with portable pumps converged on the

hangar decks. Medics began clearing the casualties. Some were burned beyond recognition; others were dead but unmarked, snuffed out by suffocating smoke. A hit like this early in the war could have destroyed the ship, spreading the fire along fuel lines to the volatile storage tanks; but these days the lines were quickly voided and filled with noninflammable gas, and by 1250 the damage control officer reported the flames contained and under control. The carrier resumed station in the task group. The forward flight deck fire was doused by 1315, although smoke still trickled through the hole in the main deck. Mitscher signaled his congratulations. But 72 *Hancock* men were dead and 82 injured.

Desultory suicide attacks continued. Repair parties kept working while the guns barked overhead. The Japanese were sending in small groups of Suisei 4YI (Judy) dive-bombers, with only their pilots aboard, to crash into the carriers. One of them narrowly missed *Essex*, hitting the sea and exploding 100 yards off her starboard beam. The pilot was blown out of the plane, his parachute opening uselessly.

Hancock was operational when her frustrated air group got back at 1630. They had flown over five hours to within 70 miles off the Kyushu coast without sighting the enemy task force. Starting off late from the farther-flung corner of Task Force 58, unable to pick up a corrected course owing to poor, possibly jammed radio communication, they had jettisoned bombs and torpedoes on uninhabited islands and struggled back on the YE/ YG homing beacon. It simply wasn't their day.

PART
VI

APRIL 7, 1945
Afternoon & Evening

SINKING OF JAPANESE FLEET, INCLUDING *YAMATO*

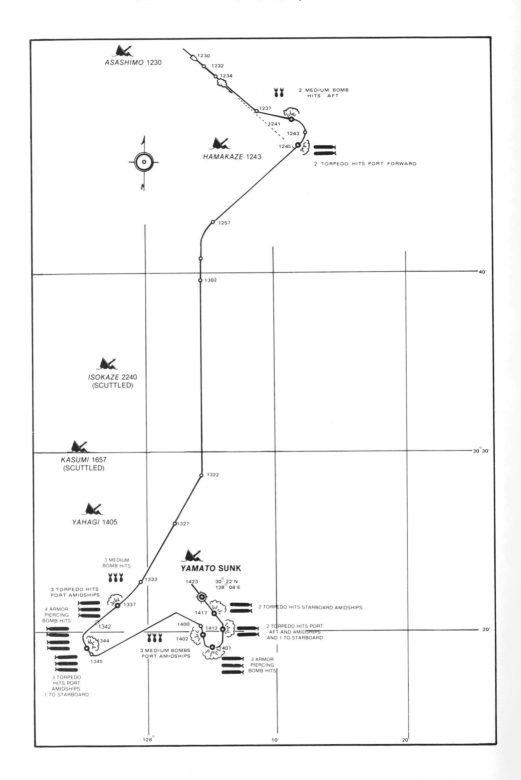

Beginning of the U.S. Attack: Wave One

1235 HOURS, APRIL 7

THE ENEMY FLAK was fierce enough to keep Hugh Wood's Helldivers dodging through the clouds. The man who first detected the Japanese task force on his radar was whipping round into 20° turns every five or six seconds. Three other members of *Bennington's* bomber group followed in deliberately loose formation. Multicolored pyrotechnics burst around them. The four planes pushed over into shallow dives from 3000 feet, just below the cloud blanket, approaching *Yamato* from astern. The great ship went hard about at the crucial moment, heeling sharply to port as her swinging bow scythed a wide semicircular wake through the China Sea. Red flashes winked from the amidships gun clusters. Glowing tracer balls curved up, slowly at first, then whipped past the diving planes.

Lieutenant Commander Hugh Wood felt the hits which severed two of his oil lines and damaged the port dive flap. But he held course, aiming his bomb toward the battleship's stern and hauling away along the length of her hull, just missing the bridge tower, before limping home leaking oil. Looking back, he saw a column of smoke shooting up abaft the battleship's smokestack. He landed back on *Bennington* with only 1 gallon

243

of lubricant left in the engine. The plane behind him lost the tip of its starboard wing. Another plane was slightly damaged in the wing slot.

Jack Fuller was not so lucky. Someone thought he saw a wing fall off the ensign's bomber as it turned into its dive. Someone else spotted two parachutes before the stricken plane exploded in the water. Neither the pilot nor his crewman, Charlie Williams, was rescued.

The group's bombs churned up huge white puddles around *Yamato*. Two exploded on the enormous hull. Wood's hit may have destroyed the main radar room. Reporting was naturally confused and exaggerated. Claims overlapped increasingly as more planes pressed their attacks. If every hit confirmed at the day-end debriefings had actually struck home the Japanese force would have been sunk twice over.

Commander Konrad felt in retrospect that the results were disappointing. It was not ideal bombing weather. Circling 2 miles to the east, enjoying a grandstand view, he vectored *Bennington's* other six Helldivers toward the escorts. It was a pity they were not carrying armor-piercing bombs. Fountains of water were thrown up around a destroyer west of the battleship (probably *Kasumi*) and another destroyer to the east.

The lone marine pilot, Lieutenant Kenneth E. Huntington, drove his Corsair after the fleeing *Yahagi*. He "didn't actually throw the switch that snuffed out the Japanese force," to quote the official marine history, "but he did race through the technicolored antiaircraft, plant his bomb on the forward turret, and silence those guns. One marine. One bomb. One Navy Cross."

Other fighter-bombers from *Bennington* followed the coordinator's instructions to smother the flak from those elusive Japanese escorts. One Hellcat claimed a direct hit aft of amidships on a destroyer. Others scored near-misses. Lieutenant Commander E. W. Hessel was infuriated when the bomb failed to release during his strafing run. He had "carried a 1000-pound general purpose bomb 260 miles to use on the Japs" and had no intention of carting it back home. The bomb, released on the second run, fell close alongside the enemy ship—without exploding.

Hornet's fighters closed in. Her 16 Hellcats had been making full use of the cloud cover while they selected their targets. Lieutenant Commander M. U. Beebe led his division down first, sections peeling off through the overcast to rake the destroyers with their guns. It was hair-raising but exhilarating. The flak stormed upward; the enemy grew from a cavorting toy to a lethal dark gray warship with real men running around its deck firing up at point-blank range. A quick burst from the fighter's 20-mm wing cannon sawed across the surface in a splatter of white foam changing to puffs of gray smoke as the explosive shells impacted on a destroyer's sides and superstructure.

Planes equipped with the still unreliable aerial rockets fired them from 1000 feet, watching for the destructive bursts that all too often failed to materialize. *Fuyutsuki* was struck several times by duds.

It still looked good to the pilots. One destroyer was left ablaze. Another *Hornet* air division, carrying bombs, claimed direct hits on a destroyer from 2000 feet. Fires broke out and shortly afterward the ship exploded. This could have been *Hamakaze*, although a torpedo seems to have finished her off. But there was no sign as yet of any slackening in the Japanese barrage. Long-range flak was consistently inaccurate, because of inadequate and outdated gunnery control. Close-in, the flak still packed plenty of punch. The 14 Helldivers from *Hornet*, hard on the heels of *Bennington's* bombers, were raked by uncomfortably accurate fire. Four of the seven planes led by Lieutenant Commander Robert M. Ward which pounced upon *Yamato*, ended as write-offs. One crash-landed in the sea on the way back. The others had to be jettisoned. Ward was slightly wounded in the left foot; he made the flight home with a flying boot full of blood. He claimed two hits, however, one on the battleship's superstructure, another on the after deck. It may have been his armor-piercing bombs which caused many casualties below decks. Two other pilots were also credited with hits on the bow and abaft the stack.

Bennington's remaining bombers spread destruction throughout the rest of the fleet. Three hits were claimed on the floundering *Yahagi* and one each on four destroyers. Most of these can be discounted, but with the battle only eight minutes old, Konrad was already satisfied that the Japanese sortie was doomed. He thanked his lucky stars there was no Japanese air cover. Even the inexperienced fliers the enemy was putting up these days would have seriously compounded the attackers' problems. The coordinator maintained constant communication with his friend, Harmon Utter, strike leader of the planes of Task Group 58.3, still circling, awaiting their turn, 20 miles to the west.

The two Mariner flying boats were by now forgotten. The Japanese were preoccupied with more lethal targets. But *Dog Eight* and *Dog Ten* remained overhead, keeping well out of range and catching occasional glimpses of the action through the cloud breaks. The pilots' chatter below came clearly over their headsets. It was like listening to 20 sports commentators reporting the same big ball game—in code:

"Hello Peacemaker 10. Hello Peacemaker 11. This is 9 V 250. 145 Chili Williams authentication is Sugar 130 Chili Williams 145 vector 040 . . ." until in clear someone said: "Cadillac 9, go get that destroyer over there."

Lieutenant Commander Ed De Garmo had hoped to muster all 14 Avengers from *Bennington*. Four got left behind in their pell-mell takeoff and another never left the traffic circle because of a fuel system failure. The hasty launching left his air group embarrassingly short of attack planes, including fighters and dive-bombers, but De Garmo reckoned he could still cope with the best the Japs could put to sea. Now it was his turn to slip out of the clouds and put torpedoes into this impudent little fleet.

De Garmo was circling clear of the flak when Konrad ordered him in. Unfortunately, his torpedoes were set to shallow depth; and in order to increase the squadron's endurance most of the radiomen had been left behind. There was no one else to readjust the torpedoes' depth settings. That ruled out the battleship. Despite all its improvements, the Mark XIII would be wasted at this setting on her heavy hull armor. So the air-group commander led a three-plane division through the flak to the bomb-shaken *Yahagi*. The upcoming fire was fierce, but they held course, dropping at 800 feet, and claimed a large explosion on the cruiser's starboard beam.

One pilot who lost touch with his division in the overcast found himself unexpectedly lined up on a lone destroyer. Pulling away after the drop he was delighted to hear a loud yell of "Bingo" from his gunner and looked round to see the target exploding violently amidships. It could have been *Hamakaze*. The ship promptly sank.

Lieutenant Norman Wiese swung from the east directly over *Yamato*. The flak was awesome. He reckoned himself lucky to survive. Pushing over at 6000 feet he headed directly across the enemy formation, passing close alongside the battleship. His plane was raked, and hit four times just as he released his torpedo at the escort screen. "An instinctive duck of his head probably saved his life as a 25-mm shell crashed through his windshield and instrument panel, driving a splinter of shrapnel into his scalp and temporarily blinding him with a spray of gasoline from the broken fuel pressure gauge," according to the official combat report. "Another shell exploded in the radio compartment, severely injuring the radioman (D. B. Blakely) with a chunk of shrapnel which lodged in his arm. Two others shredded his vertical stabilizer and rudder." A burning destroyer, sighted later, may have been hit by Wiese's torpedo.

Two other Avenger pilots jinked through the streams of tracer to renew the attack on *Yahagi*. They claimed a hit on the cruiser's port quarter that threw steam and debris high in the sky.

Time for the torpedo bombers to tackle *Yamato*. Eight of those aptly named Avengers from *Hornet*—the *Essex*-class replacement for the first *Hornet*, the gallant old carrier lost off Guadalcanal—dipped down into the storm of flak that erupted from the battleship's port side. Racing 500 feet above shrapnel-flecked water, engines dragging them forward at well over 250 knots, the pilots held course for those vital, vulnerable minutes essential for an accurate drop. The sea exploded ahead of them. Odd black objects, "dark whirling blobs" the size of a human head, spun through the smoke without apparently exploding. Six of the eight planes were hit. Large holes were ripped from wings, flaps were shot off, and perspex was shattered. Ensign Lee O'Brien slid suddenly out of formation, his engine disintegrating and afire. He splashed close to the battleship's bow. None of the three-man crew bailed out. The other seven Avengers dropped a beautiful spread despite the damage. Those planes were built for punishment.

Four torpedoes ran hot and true toward *Yamato*. All four of them hit, if *Hornet*'s combat report is to be believed, although it is more likely that only two or three did so.

Three other Avengers claimed a lethal hit on a destroyer. It is possible that in the confusion the destruction of *Hamakaze*, credited to *Bennington*, should be attributed to them. So many planes were milling about that it was impossible to decide who hit what with any certainty. No other hits were claimed. Small, shallow-draft ships were notoriously difficult to torpedo even with minimal depth settings. Several Japanese destroyer crews held their breath as torpedoes plunged harmlessly underneath their keels.

Heavy gunfire chased the retreating aircraft as far as the horizon. Great blobs of smoke burst around *Bennington's* air group as it rendezvoused 10 miles away. Only *Yamato's* 18.1-inch guns could reach that range, though, as usual, their aim was low. This was not surprising, since her turrets were never designed to fire at high elevation.

Yamato was spared further torpedo attacks from this strike wave. The combined air groups of Task Group 58.1 had dropped their last fish. *San Jacinto's* aircraft were busy elsewhere. *Belleau Wood's* small contingent of 14 aircraft, including six Avengers, carried only bombs. Flak stabbed through the clouds as they circled awaiting instructions; strange conical clouds of purple smoke shot up toward their formations. One pilot counted some 70 bursts exploding harmlessly at the same altitude. Most of the eight Hellcats were glad to peel off to bomb and strafe the escorts.

The hero of the previous day's air battles, Ensign Michele Mazzocco, was confounded by the shellfire from the battleship's main batteries. He had never faced such massive guns; nor, he guessed, had any other pilot.

"It was quite a sight," he recalled. "Like looking into a volcano."

Smoke belched from the great gray turrets as he put his Hellcat into a screaming dive. Today he was a bomber pilot with two 500-pound bombs slung beneath his fighter. But he was not going to waste them on the escorts: it was *Yamato* or nothing. The zigzagging hull grew steadily in his sights. He pulled back when the gaping maw of the ship's smokestack seemed to be opening to swallow him.

The bombs fluttered down; the aircraft shuddered as it defied the laws of mass and gravity and staggered upward through a storm of flak. Mazzocco felt sure his bombs had hit, although drifting smoke, shellbursts, and low-lying rain clouds made confirmation difficult.

The Avengers behind him were almost flying blind. Ensign Lycan stayed on his squadron commander's wing until he could no longer see his own wing tips. To avoid a collision he began letting down: "I came out in a shallow dive and by pure luck my sights were almost on a destroyer which was one of several about 1000 yards on the port quarter of the battleship," he reported. "All that was necessary was to push over and get my bomb bays open. I dropped at minimum intervalometer setting, at about 1400 feet, and I'm sure at least one of them hit. When we had pulled out and could look back, I could see the destroyer burning quite heavily amidships."

Enemy gunners ranged in on Lycan's retreating plane, but some smart spotting by his turret gunner, Anthony Dadamo, calling off the relative distance and altitude of the bursting shells, helped the plane to maneuver away unscathed.

Lieutenant Robert F. Reagan found himself mixed up with *Bennington's* dive-bombers when his Avenger emerged from the clouds. His wingmen were gone. A ship he classed as a cruiser, more likely the fast new single-stack destroyer *Fuyutsuki*, was almost directly below. He pushed over to a 45° dive and promptly caught a burst in the bomb bay. He managed to drop his four bombs, all missing the target to starboard, but the shell had burst inside his fuselage, spraying shrapnel, wrecking the radio gear, and tearing a foot-square hole at the base of the bomb-bay window. His radioman, Clarence Conner, would undoubtedly have been killed but for the fact that he was crouching aft at the time taking pictures.

The most extraordinary adventure of the day befell a young lieutenant from Detroit. William E. Delaney would have preferred to be home celebrating his second wedding anniversary with his wife, Lorraine. Instead he was pulling his Avenger out of a 250-knot dive on the battleship *Yamato*. He had lost Reagan and the other *Belleau Wood* torpedo bombers in cloud a few minutes before. He had gone in solo on this foolhardy attack, dropping his bombs wide of the ship and offering a splendid, isolated target as he dragged back the stick 500 feet from the water. He was still heading seaward when the converging flak smashed through the belly of the plane, tore off the starboard wing tip, and set the right wing tank on fire. The cockpit instantly filled with smoke. He couldn't even see the instrument panel. There was no time to gabble a farewell prayer . . .

Delaney forced back the starboard hatch, burning his right wrist, and peered out through the smoke. The blazing plane should have gone straight in the water; yet it was climbing steeply. Only his dive speed kept it from stalling. He quickly leveled off and dipped again toward the water in the hope of putting the fire out. The right sleeve of his flying suit was afire, though he did not notice it at the time.

"I couldn't tell exactly where the fire was, but it kept getting worse," Delaney reported. "I called the crew and said, 'It looks like they got us that time,' and started to climb again to get enough altitude to bail out. At about 1000 feet I told them to jump and waited about a minute for them to get their chutes on and go. By then the smoke in the cockpit was choking me pretty badly and I couldn't see a thing. The seat was too hot to sit on much longer and I knew I had to get out of there—and quick."

Radio operator William Tilley and gunner Ed Mawhinney flung back the cockpit canopy and jumped. Delaney climbed onto the port wing:

> I remember being surprised at how easy it was to stand on the wing. The slipstream didn't seem to bother me at all. I stood there and held on easily with one hand, getting smoke out of my eyes. There aren't very many of the rules for proper use of a parachute that I didn't break. Standing there on the wing, I reached over with my right hand and pulled the rip cord. I remember holding the red rip-cord handle in my hand, looking it over carefully, and tossing it down on the wing. I was facing aft and the chute, very fortunately, didn't stream immediately and foul on the tail surfaces. Nothing at all happened, in fact, until the tab began to take effect and the plane's nose came up slightly more.
>
> Then I simply walked to the trailing edge of the wing and dived off sidewise so as to miss the tail surfaces. The chute opened immediately and I did not oscillate a great deal. I never saw the plane after I left it. Mawhinney's parachute was a little below me and only about 150 yards away, close enough so that I could easily recognize his face. He was pulling on the shroud

lines of the parachute and appeared to be all right. Tilley was also in the air, about the same distance on the other side of Mawhinney. He was pulling on his shroud lines and was OK as far as I could tell. The chute was turned in such a way that I did not see them hit the water, nor was I ever able to locate either of them again after entering the water myself.

When I went in I had the chest strap unbuckled but not the leg straps, and I immediately inflated one side of my Mae West to keep me afloat while I got untangled from the harness. Some shroud lines were tangled up in my legs and I left them there until I broke out the parachute raft. It inflated without difficulty and I secured it to me, but stayed in the water alongside it for fear the Japs would see me. The wind was about 5 knots from the north. The sea was smooth with about a 3-foot swell. I looked at my watch about the time I got the raft inflated. It was 1300.

It took a little longer for the awful truth to dawn on Delaney. He had a shark's-eye view of the battle, alone in the middle of the enemy fleet . . .

The light carrier *San Jacinto* boasted a unique combat record. She had fought in more battles and steamed more miles in combat during the past year than any other carrier in the U.S. Navy. Her highly professional aircrews flew 9291 sorties between the Carolines campaign of May 1944 and the end of April 1945. They made short work of the straggling *Asashimo*. The limping destroyer was barely moving, 5 miles northeast of the Japanese task force, when the six Hellcats, one elderly Wildcat, and eight Avengers, plus a camera-equipped torpedo bomber, burst through the overcast to pounce on Sugihara's ill-fated command. Wheeling toward target at 5000 feet, showering down bundles of window, the formation passed a little too close to *Yamato* and her escorts. Pilots saw the battleship reel every time she let fly with her big guns.

The fighters went in first with their half-ton bombs. *Asashimo* looked like a light cruiser with her tripod foremast and triple main turrets. Helpless she might be, crawling slowly through the water, but her gunners put up a spirited defense. One gun crew aft was especially troublesome, the attackers later reported, and although the ship was ringed with bomb bursts nobody scored a hit. The fighters came down to deck level to strafe the gunners, crossing athwartships, fishtailing to pump in the maximum shells. Still *Asashimo* fought back, blowing a large hole in one Hellcat's port wing.

Two or three more runs and the deck began burning. The ship's guns were silenced. The bombs might have missed but they had badly shaken the ship's hull. Some of the side plates must have buckled, because a widening slick of oil trailed out across the East China Sea.

The torpedo bombers roared in from starboard at 240 knots to administer the coup de grace. The eight Avengers launched an inescapable spread almost simultaneously. One torpedo tumbled out of its bomb bay and sank. The others hit the water in textbook fashion from a height of about 300 feet at ranges between 1200 and 1600 yards. This allowed a clear, smooth run—"hot and true"—at point-blank range. The slowly moving destroyer turned to starboard in a feeble attempt to comb the wakes. She dodged two of the deadly fish; others passed astern. But two torpedoes struck, one beneath the bridge, the other close to the engine room. The explosions lifted the bow high in the air. The stern dipped into the sea and appeared to snap off. The bow slid slowly back under the water until a tremendous explosion beneath the surface blew it back up again. Then it seemed to disintegrate. In a matter of seconds all that was left was the oil slick, a miscellaneous mess of wreckage, and a handful of survivors.

Asashimo was destroyed in less than three minutes.

Aboard Yamato, *East China Sea*

SESAME SEEDS. Clumps of them, circling beneath the clouds. The young gunner Masanobu Kobayashi could not believe those were enemy planes. So many of them too. Slowly and quite deliberately he swallowed the last rice balls, grabbed from the mess hall when the alarm sounded. He slipped off his helmet and flak jacket and settled behind his gun. There was no sense in letting battle gear hamper his movements.

The small buzzing objects were still far out of range, but he tracked them automatically in the cobweb gunsight. If this was the real thing, he must have wasted a lot of training time. The only firing experience he'd had so far—apart from a few frantic moments last month defending *Yamato* in Hiroshima Bay—was aiming at a target sleeve tugged sedately past by slow-flying aircraft. Even this kind of firing practice had lately become rare.

The trick was to allow for aim-off. You fired just far enough ahead of the target to give the tracer time to catch up with it. The enemy literally flew into your line of fire. The instructors had painstakingly described it dozens of times, drawing triangular diagrams on the blackboard.

But what if a plane was heading for you from a sharp angle?

253

They had never practiced that on the firing range. The problem was simple, the instructors advised, because little or no aim-off was needed. You fired straight at the oncoming enemy and took corrections from your tracer. Nothing to it, really. Kobayashi glanced around for reassurance from the rest of the gun crew. They were staring tensely at the horizon, a group of uniformed statues.

The latest flag signal from the bridge tower streamed stiffly in the wind as the task force bent on full speed. It confirmed the obvious. Enemy aircraft sighted in large numbers. Prepare for antiaircraft action. Every ship signified readiness.

Vice Admiral Seiichi Ito made a rare visit to Ariga in his tower-top command post. He found the captain studying the enemy through powerful binoculars. "Torpedo bombers," he was saying. "Fighters, dive bombers . . . I'd say those bastards have everything!"

"Have we?" asked Ito.

Ariga shrugged.

"All we can expect," he said.

Ito pointed out the handful of Helldivers peeling off from the main formation.

"We'd better order every ship to fire independently. No sense in trying to coordinate our air defenses under this sort of attack."

Ensign Mitsuo Watanabe repeated the order over the intership radio as the admiral returned to number one bridge. He braced himself against the bulkhead as the roar of engines grew louder. One of the radar officers, Ensign Tatsuo Nishio, a Kyoto University graduate on watch in the crowded wing cabin, put his head round the door. He was saying something about rainsqualls interfering with reception when the guns let loose again
. . .

Captain Tameichi Hara tried to draw the attackers away from *Yamato*. He called for full power from the engine room. *Yahagi* surged away from the flagship at over 35 knots. The hull shuddered as he threw her into a series of convulsive turns. Two of the six Helldivers heading for the battleship turned in his direction. They came screaming down upon the port beam oblivious to the shells and tracer spitting skyward from the cruiser. As the first bombs curled down, Hara flung his ship hard to starboard.

Great geysers of dirty water crashed over the upper deck. Other Hellcats followed, almost at deck level, dropping more bombs which shook her rivets. Machine-gun bullets ripped through the upper works. The floatplane blew apart on its catapult, but no one seemed to be hit. The gunners fired back without flinching.

The oily sea was torn by scurrying ships, bursting bombs, and splashing flak and bullets. A rainsquall offered respite half a mile ahead. Hara steered toward it. The fighters closed in at mast-head height. The cruiser dodged gamely through another clutch of bombs. Ensign Yamada tied down his radio sets in the shack beneath the bridge. Successive shock waves threatened to throw them onto the deck. He strained his ears for American voices. Very little was audible; either they were maintaining exceptional discipline or he was on the wrong frequency.

One signal did come through, loud and clear. It was uncoded, from *Asashimo.* "AM UNDER AIR ATTACK," the unseen telegraphist tapped out. "AM UNDER"—the circuit went dead. A lookout on the cruiser's bridge spotted flak beyond the horizon. Gradually it died away.

Four Avengers launched a spread of torpedoes off *Yahagi's* starboard beam. Hara was caught off-balance. Too late he yelled a helm order. Three bubbling tracks were bearing down on the cruiser. The skipper swung her round to face the oncoming wakes. She was halfway through her turn when a torpedo caught her amidships just below the waterline. A column of water gushed higher than the bridge, there was a deafening crash, then silence. The stricken ship wallowed in the gentle swell, engines dead, electric power gone, and a lengthening slick of oil spreading out astern.

The lookouts were shouting again. The guns threw up a futile barrage as three more Avengers dived in from the opposite quarter. Hara watched helplessly, his ship a sitting duck. The fantail flipped out of the sea. Water and wreckage thundered down on the after gunners. The rudders and propellors were almost certainly sheered off, if not worse. Hara looked disbelievingly at his watch. It was 1246. They had been in action for precisely 12 minutes . . .

Yamato was taking much more punishment. But she was built to take it. The first Helldivers bored through a curtain of flak, scoring at least two hits with 1000-pound semiarmor-piercing bombs. One glanced off the after gunnery control, wiped out two 25-mm mounts, and exploded two decks below, killing every member of the after port damage control team. Ensign Katono heard the crash in his secluded tomb on the starboard side, but the central bulkhead shielded them completely. He thought it must be a torpedo. Another bomb hit the main radar room where Ensign Yoshida had been relaxing an hour before. When no one could raise the radar crew on the telephone, damage control ordered him aft to investigate.

Yoshida did not see how anyone could survive on the open deck. It was a madhouse, he told himself, creeping along in the peculiar crouching posture men adopt in the hope of offering the minimum target. The antiaircraft gun positions clustered so invitingly around the smokestack were being raked by machine-gun fire. The enemy was sending in his Hellcats to strafe the gunners while dive-bombers and torpedo bombers coordinated their attacks on the weaving battleship. Bullets stitched across her upper works, clanging on armored steel or crushing into helpless flesh. Men did not just topple over as Yoshida had seen in the movies; a hit from a point five bullet threw the gunners about like paper dolls. Limbs tore off. Blood splattered high up the smokestack.

The ensign crept aft through swirling smoke. Several times he flung himself flat on the deck as a Grumman howled low overhead. A gunner close to his elbow lurched over the ammunition clips clutching his stomach. His eyes glazed as he opened his mouth to scream. A nearby gun crew cheered as their tracer smashed into an approaching Helldiver's cockpit. It crashed and exploded off the port bow.

One of the 5-inch gun turrets had vanished. The radar room was split wide open. The communication ladder was gone. Yoshida slid down inside on a rope. He looked around for his friends Lieutenant (jg.) Omori, Petty Officer Hasegawa, and the others. A human torso was blown against one bulkhead. Lumps of bloody flesh lay among the shattered instruments.

More dive-bombers. Yoshida stared up desperately through the gaping deckhead. He thought: "This is not where I should die. My place is on the bridge." He heaved himself out of the shattered deckhouse and ran, head down through the confusion. Ammunition loaders with smoke-blackened faces bumped into the panic-stricken officer. Corpses cluttered his path. Several times he slipped in pools of congealing blood.

A bomb blast caught him as he was about to scramble up the outer bridge ladder. His body slammed against the rungs. He looked back, blinking, to see a pall of white smoke rising from what had once been the rear auxiliary battery. The triple 6-inch turret, big enough to provide the main armament of a light cruiser, seemed staved in by some giant hammer. Dazedly he climbed the ladder repeating aloud his report on the radar room: "All personnel killed in action. Equipment completely destroyed. Use impossible." Bullets twanged around him, gouging silver slivers from the gray steel plate. Somehow he made it back safely to the bridge.

Vice Admiral Ito still stood there, rocklike, with folded arms. He gave no further orders. Each ship had to fend for herself. He refused to flinch even when bullets sang in through the open bridge windows. One smashed the fleet engineering officer in the chest, slamming him back against the bulkhead. He slithered to the deck, leaving a long smear of blood.

The radar officer, Ensign Nishio, fell beside him. Convulsively he tried to stuff his own entrails back into his gaping stomach. He smiled bravely as Yoshida tried to help him; then suddenly he died, his smile stiffening into a gristly grin. Stretcher parties removed the bodies and sanded the blood-soaked linoleum.

Morishita let out a croaking cry. Everyone thought he had been hit. But he was staring aghast to starboard, pointing a nicotine-stained finger at *Hamakaze*. Explosions were erupting from the veteran twin-stack destroyer. She seemed to have been hit simultaneously by bombs and torpedoes. Her bow and stern snapped out of the water as the hull jackknifed. Within seconds she was gone, leaving nothing but an oil slick, minor wreckage, and many men swimming for their lives. They would be swimming a long time before anyone could help them.

Kobayashi's gun tub stood isolated and exposed on the after deck. He had been deafened but unharmed by the direct hit on the nearby battery. There was no sign of life from the dented turret, perched on its tower abaft the main after battery control. Fire licked through a gaping hole in the deck. The tower itself was gashed and dented by splinters.

The big main guns crashed and roared alongside them, cloaking the crew in choking smoke. Gunners like Kobayashi were getting off relatively lightly on the starboard side. Most of the attacks so far were hitting the opposite side of the ship. All they'd been able to shoot at so far was attacking aircraft pulling out of their dives and climbing skyward. The crew watched their tracer falling harmlessly behind several departing Grummans before deciding it was better to conserve their ammunition. Rear gunners in the retreating planes fired back, however, aiming for the bridge tower and the overcrowded gun positions around the smokestack. Bodies were blown all over the deck. A veteran warrant officer, a stickler for neatness and order in this part of the ship, strolled methodically down the port side throwing dismembered limbs into the sea. He pursued his gruesome task as if by reflex, impervious to the battle around him.

Executive officer Nomura crouched over the damage control panel in a collapsible canvas chair. At his back, through a doorway in the armored command post, Chief Quartermaster Koyama juggled the steering wheel. It was a small wheel for such a large ship, brass and highly polished, and the old man was spinning it as fast as his hands could flick the spokes in answer to the torrent of helm orders bellowing down the voice pipe.

The executive officer gave up trying to contact number seven damage control. The telephone did not answer. The ship had been hit somewhere on the port quarter. He had felt several explosions. What he needed now was detailed information. One of the nest of voice pipes shrilled. It was Yoshida on Ito's bridge reporting destruction of the main radar room. A petty officer staggered in shortly afterward, wiping blood off his face. The crewmen in number seven damage control were all dead. Several gun turrets were knocked out. A bomb had penetrated two decks on the port side and exploded in the stores section. Casualties were mounting on the upper deck.

The ship jolted violently under the shock of several near-misses. A red warning light winked on the control panel. The temperature was rising in one of the ammunition magazines. An explosion there would blow them sky-high. Nomura phoned number six auxiliary magazine, which fed the portside 5-inch antiaircraft batteries. The warrant officer in charge confirmed that the cordite store was getting hot. His men were working the hoists stripped to the waist. But the magazine itself wasn't on fire. The heat was coming through an adjacent bulkhead.

Nomura ordered a damage control party from one of the amidships divisions to find and tackle the blaze. It must be the stores section. There was still plenty of inflammable material aboard. Those supply clerks were loath to off-load everything. The ship shuddered and vibrated around him. The crash and stutter of her guns swamped out the thump of straining engines. Nomura experienced a curious urge to run out on deck, out of his steel cubbyhole, to see things for himself. Anything but this cramped inactivity. Thus far they had only been bombed. Where were the enemy torpedo planes?

The crash flung him across the room. *Yamato*'s great bulk seemed to rise from the water, squirming with agony. The unspoken question was answered. Torpedoes had struck home . . .

Ariga saw them coming. So did the lookouts. There seemed to be so many heading toward them that they had stopped their regulation reporting. Instead of shouting: "Torpedo bearing port" such and such degrees, they were hoarsely yelling: "Portside! *Gyo!* Fish!" The captain did his best. His experience in destroyers was proving invaluable. The snobs in Tokyo who doubted whether this potbellied little bulldog could handle the pride of the Imperial Navy should have watched his inspired performance. He gauged the direction of the falling bombs, altering course as they wobbled toward him—"rather like red beans," one of the lookouts remarked—and skillfully evaded most of them. But torpedoes could not be avoided so easily. While Ariga concentrated on dodging the Helldivers, the torpedo bombers crept in low on the port beam.

The ship's gunnery officer, Captain Yoshio Kuroda, had given up trying to coordinate *Yamato*'s antiaircraft fire. His entire system, including the impressive optical range finder swinging 25 feet above Ariga's head, was designed for surface targets. It was like swatting bugs with a sledgehammer! He passed control to local battery commanders, ordering them to choose their own targets. There were plenty in sight. But when the Avengers formed up, a line of menacing black shapes against the slate-colored sky, he brought the main batteries to bear. The great guns pumped shells into the sea ahead of the approaching

Avengers to whip up a defensive curtain of fragments and fountaining water.

The Avengers held course 500 feet above the churned-up water. On they came, straight through the barrage. The gunnery officer had to admire their courage. The smaller guns joined in. Black shell bursts peppered the sky. Streams of glowing tracer arced out toward the enemy. One plane was hit! It shuddered violently, staggered swiftly out of formation, and exploded in the sea. The other bombers calmly dropped their fish and broke off in all directions. The bubbling wakes plowed steadily toward them. There was only one hope of evasion. They must "comb the wakes" by swinging directly at the oncoming torpedoes. Chances were they could steer between them. Everything depended on the way the enemy had fired his spread. A group of torpedoes should, ideally, be fired to catch the target whichever way it turned. And that was what happened. One line of bubbles missed the fast-swinging bow. Another passed harmlessly astern. A third exploded abaft the bridge, shaking the ship from truck to keel and drenching the amidships guns in dirty water. A fourth smashed into the hull alongside the outer port fireroom.

Nomura picked himself up, checked for damage, and received reports of minor water seepage from the engineers. The clinometer showed zero degrees of list. Speed appeared unchecked. The executive officer found the chief of staff looking over his shoulder. Morishita had raced down the tower like a maniac. The two men looked at each other. Morishita nodded, darted into the wheelhouse, clapped old Koyama on the shoulder, and dashed topside again.

Fresh attack waves were already bearing down on *Yamato*. Helldivers came screaming in astern. Confused gunners swore there were hundreds of them. A solitary Avenger diving in from the starboard beam came into Kobayashi's sights. The pilot had just released a stick of bombs which exploded way astern. He was pulling out of his dive when tracer bullets ripped into the pale gray belly of the plane.

"Fire! Keep firing!" screamed Kobayashi. The triple gun barrels were smoking hot. Any moment now they would melt.

The torpedo bomber staggered up into the air trailing smoke and seemed to hover there while three yellow parachutes drifted down. Then it crashed blazing into the sea. The gun crew cheered madly. They had the feeling, though they couldn't be sure, that this was *their* victim. It felt good to hit back when old *Yamato* was being hit so hard.

The dive-bombers were not scared off. They pressed in even closer through the storm of steel. The battleship disappeared in a forest of splashes. Men aboard the destroyer *Fuyutsuki*, gallantly holding station to starboard, were convinced for a moment that *Yamato* was gone. She reappeared, majestic as ever, guns blazing, but with several more bomb craters in her upper deck.

One burst inside the forecastle, causing little damage. A junior messenger Nomura sent to investigate found the officer in charge of damage control seated on an upturned box waving his naked sword and screaming the samurai war cry: "Wah! Charge!" The telephone rang unanswered at his elbow. The youngster risked a shortcut back to the command post across the open deck, dodging bursts of machine-gun fire. He flung himself down behind bollards and capstans as bullets tore up the camouflaged teak planks. Ahead lay the shelter of the main turrets thundering spasmodically at the darkening sky. The thin black curtain of a line squall slanted down a mile or two away. The boy crept past the forecastle machine gunners, all of them dead or wounded, and reached the bridge tower in one last breathless sprint.

The bomb which hit just abaft the tower obliterated two triple machine guns before exploding in the senior wardroom. The chief surgeon and his staff were using it as an emergency dressing station. The room was packed with wounded. Litter cases overflowed into the adjoining companionways. Not a man survived. The messenger was still vomiting when he reported to Nomura. He had looked inside a butcher shop.

The telephones went dead. The communication trunk deep inside the central bulkhead was irreparably fractured. Two more torpedoes slammed into the port side. Nomura began activating the valves to correct a developing portside list. He breathed a trifle easier when 3000 gallons of seawater began pumping into the empty blisters on the starboard side. He had been afraid the pumps would jam. The ship slowed perceptibly, but gradually righted herself.

An unexpected source of damage caused new anxiety. Near-misses were creating almost as much havoc as direct hits. The designers' urge to produce an impregnable armored box inside the hull had reduced structural flexibility. Heavy shocks close alongside sheared rivets in the armor plating and thrust reinforcing beams through the bulkheads they were intended to support. Flooding spread rapidly through ruptured compartments along the battered port side. The outer port engine and firerooms would soon be full of water.

The attacks ceased. Nomura ran up to report to Ariga. *Yamato* was by no means crippled, but she was hurting. The skipper nodded grimly. He ordered his signal yeoman to hoist the Z flag. It was the historic signal Admiral Togo flew as he closed the Russian battle line at Tsushima. The converging triangles of black, blue, red, and yellow signified a dramatic message:

ON THIS ONE BATTLE RESTS THE FATE OF OUR NATION. LET EVERY MAN DO HIS UTMOST.

Ariga watched the Nelsonian exhortation fluttering from the starboard halyard. He leaned back against the compass binnacle. Patches of perspiration darkened his uniform, though the day was cool. Medics removed a body on a litter.

"We're still afloat and still fighting," Ariga said. "Now we've got a pause for breath."

He watched *Yahagi* falling immobilized astern. He glanced wearily at the bulkhead clock. It was 1259. The pause for breath was to last less than five minutes.

U.S. Attack:
Wave Two

THE JAPANESE COUNTED five separate attack waves. It was understandable in the confusion of battle. Actually there were only three. The formations from Task Group 58.1 pulled clear of the action to make way for Task Group 58.3. Planes from *Essex*, *Bataan*, *Bunker Hill*, and *Cabot* were circling nearby, impatient for action. *Hancock's* air group should have been there too, but it was floundering about hopelessly lost, 100 miles to the north, after a late takeoff. The *Hancock* pilots missed the target in the bad weather—and missed the battle.

Edmond Konrad, still circling over the battle, handed control to Commander Harmon T. Utter of Task Group 58.3 and lingered awhile to watch. His men had done well, but could have done better—particularly the dive-bombers. Their performance, he felt, was disappointing. It was hardly surprising in this filthy weather.

There was a brief pause before Utter's planes renewed the assault. Pilots from *Essex* led the attack. The crew of this veteran carrier, first of the new class that turned the tide of war in the Pacific, was one of the finest in the fleet. Their battle honors harked back to the Marshall Islands campaign of early 1944

263

when it became obvious even to the strategists in Tokyo that the weight of American ship construction had irrevocably tilted the balance of sea power against Japan.

Harmon Utter was an *Essex* man himself. He watched the enemy maneuvering with grudging admiration. The escorts were putting up a superb fight. Their antiaircraft fire was extremely accurate, as he soon found by flying too close to *Yahagi*. The first wave had dented but not destroyed the Japanese formation. The enemy task force commander must be an unusually capable officer, he thought. Still, it wouldn't do much good in the end. The Japs were cornered . . .

The same pyrotechnics splattered the overcast: great black blobs of smoke, ghostly white phosphorescent trails, bursts of dirty yellow. "A regular Fourth of July show," one *Essex* pilot remarked. The majority of planes directed against *Yamato* were hit by flak. Helldivers went in first to distract the battleship's gun crews as the torpedo bombers maneuvered into position. The dive-bombers dropped in from 6200 feet, taking advantage of a cloud break, gliding like rose petals through the stuttering tracer spurting from *Yamato*'s starboard beam.

"Bomber pilots pushed over in all sorts of crazy dives," Utter reported. "Fighter pilots used every maneuver in the book, torpedo pilots stuck their necks all the way out, dropped right down on the surface and delivered their parcels so near the ships that many of the planes missed the ships' superstructures by inches. The Japanese ships squirmed like a nest of snakes . . ."

Lieutenant (jg.) A. L. Mitchell came in at 65° without dive flaps, releasing both 1000-pound semiarmor-piercing bombs at 1500 feet and pulling out in a shuddering climb at 800 feet. *Yamato* sprawled out below him, guns spitting, smoke drifting out of a hole abaft the smokestack. One bomb burst on the starboard side of the bridge tower. The three other pilots of his division, banking in sharply across the target, claimed hits from forecastle to quarterdeck.

The men aboard the torpedo bombers saw some of the Helldivers' bomb bursts welling up as they began their run toward the Japanese battleship. The first division of four planes, led by Lieutenant Commander A. H. White, was forced by the clouds to come in slower and lower than he would have preferred, but this helped them approach unobserved. They were heading in at 40° on *Yamato*'s starboard bow when the ship began swinging toward them. The angle and the target size decreased rapidly as three of them loosed their fish and hauled away through the flak. Lieutenant (jg.) David Jacobs was too far off position to attempt a drop. He made an independent attack on one of the destroyers.

The big guns spouted flame and smoke. The concussion from a passing shell nearly knocked one plane into the sea. But a torpedo struck *Yamato*'s starboard bow.

The other 11 *Essex* Avengers followed in divisions at 15-second intervals. The battleship continued her wide slow turn, presenting an increasingly tempting expanse of port side. Lieutenant (jg.) M. J. Walden's division watched at least three of their fish hit this enormous target. Division three, hard on their heels, claimed it was better than a training run. They were also credited with three hits. The fourth division, three planes strong, led by Lieutenant (jg.) Mike Shumway, couldn't believe their luck. They were assigned "the cleanup job." *Yamato* continued her fatal turn in "a perfect setup for the shot." Another two torpedo hits were claimed.

These reports later proved exaggerated. But by now it was obvious that the battleship was in bad trouble. She was listing to port, battered by bombs and ablaze below decks. A huge black-rimmed crater on her port deck was pouring silver-gray smoke.

The *Essex* fighter-bombers played havoc with the escorts. Lieutenant Thaddeus Coleman, the hunting blackbird, lost touch with his Hellcat division while awaiting the order to attack. He tagged on to a group of Helldivers and Corsairs about to dive on *Yahagi*. The cruiser was drifting helplessly some 4 miles north of the main force. Coleman pushed over from 4500 feet in a 40° dive. Flak poured up at him. The plane staggered as a shell tore through the port wing. He pulled out in time to see his bomb exploding amidships. As he watched, another bomb struck the cruiser's bow. The ship vanished in a curtain of bomb splashes.

The lieutenant's missing Hellcats turned up a few minutes later. *Yahagi* received another pounding. More bomb hits reduced her superstructure to smoking ruins. A near-miss off the port quarter lifted her battered stern clear of the water. It splashed back with shocking force. The planes closed in, strafing at low level. Fighters from *Essex* fired 1.5 million rounds of point five ammunition during the battle.

A triumphant but badly battered air group headed home. One Avenger had taken so much shrapnel in the engine that the pilot did not think he could make it. He landed almost out of oil. Four others were so badly riddled that each needed a wing change. Seven Helldivers and four Hellcats limped back with damaged stabilizers or hydraulic systems, or tattered wings. Rugged aircraft construction saved many lives this day . . .

Harmon Utter was determined to get that battleship. This was the moment to strike, now that she was listing. He ordered *Bataan's* nine Avengers to close in without delay. To hell with bombs! Torpedoes would decide this battle.

Lieutenant Commander Harold R. Mazza watched the *Essex* planes attacking *Yamato* through a frightening storm of flak. The enemy fire was so intense and visibility was so poor that he swung his torpedo bombers back into the clouds to look for a less dangerous line of approach. He decided to come in from about 5 miles astern, turning broadside onto the target the moment he was abeam. Pilots would "ladder" their attack, holding speed down for a final, steeper, more accurate dive. Immediately after completing his torpedo drop, each man would whip about and high-tail it to safety. Mazza passed out his orders over the radio.

Yamato was still turning to starboard at reduced speed when Mazza led the charge. He executed a classic drop at 1500 yards, speed 250 knots, from a height of 300 feet. Lieutenant (jg.) Kenneth E. Wheeler dropped his fish a moment later. Most of the others followed, turning abruptly around for their prearranged rendezvous 10 miles away.

Ensign Jerry Schmidt could not pull away in time. He found himself flying directly across *Yamato* fore and aft, with antiaircraft gun mounts tracking him as he fled. Tracer came up like "purple popcorn balls." His gunner, William S. Armstrong, blazed back and saw his tracers bounce off the scarred superstructure. By some miracle the plane survived untouched.

Ensign George Murphy was heading out of the flak, congratulating himself on completing a satisfactory drop, when crewman Ed Mueger told him the torpedo was still aboard. He went back again, flying low, propeller wake ruffling the ocean swell, to drop the balky fish from 100 feet.

Nearly everyone claimed a hit. Conditions appeared almost perfect. Two torpedoes certainly hit *Yamato's* starboard side, one forward and one amidships, but the attackers were taking such violent evasive action that positive identification was impossible. Persistent underestimates of the battleship's speed may also have impaired the torpedo bombers' aim.

Bataan's 12 Hellcats, each carrying two 500-pound bombs, had a tougher time harassing the escorts. The clouds were so low that the Hellcats were forced into long shallow dives from about 1000 feet. They attracted more concentrated fire from the battleships and the destroyers than the Avengers. Three of the fighter-bombers went for what they believed was a cruiser but was probably *Suyutsuki*. They claimed one hit which set the ship on fire. Lieutenant (jg.) Walter Trigg was bearing down on a destroyer, probably *Kasumi*, already hit and damaged by another division, when a shell shot away his rudder controls. He eventually crash-landed safely near his carrier. Two accompanying Hellcats were similarly crippled but managed tricky deck landings.

The time was 1309. The airgroups from Task Group 58.3 had been in action for exactly ten minutes.

Next, *Bunker Hill*. Her pilots were keen. They had never attacked enemy warships on the high seas. It was still a shock to look over the cockpit sides and see a battleship and her destroyer screen dodging about below. Everyone had heard about *Yamato*. Everyone longed to sink her. But they never guessed just how big she was. Debriefing reports put her size at 45,000 tons with 16-inch guns. Perhaps the American mind could not accept the possibility that the scrawny Nips had outbuilt them.

Utter ordered *Bunker Hill's* torpedo bombers to take on the big one. The flak seemed to be slackening and ill directed. They must strike hard—and fast.

Lieutenant Commander Charles W. Swanson found a hole in the clouds just as he picked up the target on radar. The battleship was still turning to starboard, heading roughly southwest. Light rain and gloomy darkness partly blanketed the enemy force. He led the first division ahead, working southwest while the second division broke left in a southeasterly direction. It was the classic squeeze play the Japanese aviators had practiced in their heyday, designed to trap their target whichever way it moved. Attacks were mounted from every angle.

Flak erupted with renewed vigor. More multicolored bursts stained the stormy sky. The way *Yamato* kept turning ("Was her steering damaged?"), it was obvious that a three-plane split would give them a chance of firing an inescapable torpedo spread toward her bow. The wing planes broke away on each side while their leader performed a slight S-turn to avoid creeping too far ahead. They plunged straight toward the battleship's bow, the second division led by Lieutenant J. Berry close on their heels.

One of them didn't make it. The plane flown by Lieutenant (jg.) Richard Walsh caught fire and crashed before it could drop its torpedo. Crewmen Glen Heath and Clayton Whiteman died with their pilot in the explosion. Brian Berry stopped a 40-mm burst in his port wing, about 3 feet from its tip, which flipped him on his back. He recovered in time to aim his fish at *Yamato*'s starboard bow. Ensign Fred Guttenberger heard a crash behind him. A machine-gun burst had hit the fuselage just abaft the turret, injuring his radioman and knocking the gunner unconscious. Fragments hit Ensign Orville Webster's starboard wing root and started a fire. His starboard wheel dropped down, but after two or three minutes the fire went out. Lieutenant Owen Ray had flown all the way from the carrier with his starboard wheel unretracted. He was hit by a 40-mm shell. On the flight back his crew dumped everything they could lay their hands on, including guns, ammunition, camera, and radar. They landed safely aboard as did the other battered survivors of *Bunker Hill*'s torpedo squadron.

The pilots claimed 9 hits out of 13. It was an impressive if exaggerated score. Only two torpedoes hit *Yamato* during this attack—a tribute to the efficacy of her antiaircraft fire. Lieutenant John Davis spoke for most *Bunker Hill* pilots when he remarked afterward: "On the way in I was working for the navy, and on the way out I was working for myself and my crew."

The carrier's fighters and dive-bombers followed the now routine pattern of attacking the escorts. Most of the Helldivers and bomb-carrying Corsairs made a heavy attack on a destroyer 10 miles from the main force. They claimed at least three dam-

aging hits. Their detailed combat report, complete with diagrams, could have given them credit for sinking *Asashimo*; but
she was already sunk. The difficulty of establishing an accurate
position, plus the confusion of battle, may explain the error.
More likely the victim was *Isokaze*.

The 19-strong attack force from *Bataan's* sister ship, the light
carrier *Cabot*, was to strike the last blow for Task Group 58.3,
for Harmon Utter, masterminding the chaotic melee below him,
and for Mitscher himself, still fretfully awaiting confirmation of
victory. So far he had received only garbled reports, but once
the flying boats confirmed his lads were in action his last doubts
vanished.

"Sic 'em, boys. Sic 'em," he mumbled from his perch on the
walkway.

Utter had no doubt that *Yamato* was doomed. He said so, in
a flash signal to Vice Admiral Mitscher. He had watched the
torpedo wakes converging on her bulky hull through the oily
gray sea. He couldn't be sure exactly how many had hit her. But
surely the answer was "plenty." It was amazing how *Yamato*
still managed to take it. Most battlewagons would have already
gone to the bottom.

Carrier planes had been attacking for 22 minutes. Utter's
group had been in action since 1259. It was now 1312.

It was *Cabot's* fifth strike against the Japanese fleet—her aircrews figured that was a record. But this was the most difficult.
The nine Avengers and ten Hellcats, each carrying a 1000-
pound bomb, milled about in the lowering sky, vainly awaiting
orders. None came through. Radio reception was so poor and
messages were so badly garbled that they suspected, wrongly,
that the enemy was jamming their communications.

Fortunately, it made no difference. Lieutenant Jack Ander-
son, leading his torpedo bombers through the murk close behind
those from *Bunker Hill*, knew exactly what he had to do. He had
no intention of wasting his fish on anything less than *Yamato*.
The battleship had slowed, listing slightly, her six operational
escorts zigzagging around her, all filling the sky with a massive
if haphazard barrage of shells. He picked a passage through the
destroyer screen directly between two wildly maneuvering
ships and led his first four planes in shallow dives toward the
battleship.

Their aim point, he reported afterward, was the big ship's

starboard side. He was mistaken. The Avengers renewed the assault from the battered port beam—though in the excitement they did not know it—and added to the damage already inflicted. The two divisions claimed two hits apiece. That would make a total of 29 for Task Group 58.3. The more accurate figure was four or five. It is possible that on at least one occasion two torpedoes struck *Yamato* simultaneously. The fighter-bombers sought targets among the escorts. An isolated destroyer, probably *Isokaze*, came in for another pounding, but by now the softening-up process was over. Sixty planes from Task Group 58.4 were racing in for the kill. The time was 1330. The scene was set for the final massacre.

Aboard the Japanese Fleet: Wave Two

1240 HOURS, APRIL 7

"HERE THEY COME AGAIN!" yelled Rear Admiral Ariga. The speaker system was still working; so were most of the guns. The hull jumped as if stung as soon as the main batteries resumed their barrage against the clouds of aircraft swarming across the southern horizon. "Twenty . . . 50 . . . 100!" cried the lookouts. Where did they all come from? Cordite smoke smudged the great battle ensign flying from the main. Enemy bullets had torn through the heavy silk, but, like the ship herself, the flag remained remarkably intact.

The after secondary armament was a total loss, the triple 6.1-inch guns jammed mutely skyward; only one man escaped alive from that caved-in turret. He warned that poisonous fumes were coming up the ammunition hoist. The after gunnery control tower was out of action: one of the six 5-inch antiaircraft turrets was blown to bits, together with three triple machine-gun mounts amidships, and there had been terrible casualties among the unprotected gun crews.

But there was still a massive array of operational fire power. The list was corrected, the portside torpedo hits had scarcely penetrated the armor belt, and there'd been no loss of speed.

271

Ariga seemed full of confidence. He bustled about his exposed cockpit, humming absently, as the next attack wave bore down on the starboard quarter. These dive-bombers were smart, he grunted admiringly. They were approaching from astern. At that angle only the smallest concentration of the ship's antiaircraft guns could be brought to bear. The destroyers' firepower would be urgently needed. *Fuyutsuki* dashed in like a prancing stallion to provide additional cover. The waves peeled back from her glistening bow as she swung into position at over 30 knots. *Hatsushimo* closed to port, near *Kasumi*, in *Asashimo's* former position. The limping *Asashimo* was long lost from sight, presumed sunk. Damaged *Yahagi* was also falling astern. *Isokaze* was standing by to help. With *Hamakaze* gone, that left six ships to protect *Yamato*.

Kobayashi braced himself for the next round. He had hoped for a longer respite. The brief lull almost convinced him the enemy carriers had shot their bolt. The Americans must have stretched their resources to the limit, he decided, mounting that last attack after the losses they must have suffered at the hands of the Kamikaze. *Yamato* needed to survive only a few more hours before darkness cloaked the force. Nothing could then avert the decisive sea battle for which this giant ship was ultimately designed.

Rear Admiral Morishita conferred with chief of operations Captain Yuji Yamamoto over the battle plot on number one bridge. Seawater and blood spots smeared the chart and blurred the penciled tracks. The last two hours' maneuverings had cost them valuable time; the task force had hardly advanced 10 miles toward Okinawa. It was just as well that the supply officers at Tokuyama had given them more oil than ordered.

Communication with the VHF radio room had not been affected by the failure of the ship's telephone system. Ensign Watanabe kept in touch with the destroyers over the TBS. He noted the stream of damage reports from *Yahagi*. They sounded serious. How could a fine ship like that be knocked out so quickly? *Yamato's* own radiomen were in trouble. The impact of the exploding torpedoes had badly shaken the sets. Water was seeping into the two main radio compartments, deep down on the port side of the armored hull, although they were reputed to be leakproof. Battened below four layers of deck, the radiomen would drown like trapped rats if the seepage grew any worse.

The executive officer, Captain Nomura, fumed over his useless phones. A messenger came panting in to report that number eight outer port fireroom was flooding. Only a handful of engineers had managed to shin up the ladders to safety. He ordered another 2000 gallons of seawater pumped into the starboard blisters to correct the reviving list. The situation was becoming perilous. Further torpedo hits on the port side would endanger the ship's stablility. The presence of that lateral bulkhead running the length of the hull prevented the incoming water from spreading across the entire beam. It was likely to pile up on one side—as unbalanced, say, as a weightlifter's bar with a weight on only one end—and eventually, no amount of counterpumping would be able to compensate. Nomura begged Ariga to hold the ship as long as possible in a tight starboard turn to keep the damaged port side high out of the water.

The man who least expected to survive felt sorry he had not brought his book. Now he would never know how it ended. Ensign Katono gave up trying to raise damage control on the telephones and sent a man to the upper decks to investigate. The sailor made his way to the amidships section where the stores clerks were getting drunk on sake. Some of the storerooms were on fire. Others were flooding. But what was the point of wasting good booze? No one seemed to care. Reports of damage were filtering down to the clerks from the main deck. An emergency casualty clearing station was being organized farther forward and it was filling up with wounded men. Most of them seemed to be gunners.

"Here they come again!" yelled the petty officer in charge of Kobayashi's gun crew. Gunners on the starboard side had so far escaped lightly. The attackers kept hammering away at the port side. Now the Helldivers were coming straight at them. It seemed like a hundred, maybe more: crows swooping down on carrion. The triple machine guns began their insane chatter, consuming heavy 30-round magazines as fast as they could be fed into each breech. The racket mounted, assaulting the eardrums with stuttering waves of sound. There was a strong smell of burning oil. The barrels were overheating again; but they cooled off, hissing and steaming before the rifling melted, as near-misses dumped tons of muddy water into the gun tub, knocking the crewmen all over the greasy deck. The cool spring breeze bit through their sodden uniforms.

Tracer pumped up into the enemy's faces. One dive-bomber staggered, hit in the wing. Another seemed to be on fire. But the planes dropped their bombs and got away. Two of their hits penetrated the starboard deck. Kobayashi caught the heat from a burst beside the tower. The shock wave threatened to cave in his ribs. The gunlayer was flung backward from his seat and lay quite still among the empty shells, a gaping hole in his chest. Kobayashi took his place. Within moments the gun was firing again—a little wildly perhaps, the sky seemed filled with planes—but he got in one good burst at a torpedo bomber that seemed to brush his head. It leaped across the ship at mast height from the opposite beam. He got a fleeting glimpse of the enemy gunner, glinting goggles, glinting teeth, lips drawn back in a savage snarl as he poured a stream of tracer into their open tub. Bullets clanged off the gun shields; the middle gun of their triple mounting ceased firing—a recoil spring was shot away— and Kobayashi felt a stinging blow on the forehead. His eyes filled with blood. He groped around for an emergency dressing to bind the wound and found a 6-inch metal fragment lodged in his brow. He eased it painfully out, releasing another spurt of blood, and thanked his sacred luck. It must be the amulet he was wearing from the village shrine. Given a trifle more momentum, that chunk of jagged metal would have taken the top of his head off.

His friend Karuma, loading at his very elbow, had also been hit. He lay on the bloodstained deck looking very pale. A bullet had shattered his right thigh. An artery must have been severed; he was rapidly bleeding to death. Kobayashi rigged a rough tourniquet and helped him down the gun-tub ladders and into the amidships casualty station. The belowdecks companionway was crowded with limping, bleeding, vomiting men, converging in eerie silence upon the medics. Nobody complained or even moaned. Men already on the litters awaited their turn in stoic silence. The only sound was the snip of scissors and the slow shuffling of wounded feet.

Kobayashi tried to grab the attention of a doctor. There wasn't one to be seen: only overworked medics in blood-splattered rubber aprons. They scarcely glanced at Karuma. A senior medic glared accusingly at Kobayashi.

"Get back to your gun, sailor," he said. "This man's dead. Drop him out there . . ." He nodded toward an open door. It was a bathhouse. Orderlies were throwing the bodies into the great hot-water pool where he and Karuma and the other young gunners had once played "submarines." Now it was choked with floating bodies, jostling gently against one another with every gyration of the ship, some seemingly untouched, many dreadfully mutilated, suspended in a still steaming bath of blood.

The captain's messenger, Tsukamato, had been through the air attacks at Leyte Gulf. Today's were heavier, but he was not yet unduly worried. Ariga sent him up to the tower-top gunnery control as soon as a fresh wave of torpedo bombers was detected. They should be able to knock down these lumbering aircraft, the captain complained, particularly when the pilots leveled off into their steady, obligatory approach run. The chief gunnery officer shrugged helplessly. A cruiser or a battleship would be no problem. But his fire control equipment could scarcely track, let alone concentrate the guns on, the tiny groups of Grummans converging on the bow.

The main and secondary armament were proving ineffective against aircraft. At extreme range the airbursts were too low. There was insufficient elevation on the guns and no radar to direct them. Closer in, their fire was equally disappointing; it made him feel like getting up and throwing rocks at the attacking planes.

The chief gunner told Tsukamato to get word to the men inside the big turrets that they'd better set their *San-Shiki* shells to burst on one-second fuses. That would throw up a barrage less than 1000 yards away. The gunners complied. A fresh curtain of exploding water leaped up ahead of the enemy. It had no effect on the approaching Avengers. There was a remorseless professionalism about the way the Yankee pilots pressed their attacks.

Yamato continued her stately turn to starboard. The flooding eased, Nomura noted, in the outer port engine and firerooms. Ariga maintained the turn even when the torpedo wakes were bubbling toward their exposed port side. For the first time since the action began, he failed to take evasive action. The steering was undamaged, although some power loss was threatening as water began to swamp the portside steering engines. Electrical commands from old Koyama's minuscule wheel activated the big hydraulic devices which thrust 45 tons of main rudder around the slipstream of the four huge bronze propellers. If these engines failed, the ship would be forced to fall back on less powerful auxiliaries.

The only valid explanation for Ariga's numbed inactivity must have been his hope that a continued, steady turn would bring all batteries to bear. Many officers were confident of the power of *Yamato*'s broadside. It was typical big-ship thinking. Had he been able at that point to confer with his frustrated gunnery officer, the captain might have acted differently. Instead, he gripped the brass ring of the compass binnacle yelling encouragement into the ship's intercom:

"Steady, men! Steady, men! Keep fighting!"

The exploding U.S. torpedoes threw up surprisingly little water. One man thought he saw a rainbow-colored flash as the enemy fish bit into the port beam. No one could agree later on the number of hits, nor on the exact time. But as more Avengers followed in successive waves Nomura noted three, possibly four hits to port and one amidships to starboard. Water engulfed number eight and number twelve firerooms. The starboard hit quickly flooded number seven fireroom. Speed dropped to 18 knots. The list increased perceptibly.

"Hold on, men," Ariga cried over the intercom.

He clung to a stanchion as the deck canted sharply. The big guns stopped firing. The tubes could no longer be brought to bear. Ensign Yoshida found himself absently wiping the sea-drenched chart table with a piece of cloth. It helped to be doing something in a moment of crisis. Everyone on number one bridge was soaked through, but the space was less crowded now that the bullets crashing in through the open windows had taken their toll. Smoke drifted in from outside. The roar of bursting shells and spouts of flame made it impossible to hear anyone speak. Ensign Watanabe abandoned his radiophones: the antennas were shot away. The portside radio rooms were silent. His friends there must be drowned. He ordered a signalman to maintain contact by lamp with *Hatsushimo*. The destroyer would have to relay all fleet messages. As far as he knew, very few had been sent: a signal to Combined Fleet had announced the initial attack at about 1230; after that, nothing more.

"All hands work to trim ship." It was Ariga again over the loudspeakers. He called Nomura over the voice pipe demanding urgent action. The executive officer tried shifting oil fuel. The straining pumps were working at full capacity.

Confusion was spreading belowdecks. The damage parties had never been up to their jobs. Deprived now of central direction by the loss of the telephones, decimated by bomb hits and burns, they feebly fought the spreading fires along the port side. A warrant officer smelled his skin frying as he threw himself against a red-hot door to seal off the after magazine. A petty officer automatically donned a gas mask when a bomb crashed into the gunnery flat. It saved him from the toxic smoke which killed everyone else around.

Men began escaping through an air vent from the fast-filling auxiliary steering compartment. They groped their way through unlit stretches of deck, climbing over what appeared to be heaps of damp blankets. Some screamed hysterically when they realized that the blankets were bodies. Many just stayed put. No one ordered them to leave. They sat quietly smoking—and drinking when they could get something to drink—calmly waiting their turn to die. An elderly warrant officer snored, dead drunk, in a corner of the gunroom, an empty bottle of Black Label between his knees.

"All hands work to trim ship."

Ariga's voice reached Ensign Katono in his ghostly isolation. It was as if he was already dead, waiting in dim, steel limbo for his triumphant translation to heaven. The deck was canting, that was all he knew. The telephones has been out for what seemed hours. A messenger clattered down the ladder.

"Commanding officer's orders. Seventh damage control is to flood starboard compartments 331 through 350."

"What's the trouble?" asked Katono. There was a great deal he would have liked to ask, if they had time.

"Flooding heavily portside," snapped the messenger, fleeing promptly to the safety of the upper decks.

The ensign led the way three decks down into the bilges. He opened a manhole and took down two men with flashlights who knew where to find the sea cocks. Things must be desperate, he thought: whatever had happened to the counterpumping system? He waited five, ten minutes, with one foot on the ladder. The propellers thudded close around him; the metal walls vibrated and groaned.

The torpedo hit, when it came, boomed like a temple gong. Katono called his men back. No answer. Water flooded round his feet, rising faster by the second. He yelled and waved his flashlight, retreating step by step up the ladder. A petty officer hauled him clear and slammed the cover. The ensign sat muttering a sutra for his lost men—and for himself.

Morishita was conferring with Ariga when a lookout sighted a torpedo approaching the starboard beam. He dashed to the side rail, yelling exultantly.

"This way, little fish. This way!"

Morishita slapped Ariga on the shoulder as the torpedo struck amidships.

"I never thought I'd welcome a torpedo," Morishita chuckled. "But this is better than all of Nomura's pumps."

It was a costly way of correcting the list, in the executive officer's view. This latest hit quickly flooded number six fireroom. The adjacent engine room was threatened by seepage. The ship righted herself, nevertheless, to a bearable 5° to port. The main batteries began to fire again.

The machine gunners were hitting back meanwhile with reckless courage. More than half were dead and wounded; others were still falling, but no one deserted his post. A few fought on single-handed, despite the twanging, clanging barrage of bullets that periodically swept the upper deck. It never occurred to Kobayashi to duck for cover. He was little more than a boy, scarcely trained by prewar standards, fighting his first and last real battle with a ferocity worthy of a veteran. The iron discipline of the Imperial Navy and, it must be added, his total absorption in the surrounding excitement kept him glued to his guns. Only two tubes were still firing, but that was enough. He grunted with satisfaction as a dive-bomber exploded in the sea. He fired wildly at a torpedo bomber which rashly roared down the length of the ship, raising a shower of tracer.

This low cloud cover undoubtedly aided the enemy. Planes darted out so unexpectedly that it was difficult to draw an accurate bead on them. Kobayashi found himself blazing off in the hope that something must eventually hit home. Dozens of Grummans were flitting through his sights. Their falling bombs sounded to him like flutes. They must be the third (or was it the fourth?) attack wave. All sense of time and sequence had long melted into a single nightmare montage—something quite different from his innocent heroic fantasies.

Somebody was screaming. It was Leading Seaman Uchiki. He begged Kobayashi to pass him a wrench from the toolbox. A bomb fragment had smashed his right knee. He bound his belt round the pressure point on his thigh and twisted the wrench to stanch the spouting blood. He sat back heavily among the ammunition boxes operating the tourniquet. Gradually he lost consciousness.

Kobayashi was hit a few moments later. A long piece of jagged metal whipped under the gun shield and struck him in the knee. The metal burned his fingers when he pulled it out. He began to bleed so badly that he took the bandage off his forehead and transferred it to his leg. Blood began trickling into his eyes again. He searched the dead gunlayer's pockets for a fresh emergency dressing. Unnoticed, Uchiki quietly died . . .

The ship's loudspeaker was crackling out some message. He could barely hear it above the din. Something about repairing the ship. He realized the deck was listing. There was a fire over on the port side. He limped back to his seat at the gun mount. Most of the nine-man crew were gone. The petty officer was still on his feet and so were two other men, looking shocked and dazed.

"Don't worry," he told himself. "We'll get through. *Yamato* will never sink."

Kasumi was badly hit. Black smoke poured from a bomb crater on her quarterdeck. The small triangular signal flag flying from her main halyard announced temporary loss of steerage. She came yawing up to *Yamato*, plainly out of control, and narrowly escaped collision. The two ships lay close abeam, eyeing each other's awesome damage, before the crippled destroyer fell away on the port quarter. *Hatsushimo* hesitated, wondering whether to offer help, but another air attack sent her scurrying off to support the flagship.

Bombs hit *Suzutsuki's* forecastle, pulverizing the bow section, knocking out her main turrets, and heaping the weather deck with corpses. Rockets hit the gallant *Fuyutsuki* but failed to explode. A torpedo passed harmlessly beneath her. Time and again this superb ship was saved by her extraordinary turn of speed. The older but equally nimble *Yukikaze* was also virtually unscratched.

Ensign Shigeo Yamada sadly discarded his headset. *Yahagi's* after radio room was already hit and flooded. His nisei friend Kuramoto died there. The former college footballer had thrown his last forward pass. Now a series of explosions had reduced Yamada's radio sets to rubble. Someone ordered the radiomen to take shelter in the companionway beneath the bridge. But they clustered too close to a nearby hatchway leading to the magazine. A huge burst of flame caught the radiomen as they took shelter. "Some of us were thrown to the deck," Yamada recalled. "Some died right there. Some people inhaled the flames and died. I was just bruised and burned on the back of the neck. There were people killed all around us and bodies were floating by, or lying all over the deck. There were explosions and fires all over the place."

Captain Hara wondered how long *Yahagi* could take this sort of punishment. Near-misses thumped the hull. Planes dived from every angle. A hit on the forecastle blew six bodies into the air. He thought of the mighty British ships *Repulse* and *Prince of Wales*, sunk by a far smaller force than the one now attacking them. Everyone was dead in the engine room. The cruiser was listing noticeably to starboard. Young Lieutenant Hatta was dashing about the deck, his face begrimed with soot or oil. He cut loose the starboard anchor to help correct the list, dragged the wounded under cover, and assigned fresh hands to the guns. For the first time their fire seemed to have some effect: the crew cheered as two of the attackers spun into the water.

A tremendous explosion flung the stern out of the water. Hara saw three mangled bodies soar 60 feet off the deck. Another torpedo hit the starboard bow.

"*Yahagi* quivered and rocked as though made of paper," wrote Hara. "Clinging to the rail of the trembling command post, I saw that the torpedo hit had blasted a huge hole in the bow and the ship's list was increasing. Still another group of fighters and bombers came to concentrate on that shattered bow. The deafening drum of machine-gun bullets was climaxed by a direct hit on number one turret which wiped out its entire crew and smashed men on the forecastle. Strangely, no one on the bridge or in the command post was hit. But rivets popped as steel plates worked loose and the bridge shook so violently that it might collapse at any moment."

Yahagi was falling to pieces. The main forward turret was still intact, although acrid yellow smoke was seeping out around it through the cracked deck. The captain heard young Hatta yelling for someone to flood the magazine. The fire was doused in time, but the list increased.

A voice pipe shrilled. It was the torpedo officer, Lieutenant Commander Takeshi Kameyama, requesting permission to dump the fish. Their load of type 93 torpedoes would be their deadliest weapon off Okinawa.

"If they're set off," warned Kameyama, "it will blast everything."

"OK," yelled Hara.

The amidships crane had just dropped the last torpedo overboard when a clutch of bombs burst among the torpedo tubes, bringing down the mainmast and wrecking the aircraft catapult. Avengers followed up with a torpedo attack which shook the dying ship with three, four . . . no one was certain how many hits.

"I looked around," wrote Hara. "All the gun posts lay in ruins. My proud cruiser was but a mass of junk, barely afloat. Strangely, I thought, there were no fires."

Ensign Yamada did not recognize the ship when he made his way painfully and cautiously onto the open deck. The upper works seemed to have been hit repeatedly by a giant battle-ax. Few guns were firing. Scarcely anyone survived to man them. His personal steward was still standing behind a machine gun. The man was dead. Half his head was missing. A seaman was running about the deck screaming in agony. He had been scalded by a burst steam pipe.

"Guess we'd better got out of here," said Rear Admiral Komura. It would be better to shift his flag to some ship which stood a better chance of reaching Okinawa. Hara bowed and mumbled his apologies. He gave the order to abandon ship. A signalman flashed *Isokaze* to pull alongside. She had been keeping a watch on the cruiser throughout the action from about 3000 yards away. The destroyer raced to close, knifing eagerly through the swell, and was almost upon them when still more aircraft dived out of the clouds. They promptly switched their attentions to *Isokaze*.

Too late, the destroyer tried to evade. Her engines roared frantically as she dodged away from the men she had come to rescue. Near-misses burst around her. Explosion after explosion wracked her hull. Clouds of black smoke hid her from view. She reemerged, still racing for safety, only to disappear behind the smoke of a fresh attack.

Komura gripped Hara's arm and pointed. A fresh attack wave was forming up in the east. Over 100 planes! Some were heading toward them. Men began jumping overboard as water lapped over the bloodstained starboard scuppers. An unaccustomed silence fell, broken only by the growl of approaching engines . . . the clock in the command post stood at 1342.

The End of the Battle: Wave Three

1342 HOURS, APRIL 7

LIEUTENANT COMMANDER Herbert N. Houck wasn't sure he would make it. His Helldiver began to give trouble as soon as he left *Yorktown*. The engine kept cutting out every two or three minutes because of an air leak in the gas line leading from the belly tank. He refused to go back, flying first on his starboard wing tank, then on the belly tank using an emergency fuel pump, until *Yahagi* appeared below him, dead in the water, ripe for destruction.

The lanky 30-year-old Minnesotan, a prewar professional, had flown combat in every important Pacific campaign of the past 2½ years. He had won so many medals it was no longer easy to keep count. Now he was about to earn his fourth Silver Star in lieu of a second Navy Cross for directing the deathblow against the stricken cruiser.

Houck gathered together a stray assortment of Avengers, Hellcats, and Helldivers from passing air groups—the situation was this confused—while the strike coordinator blundered around in the overcast cursing the radio, the radar, and the weather.

The man who should have been running the show, Lieutenant Commander W. E. Rawie, was forced to leave the 115 attack planes of Task Group 58.4 much to their own devices. As the farthest-flung unit of Mitscher's force, they'd had a longer, more disorganized flight to the target area. Air groups which lost touch on route had difficulty reestablishing contact. The rain clouds were so low now that Rawie could seldom see below 500 feet. The Japanese ships were too widely scattered for him to spot them all; in this failing light only the flashes of their antiaircraft guns betrayed their positions. The coordinator's communications channel was jammed with a cackle of conversation. Every pilot seemed busy babbling over the command wavelength. His radar picked up reefs and islands but failed, for some mysterious reason, to detect the enemy warships. Everything was conspiring to frustrate him.

The preceding attack waves had obviously done a good job. It was probably just as well in the circumstances. His own boys' efforts were haphazard, to put it mildly.

A torrent of bombs and torpedoes quickly sank *Yahagi*. Urged on by Houck, pilots from every group jostled to get in on the kill: Avengers from *Intrepid* and *Yorktown*, fighter-bombers from *Langley*, dive-bombers from all over. Coordinator Rawie found himself lining up with clusters of planes trying to find a convenient gap in the clouds. Nimitz's order banning strike leaders from launching their own attacks did not apparently apply to this task group. Rawie's Hellcat carried bombs and he was determined to use them.

The Japanese still packed a punch. A shell from fatally damaged *Isokaze* killed a Helldiver pilot from *Yorktown*, Lieutenant Harry Worley, and his crewman, Earl Ward. But the carrier planes' ragged attack was more than their battered targets could bear.

A glancing bullet knocked Captain Hara on *Yahagi* off his feet. He sat staring stupidly at the nick in his left arm. Rear Admiral Komura leaned over him.

"You all right?" Komura asked calmly. He took a last quick look at the floundering wreck. "Well, Hara, shall we go?"

The captain checked his watch as he pulled off his shoes. It was 1405. Waves were lapping the steel deck of their command post. Lieutenant (jg.) Yukio Matsuda, a navigation officer, was trying to launch the only lifeboat. A strafing burst cut the boat in two, killing Matsuda and 12 men, most of them wounded, as they climbed aboard. Planes roared overhead, raking the submerging decks. A single gunner kept firing, somewhere aft, before the sea closed over him. The water was up to their knees when the senior officers and their staff leaped into the sea. Hara had swum a scant 5 yards before the undertow dragged him down. The water closed over his head. How ironical, he thought, to survive the worst the Americans could do—only to be drowned by his own sinking ship!

A U.S. ensign named Brewer was photographing *Yahagi's* death throes. When the survivors tried to launch a boat he dived his plane across the listing hull. A short burst from his guns smashed the boat to splinters and tossed its occupants into the sea. The cruiser quickly capsized and appeared to explode under water. A great ball of black smoke shot up. Very soon there was nothing left but an oil slick, a lot of floating wreckage, and the heads of men struggling to keep afloat. Houck dived on *Isokaze*, planted a bomb on her blazing deck, and methodically machine-gunned the survivors in the water. Other pilots joined in. Long white bullet trails slashed across the ocean swell, rapidly reducing the numbers of heads bobbing around in the oil.

The Americans felt no compunction about slaughtering their helpless foes. They had always fought a blatantly racial war in the Pacific—and so had the Japanese. Headline-seeking brass hats openly declared that killing Japs was no worse than killing lice. Reports of Japan's atrocities against war prisoners and even the unnatural fanaticism of the Kamikaze combined to convince the Americans that these were inhuman freaks, deserving little mercy. The apogee of brutalization was to be reached, four months later, at Hiroshima . . .

Tameichi Hara found himself kicking and writhing in total darkness. But it grew lighter when the undertow from sinking *Yahagi* suddenly loosed its viselike grip. Bubbles floated up before his face. Bluish beads of air were streaming from his lungs and clothing. He gagged down a throatful of seawater before bursting back on the surface. Somehow he stayed afloat, dazed and blinded. When his eyes cleared he saw heads around him. Black heads. The buzzing died out of his ears. The heads were talking. A black-faced man shouted: "Hara! Are you all right? Hara! Do you hear me?"

It was Rear Admiral Komura, almost unrecognizable. They were afloat in a sea of oil.

"I'm all right," Hara choked. "How about you?"

"I'm quite all right," replied Komura.

It was a surprise to find so many men clinging to bits of wreckage. He had not expected anyone to survive. The rolling swell raised him momentarily to his crest, offering a glimpse of *Yamato*, 6 miles away, impressive as ever but harassed by a gnat-like swarm of planes. He grabbed a passing log and hung on. A voice from behind yelled, "Hey, you, move over, make room for me." He offered the man a handhold.

"Who are you? What's your name?" asked the breathless intruder.

"My name is Hara. I'm from *Yahagi*."

It was a young seaman named Daiwa. He was abashed at his impertinence. Ships' captains were gods in the Japanese navy. "I'm very sorry, sir," he mumbled. "Forgive my rudeness. I'd better find another log, captain. This isn't big enough to support both of us."

"Don't be foolish, son," said his commanding officer. "Hang on tight. We can manage. Are you hurt?"

"No, sir, not at all. My friend Asamo and I decided to die quickly when *Yahagi* was doomed. We went down to number three magazine and mounted the shells, waiting to be blown to bits. But Petty Officer Yamada came and ordered us up on deck. He said, 'This is my place.' He was so furious that we raced up the ladder. I stumbled once and sprained my ankle, but that is nothing. I wonder what happened to Yamada and my buddy Asamo?"

"Don't worry, Daiwa. Now think only of survival. You will get out of this if you don't give up."

They both ducked as a Grumman hurtled above them, churning the oil slick with bursts of machine-gun fire. Men's heads burst like watermelons. Others, hit in the throat or chest, arched their backs half out of the water before sinking back forever. Blood mingled with the cloying oil . . .

Lieutenant William Delaney was still alive, floating in the middle of the Japanese fleet. He had given up thinking of his wedding anniversary. The way things were going, his wife would soon be a widow. The downed pilot clung to the side of his yellow life raft, slipping under the water every time an enemy destroyer dashed past. The Japanese ignored him. They had too much else to worry about. He could see planes making spasmodic attacks on the battleship. The concussion from exploding bombs could be felt underwater even at this distance. *Yamato*, about 5 miles to the southwest, seemed immobile to him.

A big pool of orange dye was spreading around the raft. Delaney could not imagine where it had come from, because he had saved both his dye packets. Perhaps another plane had dropped a marker when he crashed. Sometime between 1400 and 1415 he watched one of the Japanese ships go up in a tremendous explosion.

"There was one huge orange ball of flame that seemed to come straight out of the superstructure. I couldn't see any more of this ship after that explosion."

The downed pilot thought he had witnessed the destruction of a destroyer. He had in fact watched *Yahagi*'s demise. Ten minutes later a Helldiver spotted him. The *Yorktown* pilot rocked his wings and advised the two flying boats still watching the battle from the grandstand in the clouds. A Japanese destroyer suddenly turned toward Delaney at high speed. Her wedge-shaped bow grew rapidly larger. The shivering survivor hid behind his raft and prayed . . .

Intrepid's 14 dive-bombers headed instinctively for *Yamato*. The battleship presented an easy target, large and slow-moving, although her main turrets were still firing and accurate flak was coming from the three escorting destroyers. One plane nearly went out of control when a 5-inch shell clipped its starboard wing tip. Three other Helldivers received minor damage. Twenty-seven bombs were dropped, "with excellent results" according to the official combat reports—although there were probably few hits. It did not matter. A near-miss could do almost as much damage at this stage.

There had been a remarkably long pause before the Americans renewed their attack. Or so it seemed to the men aboard *Yamato*. The staff officers on number one bridge reckoned it lasted a full 15 minutes. The new attack wave was sighted almost as soon as the last one left. Then there was this lull. The Japanese had no inkling of the disorganization overhead. They felt they were being put through a meat grinder with appalling efficiency. But now there was unexpected time for a breather. Kobayashi enjoyed a cigarette. Watanabe readied the code books for destruction. Nomura stared grimly at the clinometer. It would not be long before water seepage revived that heavy list to port. Next time the problem would not be so easily solved. Yoshida felt hungry: he ate the packet of rice crackers from his raincoat pocket. Morishita was running up and down the bridge tower again, checking instruments and chaffing sailors as if activity was the cure for his anxiety. Ariga crammed his steel helmet harder on his head and sadly surveyed *Yamato's* ruined upper works. He was still humming quietly when the dive-bombers pounced from nowhere.

The bombs wobbled down again. Most of them fell wide of *Yamato*. Near-misses loosened more plates and the flooding increased. A direct hit beside the smokestack blew two more machine-gun tubs over the side. Another destroyed the port anchor capstan, cut the cable, and sent the massive anchor splashing to the bottom. A trickle of wounded men emerging onto the forecastle were mowed down by the passing Helldivers. Three men on the bridge were hit simultaneously and fell on Yoshida, knocking him to the deck. Ensign Katono and his party retreated farther and farther up the hull, securing watertight doors behind them. It was time he went up personally to see what was happening.

Yamato was heeling over again, with 15°, then 20° of port list. "Hold on, men. Hold on," yelled Ariga over the loudspeakers. On the voice tube to Nomura he again demanded urgent action. The executive officer could do no more. The intricate system of pumps and valves was breaking down. All the stabilizing blisters on the starboard side were partly filled. The blisters were too far out of the water for the pumps to flood them completely. The equipment had never been designed for such heavy duty.

Ariga reached his most heartbreaking decision. In a choking voice he ordered the starboard outer engine room flooded. That would correct the list, but with further loss of power. And what about the engineers below? What happened next is subject to dispute. Some sources insist that there was insufficient time to get the men clear before the water rushed in, snuffing out 300 lives. The story was accepted by Japanese filmmakers who reenacted the saga in 1951. Nomura insists that the engineers were given time to escape. The one certain fact is that the engine rooms were flooded and the ship's list partly checked, though speed dropped to a shaky 8 knots. At that rate, driven by the last operational propeller, the crippled ship faced another full day's sailing to Okinawa.

Morishita remembered the angry confrontation with Vice Admiral Kusaka at Mitajiri. It seemed days since the naval chief of staff had reluctantly issued his fatal orders. What was it he had said to Seiichi Ito? It would be up to Ito to decide on his course of action if *Yamato* suffered severe damage before she could reach Okinawa. But it was too late now to think of turning back.

So far there had been relatively few successful torpedo attacks. But at 1410 a random shot, probably from a *Langley* Avenger, hit the stern. The rudder jammed hard left. All power failed. The turrets jammed. The great ship spun helplessly counterclockwise, her port side awash, her high bridge tower teetering over toward the waves.

The shock flung everyone on number one bridge into a heap. Officers disentangled themselves, regaining a shaky footing on the canted deck as Nomura blundered up the ladder shouting, "There's nothing we can do." He clambered up higher, hand over fist, to report to Rear Admiral Ariga.

Vice Admiral Seiichi Ito drew himself slowly and deliberately to his feet. One white-gloved hand gripped the binocular stand for support. Gravely he saluted his bedraggled staff. The officers saluted back. The fleet commander shook hands all around. "Save yourselves," he said. "I shall stay with the ship." Then he made his way one deck below to his sea cabin. He disappeared inside and locked the door.

Nomura found Ariga steadying himself against the compass. He had thrown off his helmet and a light drizzle glistened on his bald head. He was staring down at the sea, smoking a cigarette.

"It is no longer possible to correct the list," panted the executive officer.

Ariga did not seem to hear him.

"The ship is sinking, sir," Nomura found himself shouting. "There's nothing we can do."

Ariga nodded vaguely. His eyes were full of tears.

"Please, sir. Give permission to abandon ship. Get the hands up on deck. There isn't a moment to lose."

No reply. Shouts echoed up from the weather deck. A solitary gunner fired a short burst.

"Sir!"

"Very well," Ariga said at last. "Abandon ship. And see you go too, Nomura. Someone has to survive to tell our story."

"You, sir?"

"Carry on, please, Nomura-san."

The executive officer grabbed the microphone. "Attention all hands. Prepare to abandon ship. This is the commanding officer's order. Abandon ship." He sent messengers belowdecks to pass the word. They would not get far with so many closed watertight doors. Well over 1000 men had virtually no chance of escape.

One of the few engineers to make it to the top deck decided to call it quits when water poured in from the auxiliary steering department. Later he felt ashamed. All over the ship men were refusing to desert their posts. Magazine crews stayed where they were until they drowned. The starboard inner engine-room watch kept working to the end. A gunnery officer knelt down amid the ruins of the portside gun batteries. As the waves lapped into the gun tubs he tore open his tunic and slit his stomach with his sword. Three young seamen huddled together in a corner of the auxiliary radar room as they lay awaiting the end, too paralyzed to move.

Jiro Nomura worked hard to prevent a panic. Yoshida saw him distribute candies, cookies, and packets of the emperor's cigarettes to the dazed and frightened men pouring onto the weather deck. To deter a rush for the side, the executive officer called on the men to relieve themselves before they entered the water. The ensign saw him lined up with a crowd of laughing sailors on the sloping deck, solemnly urinating into the scuppers.

"The emperor's portrait! Save His Imperial Majesty's portrait."

It was Ariga shouting. The assistant gunnery officer, Lieutenant Hattori, groped his way down to the senior wardroom where the portrait was kept and locked the door. He would die to ensure that this sacred object did not float accidentally to the surface and somehow fall into enemy hands. The navigating officer tied himself to the chart table down in the command post, determined to go down with the ship. Nearby, old Koyama stood gripping the steering wheel.

"Helm is not answering, sir," he kept repeating to the bridge. He stayed at his post as the sea came flooding in. The quartermaster's voice pipe fell suddenly silent. Koyama had drowned at his post.

A signal yeoman hoisted the same STEERING DAMAGED flag fluttering from stricken *Kasumi*. The main battle flag still flew from the main, but it was torn and shredded. The lookouts had seen pictures like it in their schoolbooks, depicting gallant moments in the Russo-Japanese War.

The younger officers started tying themselves to fixtures as soon as the loudspeaker began to squawk. Morishita rushed among them flailing about with his fists. "You know an order when you hear one?" he was shouting. "Abandon ship! Get out! Save yourselves!" He tossed his binoculars into the chartroom and found Watanabe roping himself to the table. The great globe presented by Fleet Admiral Yamamoto lay smashed in a corner. The chief of staff punched the ensign behind the ear. "Out! Out!" he yelled. Yoshida also gave up thoughts of suicide. He fled with the others before the raging rear admiral.

Lieutenant Tom Stetson's torpedo bombers were supposed to attack *Yahagi*, but she was as good as gone by the time they reached the target. He detached six Avengers to attack the cruiser and other escorts and decided to go for *Yamato*. Herbert Houck gave the go-ahead. Stetson could take four planes. His entire division, six strong, finally tagged along.

The *Yorktown* pilots took their time. They circled in thinning cloud while crewmen leaned down into the torpedo bay to readjust the depth settings. Their torpedoes were due to run at 10 feet, ideal for the cruiser but too shallow for a heavily armored battleship. Stetson ordered settings between 18 and 22 feet while he made his attack plans.

Yamato was listing and circling helplessly to port. Her list was so severe that the red-leaded starboard underbelly protruded well above the waterline. Hits here would tear the bottom out of her.

Stetson made two approach runs before he was satisfied. The setup had to be perfect. He gunned the engine to a full 300 knots. Four planes spearheaded the attack in line abreast. The other two, led by Lieutenant (jg.) William Gibson, were close on their tails. They released at 800 feet, range 100 yards, unseen by the enemy. No flak flew up and they pulled up and away toward the protective clouds.

Stetson saw at least four torpedo wakes streaking toward the unsuspecting battleship. Whose they were he never knew. One or two, maybe more, hit, smashing into the exposed underbelly below the armor belt.

Messenger Tsukamoto, who was helping Rear Admiral Ariga tie himself to the compass binnacle, wanted to take off his shoes to get a better grip on the slanting deck. The linoleum was slippery with blood. Ariga thought the young man was preparing to commit suicide. Removing the shoes is part of the ritual. He ordered his messenger to keep his shoes on. The unexpected blast threw Tsukamoto off his feet. It seemed as if a magazine had exploded.

"Long live the emperor!" cried Ariga.

It had become a tradition in the Imperial Navy for a commanding officer to go down with his ship. Apologists claimed that they were following British practice. If so, the Japanese were mistaken. Royal Navy tradition only required a commanding officer to be the last to leave his ship. More likely the Japanese were following an ancient tradition of their own. A commanding officer felt impelled to atone for the loss of his ship. This misconceived concept may have saved much face but it wasted countless valuable lives during the Pacific war.

Ensign Katono emerged on deck to see a bullet snap off the flagstaff on the fantail. The flag fell into the water: a half-naked seaman tried to retrieve it. Katono couldn't believe his eyes. Their proud ship was unrecognizable. She was sinking fast. He went back to his damage control party swimming along the fast-filling companionway. The ship lurched further to port—no doubt about it, *Yamato* was doomed. He thought sadly of his Tolstoy novel somewhere down in the flooded hull. Now he would never know how it ended . . .

The time was 1420. They had been under direct attack since 1237. The force was still less than 100 miles from Japan.

A signalman tried to call *Hatsushimo* alongside, but the lamp was not working. The destroyer hovered 1000 yards away on the beam, her deck crowded with horrified onlookers. *Kasumi* and *Suyutsuki* both drifted burning about a mile astern. A smudge of smoke marked *Isokaze's* postion on the northern horizon. *Fuyutsuki* began to close the sinking battleship until her skipper changed his mind. He did not want his ship dragged down as well.

Kobayashi wondered what it was like to drown. The sea was bound to be cold. Three minutes under water were all you needed, he was told; then your lungs filled and you drifted off into unconsciousness. Or was it that easy? Surely you flailed about desperately, fighting automatically for life, even when you were determined to die? At least there'd be no sharks.

The splintering of wood, the twang of snapping metal warned him that the end was near. His bloodstained gun tub lurched sharply to port, showering the deck below with empty shell cases. The corpse of the spare ammunition loader, a fellow member of the gun crew, a burly youngster from Kobe, slithered toward the break in the waist-high casement and hung half out over the ladder. Another tearing sound from the deck and the gun platform lurched again, tumbling the body down on top of the others. The deck was carpeted with men cut down by bomb fragments or aerial strafing.

The Americans' faces could be seen quite clearly now as their Grummans howled low over the stricken ship, spraying the acres of sloping open deck, the bomb-pocked upper works, and the great steel bridge tower with cannon and machine-gun fire. Scarcely anyone fired back. The great amidships cluster of anti-aircraft guns was choked with dead or jammed for lack of electric power. Strafing bullets ripped into the soaked and half-blinded survivors scrambling from the depths of the flooding hull. Some men fled below again to certain death. Most died where they stood. A few huddled together in sheltered corners under the after aircraft catapults or around the shattered radar cabin where an unseen loudspeaker, miraculously fed by emergency current, monotonously squeaked: "Abandon ship. All hands abandon ship. This is an order . . ."

The gun tub began to tremble. It felt like the start of an earthquake. The triple machine guns swung helplessly on their mounting. Kobayashi gave up trying to fire them and joined the petty officer, who was staring down disbelievingly at the deck.

"We're going," he gasped.

It was true. *Yamato* was listing so sharply that their gun platform was tearing loose from its mounting. Surely it couldn't mean they were sinking? Nobody could sink this ship—not even the Americans. She was unsinkable . . . the biggest battleship in the world, the pride of the Imperial Japanese Navy.

The loudspeaker fell silent. So did everything else. The lowering gray skies were temporarily clear of diving planes. The whole world seemed to be holding its breath.

The tall bridge tower was tilting sharply toward the sea. The shredded and blackened battle ensign would soon be touching the water. The list increased relentlessly. It was like watching a mountain fall into the sea—in slow motion.

"Kobayashi," said the petty officer. "There's nothing more we can do here."

They were both wounded. The petty officer looked in bad shape. A third survivor of the original nine-man gun crew, who'd been crouching, terrified, behind the gun shield, clawed his way toward them. Everyone else was beyond help. The man who operated the gun traverse slumped headless in his seat. Other crewmen were heaped about the platform in puddles of blood, oil, and the muddy seawater thrown up by near-misses.

A final warning shudder and the three men shinned down the metal ladder. The petty officer came last, painfully. He limped clear just as the remaining legs supporting the platform snapped loose from the deck and the entire contraption crashed and bounced across the upper works, spilling bodies, guns, ammunition boxes, and another shower of shell cases into the sea. Their companion gun, about 15 feet farther inboard, tore itself clear a moment later. A single corpse cartwheeled high in the air. No one jumped clear.

The battleship's tower was almost level with the water. Men were being flipped over the side from the canting deck. A stores clerk struck out madly as the tower descended on top of him. Dozens of men already in the water were sucked into the smokestack as the battleship settled on her side.

Messenger Tsukamoto felt himself sliding into the sea. The tattered main battle ensign was touching the waves. He pulled a cracker from his pocket and put it in Ariga's mouth. The commanding officer nodded gratefully, still tied to the binnacle. Tsukamoto's gesture was a traditional farewell to a man about to die. Next moment the messenger was in the water. He did not realize it would be so cold.

Some, like Kobayashi, postponed their swim. The deck canted steeply beneath the young gunner's feet until he was scrambling up it like a mountain goat, grabbing a fairlead in the scuppers. A great rumbling from deep inside the hull told of bursting bulkheads and shells and heavy fittings tearing adrift. The aircraft catapults swung loose and crashed overboard. Men sheltering around them were swept into the sea. The wildly spinning range finder atop the tower flailed the water.

Kobayashi dragged himself painfully up the starboard side as *Yamato* slowly capsized. He skinned his hands and knees as he crawled as far as the barnacled starboard bilge keel, now well clear of the water, and propped himself up against it, waiting to die. He stared numbly across the upturned bottom of the ship, red-painted and heavy with marine growth, now swarming with survivors like himself. The petty officer from his gun tub hadn't made it, nor had the frightened ammunition loader. One of the four huge bronze propellers came into view, still slowly revolving.

Some of the men were singing "Kimigayo," the national anthem. Others were chanting the gruesome naval lament: "If I go to sea, I shall return a corpse awash ... Thus for the sake of the emperor I shall not die peacefully at home." It was all typically Japanese. Johnny never came marching home. The martial songs left him rotting on some foreign field, or dying hopelessly, as now, in a futile suicide charge. A half-naked officer with a white Hachimaki around his head hysterically screamed "Banzai!" and waved his samurai sword in impotent defiance at the circling American aircraft ... a symbol, somehow, of the whole futile mission. What were Admiral Toyoda's words before they sailed? "The fate of our empire truly rests upon this one action." Only the gods could help the empire now.

Kobayashi tightened the bandage on his head, but blood still trickled into his eyes. He fished the last scrap of combat ration from his pocket: a single seaweed-coated *osembe* rice cracker. There was also a crumpled cigarette, one of the emperor's cigarettes with the imperial crest, issued specially to all hands on the eve of battle. He munched and smoked as a light drizzle curtained the combat area.

A tremendous explosion flung him way out into the sea. His last thoughts as the water closed over his head were of his mother. As he slipped into unconsciousness, he distinctly heard her calling his name . . .

Everyone was dragged down by the undertow. Some went down two or three times. Underwater explosions killed dozens of them, many of whom floated to the surface, entrails curling from burst stomachs, blood pouring from the nose and ears. The executive officer, Captain Jiro Nomura, suffered for years from internal injuries. He was found floating in a coma. Mitsuru Yoshida felt crushed. He kicked and fought his way upward, lungs bursting, toward a gray-greenish glow above. Oil from the ruptured tanks made his eyes smart as he floated on the surface. He wiped his face and gasped for air. Around him were groups of swimmers, floating corpses, and patches of charred debris. It was all that was left of the world's biggest battleship after 102 minutes of hopeless combat.

Tom Stetson circled 2 miles away. Herbert Houck stood off in his Hellcat taking photographs with the wing camera. They watched *Yamato* flip completely over. Her dull red bottom seemed to be crawling with men. And then she exploded. The time was 1423.

"It made a mighty big bang," said Houck. "Smoke went up— the fireball was about 1000 feet high."

"The prettiest sight I've ever seen," said air gunner Jack Sausa. "A red column of fire shot up through the clouds and when it faded *Yamato* was gone."

"She had been hit pretty well by the time we got there," said Stetson. "She was listing. She might have gone over anyway. She blew up in a great ball of flame and smoke. And then we went home."

The last American planes departed at 1443, making a few

farewell strafing runs across the *Yamato* survivors. Bullets churned up the oil. Men sank suddenly in pools of their own blood. Others quietly gave up as exhaustion, wounds, or the penetrating cold sapped the will to live.

A mushroom-shaped cloud slowly rose thousands of feet in the air. The funeral pyre of the Imperial Japanese Navy was clearly seen by coast watchers in Kyushu. The pride of the navy, the supersized folly that should never have been built, sank 450 fathoms to her final resting place in the East China Sea. With her went over 2000 men, but many more were yet to die.

Rescue Operations

THE SURVIVING JAPANESE destroyers drifted aimlessly in the swell. The Americans were gone. The rain was closing in. The sighing splatter of raindrops and the muffled thump of idling engines were all that broke the unaccustomed silence. Deckhands conferred in hushed voices, awed by what they had seen. The officers were stunned. Keyed up for certain death, they were numbed by the massacre. The senior officer afloat, Captain Masayoshi Yoshida, commanding what was left of the 41st Destroyer Group from the bridge of *Fuyutsuki*, felt like a charging cavalryman whose troopers have been wiped out around him. Was he supposed to continue the charge all the way to Okinawa? Vice Admiral Ito had not canceled the operation. Orders presumably stood unchanged.

"Of course they're unchanged. Let's head south. We're wasting time."

It was Commander Masamichi Terauchi, hotheaded skipper of *Yukikaze*. He was assailing Yoshida's ear over the TBS.

"We've come this far, we can't turn back," he bellowed. "This is a suicide attack. Even without *Yamato* we should continue."

298

Terauchi had showed little enthusiasm for the sortie at that raucous conference aboard *Yahagi*. The smell of cordite must have stimulated his adrenaline. Having accepted an impossible order, he was determined to see it through. Yoshida looked out of the bridge at the driving rain. It would soon stop, although visibility was getting worse. The barometer was falling.

"I propose," he said hesitantly, "that we pick up survivors, resume formation, and head for Okinawa."

"But no wounded," yelled Terauchi. "Only men who can fight. Can't have the decks all cluttered with bodies."

He countermanded an order to launch the ship's boat. Survivors would have to haul themselves up on heaving lines. If they weren't strong enough, they weren't fit to fight.

Another voice broke in on the circuit. It was Commander Masazo Sato of *Hatsushimo*. He was normally a cheerful little man, but his voice was cold.

"I would respectfully suggest, Captain Yoshida, that we report the situation to Combined Fleet and request fresh orders. We could meanwhile start picking up those men in the water."

Terauchi complained, but Yoshida got the point. He had completely forgotten to update headquarters. Their last signal had gone off at 1350 on *Hatsushimo*'s radio after *Yamato*'s antennas were shot away. It advised of heavy damage in the fleet. But the top brass did not yet know *Yamato* was lost. The captain ran a quick check over the rest of the force.

"Where's *Suzutsuki*?" he asked.

"God knows," said Terauchi. "When we last saw her she was on fire with her bow blown off. She must have sunk."

"*Asashimo*?"

"Almost certainly a goner. We all heard her last message."

"What's happened to *Isokaze*?"

"That looks like her on fire to the northeast," Sato chipped in. "And that's *Kasumi*, also burning, bearing 060. She seems to be finished."

"*Yahagi* sunk?"

"No doubt about it."

"I shall recommend we proceed as planned," said Yoshida. He would have much preferred to follow Hara's plan and raid the enemy's lines of communication.

"Are you sure there won't be more air attacks?" Sato queried.

"The American flying boats are still overhead." The two Mariners which had been stalking them all day were coming down quite low now, apparently searching for ditched pilots.

"We've got to risk it," said Yoshida. He dictated an urgent signal, full priority, for officers' eyes only, to headquarters at Hiyoshi, Navy Minister Yonai, the chief of the naval staff, and Vice Admiral Kusaka at Kanoya:

> SPECIAL ATTACK FORCE SUSTAINED CONTINUOUS AIR ATTACKS FROM ENEMY CARRIER FORMATIONS. YAMATO YAHAGI HAMAKAZE SUNK. ASASHIMO AND SUZUTSUKI MISSING. ISOKAZE AND KASUMI SEVERELY DAMAGED. ALL OTHER FLEET UNITS OPERATIONAL. SUGGEST RESCUE OF SURVIVORS AND CONTINUATION OF MISSION.

The message was repeated by each ship at half-hourly intervals as they began their rescue efforts. *Hatsushimo* raced back to the spot where *Hamakaze* had gone down. Those men had been in the water longer than anyone else. Lieutenant Commander Sato was delighted to find so many still afloat. The destroyer had gone down so fast he had not expected to find more than a handful alive. He picked up 257 officers and men and headed back southward in search of *Yahagi* survivors.

William Delaney watched the destroyer bearing down on him. His life raft was intentionally conspicuous. It floated like a colorful tropical water lily upon the empty gray ocean. Surely the Japs would not be able to resist a look, just to see if anyone was hiding inside? He imagined the kind of reception those sailors would give him after the bashing they had taken from his fellow pilots. Tied up, kneeling on the forecastle, a samurai sword slashing down toward his neck . . . when he could have been home, having a ball.

Hatsushimo turned away 300 yards from the raft. Her wake rocked Delaney's frozen body. He stopped praying, cautiously raised his head, and watched the veteran twin-stacker sweep past. Her guns were fully manned; her rising-sun ensign streamed stiffly from the gaff. At this distance she looked more menacing than any shark.

About a mile farther off the destroyer stopped. The pilot felt quite sure she was watching him. He was not to know that she was launching lifeboats to pick up Japanese survivors. Another half hour went by. It seemed to be getting dark. His watch said 1500 and he thought it had stopped, but it was merely the thicker weather moving in. The sound of airplane engines rumbled from the north. Circling beneath the rain clouds were two Mariner flying boats.

Dog Eight and *Dog Ten* had watched the entire battle, but they had kept well clear. With so many planes milling around in the overcast, there was too much danger of a collision. Now they had the sky to themselves. The sea below seemed almost as empty, following the destruction of the enemy task force. Three destroyers were still afloat, as far as they could see, two of them dead in the water. A huge oil slick bobbing with human heads was all that remained of *Yamato*. The pilots circled lower, warily watching the destroyers, while everybody with binoculars scoured the surface for American airmen.

Yes, there was one. An aviator floated face downward in the water, his parachute billowing around him. Nothing they could do for that man. But hold it! A yell from one of the gunners. Someone was standing up in a rubber life raft, wildly waving a yellow bailing bucket. That must be the guy the *Yorktown* pilot had reported. Lieutenant Jim Young on *Dog Ten* volunteered to try a rescue. He discussed it over the radio with Lieutanant Dick Simms, piloting *Dog Eight*. Landing a flying boat wouldn't be easy in this heavy swell. Both planes were heavily loaded. There was also that destroyer lingering suspiciously close.

Simms offered to create a diversion. He would fly over the enemy ships to attract their fire. His plane buzzed at least one ship, probably *Fuyutsuki*, without being hit, while Jim Young braced himself for the impact. The length between wave crests was about 25 feet—quite enough, if mishandled, to break the flying boat's back.

When the Mariners flew on past, Delaney thought they had missed him. He had broken open another dye marker and climbed into the raft, waving like mad. One of the planes landed safely, to his great relief, and taxied toward him. He paddled desperately—enemy destroyers had spotted what was happening and were firing in their direction—but raft and plane kept drifting apart. On the third approach Jim Young cut his engines to avoid hitting Delaney with a propeller and drifted down toward him. The frantic pilot dived off the raft and tried to swim the last few yards. His heavy flying gear impeded his progress. Two crewmen clambered out onto the port wing tip and hauled him aboard.

Shells were bursting 200 yards away. Young quickly started all engines, gunned them to full throttle, and took off with the aid of one of those newfangled booster rockets. Delaney asked after his crewmen. Nobody aboard *Dog Ten* had seen any other Americans alive. They filled the tired pilot with hot soup, eggs, and coffee and provided a dry change of clothes. Delaney told them: "I thought I was cooked."

Captain Tameichi Hara watched *Yamato* die in a cloud of smoke. Tears streaked his oil-blackened face. A sudden chill reminded him that it was raining. He clung to his log, savoring the sour taste of defeat: his cruiser was gone and now the world's biggest battleship. When he next looked around, he was alone. Komura had disappeared. Young Daiwa had dropped off the log. Somewhere nearby Hara heard men singing. It was against regulations. Men were urged to husband their strength while awaiting rescue. Singing and shouting were exhausting. Perhaps these men no longer cared. Occasional hoarse shouts of "*Tenno Heika*, banzai!" ("Long live the emperor!") indicated that the tired or wounded were sinking to their deaths.

A burst of machine-gun fire cured Hara of his creeping numbness. American fighters were spraying the sea with bullets. They concentrated on the larger groups of survivors, floating 200 to 300 yards away, but a few shots hit the water close by. Burning hatred of these murderers gave the captain new strength. Twisting and ducking round his log, roundly cursing every apple pie-eating, mom-loving American son of a bitch brought his chilled limbs back to life.

A flying boat landed about 300 yards away. Hara watched with grudging admiration as an American pilot was plucked from the water. If only Japan had looked after its fliers this well, the captain thought enviously. He grew anxious when a Japanese shell burst nearby. To hell with the flying boat! There were Japanese survivors out there in the water. Ensign Shigeo Yamada, the nisei interpreter, was scared for a different reason. If he got picked up now, he might be shot for treason! Floating only a few yards from the rescue plane, he tore all rank badges off his uniform. That's how Hara saw it; Yamada himself denied the story. He removed his badges, he still insists, to avoid getting preferential rescue treatment.

Isokaze contacted Hatsushimo by signal lamp. About 100 of her crew were dead. Most of the casualties were in the two firerooms, which were wrecked by bombs. With the engines dead, all power had failed. The radio was out. The steering was shot. Auxiliary pumps were holding back the flooding aft.

Isokaze's skipper, Commander Saneo Maeda, plaintively inquired, "What are we going to do now?"

"How long can you stay afloat?" said Sato. It was clear that the ship was beyond help.

"We are in no imminent danger of sinking."

"Very well," signaled Sato. "Hold on while we pick up survivors."

Fuyutsuki loosed off a few salvos at the American flying boat which landed on the water. But the crewmen were too busy launching rescue boats to pay much attention to the intruder. After several unsuccessful attempts to raise Kasumi on the TBS, Captain Masayoshi Yoshida flashed the shattered destroyer. The shutters of the powerful 5-inch bridge lamps clicked and clacked as the two ships conversed in Morse. Bomb hits had wrecked Kasumi's firerooms and jammed the steering. A salvage tug would be needed to get her home. But before one could arrive, the Americans would be back ...

Ensign Mitsoru Yoshida saw Fuyutsuki firing at the flying boat. He thought the destroyer was still fighting off air attacks. A signalman on her weather deck semaphored them: "Wait awhile." Officers tried to quiet the excited men in the water. Already the biting cold was causing the weaker ones to slip beneath the surface. When the destroyer finally hove to, 400 yards away, there was a mad scramble for safety. It was no use urging caution upon frantic men struggling through the caramellike oil layer. By the time they reached the ship's side, many were too weak to grab the trailing lifeline.

"A clamor of voices could be heard on all sides," the ensign wrote afterward:

The first two men to reach the rope grasped eagerly, but no sooner had they clenched it than both men slipped back into the water, never to appear again. Another man was being pulled up by the rope when a frantic shipmate in the water sought to hang on to his shoes, with the result that both of them slid into the oily sea forever.

As one man was being lifted up, I saw a long arm reach out to grab him and I knocked the arm quickly aside. All of us in the water were desperate and I was trying to rescue as many men as possible. It was, therefore, a great shock to me to suddenly find myself alone in the water. Where were they? How many had been rescued? Only four? The majority had vanished helplessly beneath the waves.

From the deck above voices shouted, "Hurry up!" as the ship began to move. I saw a rope ladder hanging down crazily from the ship's side, but it was near the stern where the screws were churning the water to a froth. This, however, was my only chance. I lunged forward and hooked my hands onto the ladder, which went taut with the weight of my body. It felt like I was being torn apart by the drag of the waves. My hands started to slip. Desperately and stubbornly I braced myself and hung on.

Smeared with blood and oil, I dangled precariously from the ladder, which was gradually raised until two men on board could grasp my hands. On the deck I lay prostrate, too exhausted even to lift my head. Men removed my uniform and thrust fingers down my throat, forcing me to vomit the oil I had swallowed ... Then they wrapped me in a blanket and said, "Your head is wounded, sir. Hurry to the dispensary." I had been unaware of any wounds, and though they mentioned a wide gash in my scalp, I felt no pain whatsoever ...

Masanobu Kobayashi could not believe he was alive. The last thing he remembered was his mother's voice as he hit the water. Now he was paddling about in oil. A huge slick a foot deep undulated on the ocean swell. Together with three or four other men he found a hammock board and clung on.

But after two hours the cold was killing him. It seemed to eat into his muscles—and his mind. The cold induced lethargy, then drowsiness, then death. His wounds were forgotten in the desperate fight to survive. He huddled together with other shipmates, hugging the pitifully few bits of flotsam, singing and shouting to keep awake. Songs, any songs—the national anthem, "Tokyo Nights," "Goodbye, Rabaul"—anything that came into their heads. And still it was not enough. The singers grew steadily fewer. A few yards away from the group a friend was waving and shouting. He was on the point of drowning.

Kobayashi swam over and reached out with his right hand to grab him. His arm would not move. The bone was sticking out in a compound fracture of his upper arm. Although he had not noticed it before, the discovery suddenly impaired his swimming. He paddled back to the group, calling for someone else to rescue the drowning man. But the man was gone. None of them felt like singing again . . .

Captain Masayoshi Yoshida paced *Fuyutsuki*'s bridge. Still no reply from headquarters; he was getting worried. The Americans might have called it a day—he felt sure of that—but they would be back in the morning. He checked and rechecked their position. Some 160 miles southeast of Sasebo. The ships should head south now if the remnants of the attack force were to hit Okinawa on schedule. Just how much four destroyers could achieve against the entire U.S. fleet was an open question. That was for Combined Fleet to decide. Some men on the deck below were asking each other what it would be like to turn themselves into infantrymen once they managed to get ashore.

Yoshida reasoned that if the operation was caneled they must leave the area by 1900 at the latest to reach Kyushu by dawn. About 100 miles would have to be covered before they could count themselves safe. One way or the other, he had better evacuate *Kasumi*.

At 1622 *Fuyutsuki* pulled alongside the crippled destroyer. *Kasumi* was battered beyond recognition. The nine-year-old veteran, last survivor of a class of ten prewar vessels, had lost a smokestack and her after battery. Smoke was still rising from the bombs which had caved in the superstructure before bursting among the engineers below. The ship's ensign was ceremonially lowered at 1630. All hands mustered, at the salute, on the buckled upper deck. Fifteen officers and 270 men transferred to *Fuyutsuki*; the last men off were the skipper, Commander Hiroo Yamana, and his executive officer, reverently carrying the emperor's portrait in its protective box. Bosun's calls trilled as the box was ceremonially transferred.

At 1655 *Fuyutsuki* sank the derelict with two torpedoes fired at point-blank range. She went down rapidly, stern first. The sea spewed up oil, wreckage, and corpses. Yoshida and Yamana watched glumly. Scuttling a ship was frowned upon in the Imperial Navy. You were supposed to go down fighting.

Captain Tameichi Hara heard the singing fade away. The

current was carrying him clear of the other *Yahagi* survivors. Occasional bursts of song wafted down on the wind. He clung, shuddering with cold, to his life-saving log. He found a 4-inch piece of rope inside his waterlogged raincoat and tied himself in such a way that the log would hold him up even if he passed out. Way off in the distance his crewmen were singing "The Song of the Warrior."

"I knew I was going to die," Hara wrote. "The distant melody, wavering like a lullaby, brought back my childhood and my mother's songs, my grandfather, school days, the academy, our world cruise, shopping in a New York department store, young officer days, my affair with the geisha girl. This kaleidoscope changed into a vivid picture of my mother, overlapped by one of my wife, and then my first formal officer portrait, which was replaced by the faces of my children."

At the thought of his family he began to weep again. He was leaving a widow and three youngsters. Could his wife every forgive him? He cursed himself for allowing *Yahagi* to be sunk so easily. Perhaps he had blundered somewhere? But no, the blunder was in Tokyo where those imbeciles first thought up this grotesque gamble . . .

The light was fading when the destroyers' radios sprang to life. Secret fleet signal 616 had been dispatched by Combined Fleet at 1639, only to be delayed by the usual communication foul-ups. It came in, coded, at approximately 1750. The operation was canceled. Survivors were to be rescued wherever possible. Crippled vessels should be sunk before withdrawal to Sasebo. The destroyers redoubled their rescue efforts. Everyone now wanted out—as far away as possible—from this ill-omened patch of ocean.

Yukikaze concentrated on picking up *Yamato* survivors. Orders were orders and Terauchi grumpily complied. Morishita and Nomura were found floating unconscious. Several staff officers of the now defunct Second Fleet were still alive, among them the chief of operations, Captain Yuji Yamamoto, who had been washed off the tower when the battleship capsized. Ensign Sakei Katono, resigned to dying deep inside the hull, was hauled aboard together with the officer who worked the TBS, Ensign Mitsuo Watanabe. Ariga's messenger, Tsukamoto, also survived, somewhat to his surprise.

Lookouts spotted Masanobu Kobayashi's group. The destroyer approached cautiously: too many men had already been sucked accidentally into the screws. Forty yards away, deckhands threw out heaving lines. Most of the sailors hauled themselves up the side. The young gunner splashed about awkwardly. He was cold and tired, with only one good arm. It was nearly dark. The men on deck were impatient to get moving. Kobayashi knotted the line round his waist and was dragged aboard. He had been in the sea 4½ hours and was one of the last to be rescued.

Captain Hara was dozing on his log when a strange sound aroused him. It was a ship's launch riding the wave crests about 200 yards away. It disappeared in a trough to reappear 50 yards away, circling around in search of survivors. So far the crew had failed to notice him. He freed himself from the log and thrashed around to attract attention. The launch turned toward him. Strong hands lifted him aboard. There were no other survivors. The coxswain explained that he had picked up many boatloads but that this was his final trip. They searched unsuccessfully for another 15 minutes before heading back through the gathering darkness to *Hatsushimo*.

Commander Sato came down from the bridge to greet his bedraggled colleague. "Welcome home, Captain Hara," he said. "We had almost despaired of finding you. Rear Admiral Komura is resting in my cabin."

The commanding officer of Second Destroyer Squadron had been fished out of the water half an hour before. Keizo Komura had come a long and painful road since he sent the first search planes over Pearl Harbor.

"I've fought my last battle," he announced firmly.

Hara sat sipping sake in the dispensary. He followed it down with a bowl of hot soup. Very slowly his body began to thaw.

"By the way," he asked. "Did you pick up a sailor called Daiwa?"

The medic checked his list and nodded. "Yes, sir. His name is here. In fact he has been asking for you ever since we picked him up two hours ago." An orderly was sent off to reassure the youngster.

"How about Lieutenant Hatta?"

The medic shook his head.

"No one of that name here."

"He could have been picked up by another ship?"

Commander Sato came in to escort Hara to Rear Admiral Komura.

"No hope of that, I'm afraid," he interjected. "We were the only ship combing your area."

A signal reached Rear Admiral Komura from Kanoya. It was from Kusaka. He praised the valor of the special attack force, whose diversionary efforts had enabled the air fleet to strike crippling blows against the enemy. Komura handed it to Hara. Neither man spoke.

Captain Nomura recovered consciousness at 2030. "From that moment," he wrote "I started a second life." He discussed with the officers the cause of the final explosion which destroyed the battleship. Could those unstable *San-Shiki* antiaircraft shells have rolled off the storage racks and exploded? The theory led to the myth, still current in Japan, that *Yamato* committed suicide. A postwar American inquiry came to the less dramatic conclusion that the moment the ship capsized, the unextinguished belowdecks fire abaft the smokestack touched off the main after magazine.

The inquiry criticized *Yamato*'s design flaws: the lateral bulkhead, the overrigid armor reinforcement, the poorly conceived pumping system for correcting the ship's list. But the presiding officers admitted that no ship could have been expected to absorb so many bombs and torpedoes and survive. How many? It was difficult to establish. The final report estimated a very conservative minimum of 11 torpedoes and 8 heavy bombs. Survivors put the total nearer to 16 torpedoes and 18 heavy bombs, with the torpedoes responsible for sending the great ship to the bottom.

At final count 269 officers and men were saved from *Yamato*, according to her executive officer. The dead numbered 3063, including the fleet commander and the ship's commanding officer, both of flag rank. In the escort force, 1187 officers and men lost their lives.

Americans losses were 10 planes and 12 men.

The ship's crew could smell the blood as *Yukikaze* approached her sister ship's mutilated port side. *Isokaze* rolled heavily, beam-on to the swell, a total wreck, red stains from the scuppers streaking her buckled hull plates. Guns bristled erratically skyward from her powerless turrets. Machine-gun tubs were stuffed with stiffening corpses. Bodies and bits of bodies draped the demolished superstructure. *Isokaze* struck the colors and transferred the imperial portrait together with 15 officers and 270 men. *Yukikaze* tried to scuttle the wreck, but the torpedo passed harmlessly under the hull. Gunners then poured shells into the wreck. Bodies were seen flying into the air as the shells tore the ship apart. Watching sailors later swore they had seen the souls of *Isokaze*'s dead ascending to heaven. The half-light can play weird tricks on the imagination when nerves are at full stretch.

Fires spread throughout the doomed destroyer's hull. She was aflame from stem to stern when *Yukikaze* pulled away. The fire was seen as far away as Kagoshima before *Isokaze* foundered, hours later.

Captain Yoshida had a hunch that *Suzutsuki* was still afloat. She was said to be the luckiest ship in the Imperial Navy. She was a relatively new ship, completed on March 4, 1942, when her bow and stern were shot off by torpodoes off the Japanese island of Shikoku on January 16, 1944. The center portion of the ship refused to sink and she was rebuilt at Kure. Nine months later her bow was blown off again by a torpedo, also off Shikoku near the Bungo Strait. She had only recently been rebuilt a second time and returned to service.

Fuyutsuki paused first at the spot where *Asashimo* had last been heard from. It was too dark to see anything, and too risky to use searchlights. Any survivors would have been in the cold water for over eight hours by now, Yoshida calculated, and there was little hope for them, assuming that anyone had survived the sinking. He turned onto a northeasterly search pattern at 20 knots.

There is a Japanese proverb that "a thing repeated will occur a third time." The crew of the missing *Suzutsuki* were saying it grimly to themselves as they fought to keep their ship afloat. History certainly had repeated itself—20 feet of the destroyer's bow had been blown off by yet another torpedo. The foremost 3.9-inch turret teetered over the sea. The radio was out; so was the gyrocompass. Fires burned through a section of the amidships upper works. But the shattered forecastle was effectively sealed off. To ease the strain on the bulkheads the destroyer steamed slowly backward—stern first. This made it impossible to steer by rudder, so the skipper, Commander Shigetaka Amano, relied on his engines. By varying the speeds of the port and starboard propellers it was possible to keep groping forward (or, in this case, backward) on a rough heading. They might make landfall somewhere along the Kyushu coast by early morning.

Meanwhile *Fuyutsuki* continued her fruitless search. At five minutes past midnight she was close to Koshiki Island, off Kyushu. Messages urged her to sink *Suzutsuki* if necessary. At 0123 Combined Fleet ordered Yoshida to break off the search and head for Sasebo. Operation Heaven Number One was over.

Return from Battle

APRIL 7 – 8

THE FIRST PLANES arrived back at 1456. *San Jacinto's* air group came in slightly ahead of *Bennington's*. The lost patrol from *Hancock* checked in shamefacedly at 1630. They had been flying since 1100 and were down to their last 30 gallons of gas. It was a relief to find their damaged carrier functioning almost normally again. All over the task force landing crews held their breath as the occasional damaged plane wobbled onto the deck. There were no serious crashes or fires. Eight of the most damaged aircraft were pushed overboard after being stripped of important spares.

Medics helped the handful of wounded onto litters and rushed them off for treatment. None of the wounds was serious. Most pilots complained of stiffness or bursting bladders as they climbed from their cockpits. Their limbs ached intolerably after five hours in the air. They looked forward to a shower and a massage after debriefing. For some, perhaps, a "medicinal" shot of whiskey.

Edmond Konrad wouldn't even take a Coke; he was perpetually worrying about his weight. As far as he remembered, nobody celebrated. There was a vague feeling that Japanese naval power was broken, but that it would not necessarily shorten the war. And that was all anyone cared about. "It was no use getting excited," Herbert Houck commented dryly. "After so many operations, this one didn't make much difference." His film was rushed to the darkroom.

Mitscher sent a congratulatory message to his beloved aircrews. Now that it was over, he seemed tired and strangely subdued. At 1632 the intelligence officers rushed in with aerial photographs of the action still wet with fixer. They plastered them across the bulkhead for the vice admiral's inspection. He examined them in detail, a cigarette drooping from his lips. Then he stepped back, still staring, arms akimbo. His staff crowded round, awaiting some historic pronouncement. The years of frustrating struggle were over. The airplane had triumphed, once and for all, over the battleship.

The Pensacola pioneer surprised his expectant audience. He turned on his heel without a word and walked off to his cabin. Within ten minutes he was asleep.

The summing up must therefore be left to Edmond Konrad. "It was glorious, it ended all right," he mused 34 years afterward. "But we still let four destroyers get away . . . with all the planes we had, we should have sunk them all."

Spruance received the news with relish. A pity there had been no surface action. Still, a passing threat to the Okinawa operation had been eliminated, and with it the last strike force of the imperial fleet. The Dvorak symphony on this phonograph sounded so good, he clean forgot to inform old Rear Admiral Deyo, who was still exercising his antique battle line out in the East China Sea. *Yamato* had been on the bottom for eight hours before the disgruntled sea dog broke off and resumed his dreary bombardment routine.

The war correspondents missed the full implications of the story. Their attention was riveted on the land battle for Okinawa. Even the destruction of an enemy battleship did not grab big headlines these days. Even in the U.S. Navy the incident was soon forgotten.

Vice Admiral Ryunosuke Kusaka first heard the news by telephone at Kanoya. The fire-eating Captain Kami was on the line from Combined Fleet headquarters, Hiyoshi. "They fought in the greatest traditions of the Imperial Navy," he declared. He sounded as if he was reading an official communiqué. Kusaka hung up. He went outside to meet the commander-in-chief's plane, which had been delayed by bad weather. Admiral Soemu Toyoda was genuinely shocked. "I should have let Kami join *Yamato*," he muttered. They agreed on a suitable message to the survivors over the chief of staff's signature. There was no question of continuing the operation. Further losses would be inevitable and would only make the Americans crow louder. Every effort must be made to keep news of the disaster secret until the public was ready to receive it. Once the tide of battle began to turn . . .

But rumors spread. Journalists at the leading Tokyo newspaper, *Mainichi*, heard the news from America on a radio hidden in their editorial lavatory. Word leaked out of Sasebo where the survivors were kept segregated for the next two weeks. Death notices did not begin reaching bereaved families until a month later. Weeping wives and children from Hiroshima to Osaka threw flowers onto the empty waters of the Inland Sea.

A signal was received by Lieutenant Commander Mochitsura Hashimoto ten hours after *Yamato* sank. He was cruising some 100 miles east of Okinawa around the spot where the battleship should have begun her dash toward the American beachhead. A coded message ordered *I-58* to head for the west Pacific and attack enemy supply ships. This was just what the submarine commanders had been demanding for years. But getting there was no easy matter. The waters round Okinawa were thickly infested with antisubmarine pickets and aircraft. He was forced to spend days sailing southward around Taiwan to reach the open ocean. By that time the confused and hesitant headquarters staff had changed their minds again; Hashimoto was ordered back to Japan. He reached Kure, evading over 50 air attacks during his abortive 29-day voyage.

Navy Minister Mitsumasa Yonai was left the distasteful task of informing the emperor. It was the painful climax of a thoroughly nerve-racking day. A cabinet of sorts had been cobbled together under old Admiral Kantaro Suzuki, dedicated to ending the war but still publicly committed to continuing it. Anything more forthright would provoke a bloody reaction from the young hotheads who refused to accept the notion of surrender. The prime minister did not want another bullet in him.

An air-raid alert had sounded when Yonai entered the palace bunker. Searchlights were flickering in the southern suburbs.

Hirohito appeared from behind the screen. He looked tired and worried. His privy seal, Marquis Koichi Kido, the peace faction's most valuable ally inside the palace, had been drawing the imperial attention to some of the franker appraisals now being covertly made of the strategic and economic situation. This was no time for bad news.

Admiral Yonai bowed, wondering how to begin.

"Imperial Highness," he said at last in a shaking voice. "I regret to report that the *Yamato* sortie has failed. *Yamato* and most of the special attack force were sunk today by American carrier planes some 90 miles south of Kyushu."

Hirohito listened aghast.

"I must regretfully report that the operation was ill conceived," Yonai went on. "We had not expected enemy air action of such intensity."

Hirohito was still trying to grasp the meaning of his minister's news.

"The fleet," he said. "What is the status of the fleet?"

Yonai bowed again. The tears streamed down his pudgy face.

"There is no fleet, Imperial Highness," he choked. "The Imperial Navy no longer exists."

How symbolic, he thought later, to break this disastrous news just as his allies within the Japanese leadership were beginning their four-month-long battle for peace. The impact on the emperor was heartbreaking.

"The fleet," he muttered disbelievingly. "Gone? It's gone?"

Hirohito swayed slightly, a hand to his temple. Yonai stood bowed in silence until the August Presence disappeared behind the screen.

Word eventually reached Lieutenant General Mitsuru Ushijima, defender of Okinawa, deep below the bomb-torn face of the island. He had postponed his counterattack until April 12, when another great Kikusui assault was scheduled.

"What an infernal waste!" the general snorted. "I advised the navy not to try it. Banzai charges should be left to soldiers!"

The cherry blossoms were still blooming around Sasebo on April 8 when the destroyers straggled into port. *Fuyutsuki* docked at 0845; *Hatsushimo* and *Yukikaze* arrived together just over an hour later. At 1430 *Suzutsuki* eased her way sternfirst into the bay, still under her own power and still ablaze. Ambulances were lining up to evacuate the wounded. Those who could walk were shepherded up the hill to the naval hospital. Vice Admiral Kusaka was waiting on the dockside. When Rear Admiral Komura stepped ashore, the chief of staff came over to greet him. The destroyer squadron commander brushed past without a word.

Ensign Mitsuru Yoshida found himself toiling uphill among a mob of limping men. A band of pigtailed schoolgirls, drilling with bamboo spears, bowed respectfully to the passing officer. He bowed back and saluted, overcome with grief. These girls had faith in the navy. Now he felt the navy had failed them. He sobbed quietly to himself, hobbling into the hospital grounds. Cherry blossoms were falling everywhere. And yet there was no wind . . .

Epilogue

THE ATOMIC BOMBING of Hiroshima and Nagasaki and the sudden Soviet entry into the Pacific war, which followed the collapse of Japanese military resistance on Okinawa and the growing threat of invasion of the imperial homeland, prompted Emperor Hirohito to order Japan to surrender. His historic broadcast of August 15, 1945, persuaded a people intent on suicidal resistance to meekly lay down their arms. It was as if a switch had been thrown, quenching the fires of nationalism and channeling all future aggression down peaceful paths. Militarism was shunned. The Japanese redirected their vast, disciplined energies toward commercial conquest. A rich, money-making empire was carved out, infinitely less painfully, by electronics, automobile, and other manufacturers. It was to be a worldwide empire bigger by far than the misnamed "Co-Prosperity Sphere" in eastern Asia seized by the military at bayonet point.

The dry dock designed for *Yamato* in Kure became the birthplace of still bigger ships, but they were supertankers and bulk carriers. The shipyards which had failed to keep pace with Japanese wartime losses began to outbuild their international competitors. Great new factories sprouted from the wartime ashes. Modern cities replaced the old.

Conservatives might bewail the loss of "national spirit" in the midst of newfound affluence, but the better educated, more internationally minded postwar generation recognized the new realities.

The world was now dominated by two antagonistic super-powers, armed to the teeth with nuclear weaponry. The Japanese were more aware than most of their dangerous vulnerability; it was safer and more profitable to forget past pretensions and remain a nation of traders. Japan accepted American protection. The nuclear umbrella obligingly provided by their former foes enabled successive Japanese governments to eschew expensive defense budgets and politely resist American pressure to rearm. The minuscule Japanese armed forces, reborn during the Korean War, were treated for many years with contempt. Officers and men found it less embarrassing when off duty to doff their uniforms. The days of adoration were over.

Yet these sentimental people never forgot *Yamato*. The saga of her last sortie slipped into folklore. It contained all the elements of the hopeless heroism the Japanese admire. The sheer magnitude of the failure made it especially endearing. Like Masashige Kusunoki and his doomed warriors, the battleship's brave crew had lost—magnificently. The Japanese and the British must be the only nations in the world to prize heroic defeat beyond the greatest victories.

The Imperial Navy played no further part in the Pacific war. The few surviving units of the fleet were sunk ignominiously at anchor, as the hard-liners prophesied; most of them by carrier raids on Kure three weeks before the surrender.

Hatsushimo's luck ran out at last. A mine sank the veteran destroyer in the Japan Sea on July 30, 1945. She was the 143rd and last Japanese destroyer lost in the war. *Fuyutsuki* and *Suzutsuki*, both damaged, were scuttled after the surrender to serve as harbor breakwaters. *Yukikaze* was handed over to Nationalist China and renamed *Tan Yang*. Her anchor is preserved today on the grounds of the Etajima Defense Academy.

Some were spared the final humiliation. Lieutenant General Ushijima, valiant defender of Okinawa, chose the samurai's way out when all was lost on June 22, 1945. He and his fiery sidekick,

Lieutenant General Isamu Cho, slit their bellies in their head-quarters cave while nine members of their staff blew their brains out. The coast watcher Matsuoka was captured uncon-scious but alive, half buried by a shell burst, on the slopes of Yaeju Hill, where some of the surviving Japanese troops made their last stand. Radioman Tanaka, first name unknown, lay dead beside him.

Vice Admiral Takijiro Onishi, so-called father of the Kami-kaze, committed ceremonial *seppuku* when Japan surrendered. He took 18 agonizing hours to die. His field commander, Vice Admiral Matome Ugaki, led his own final Kamikaze raid. "I am going to make an attack upon Okinawa," he announced, "where my men have fallen like cherry blossoms." He took off with 11 carrier bombers (4 of which broke down) in direct defiance of the emperor's broadcast three hours before. If his force had slammed into the now celebrating U.S. fleet, hostilities might have been rekindled, but the raiders vanished harmlessly some-where in the Pacific. It was a strangely appropriate epitaph for the Kamikaze effort, which claimed so much and achieved pathetically little for the loss of so many pilots' lives. Admiral Soemu Toyoda struggled fiercely to keep Japan fighting to the bitter end, much to Minister Yonai's fury, but he did not join the roll call of face-saving suicides.

The militant Captain Shiganori Kami died mysteriously and ironically after being sent on an official mission to the northern island of Hokkaido to urge Japanese naval forces there to sur-render. His plane crashed on the way back in the Sugaro Strait. The crew was saved but Kami, a strong swimmer, disappeared. It was widely believed that he deliberately drowned. After demobilization, impoverished and without pensions under the American occupation, some of the ex-officers joined the Mari-time Self-Defense Force in 1951. To this day it is never referred to in Japan as "the navy."

Most of the older men refused to join. Their allegiances lay with the past. Captain Tameichi Hara joined his brother-in-law's printing business. Like most of the senior officers featured in this story, he is now dead. So are such leading figures as Yonai, Toyoda, Kusaka, and Komura. Morishita regretted being saved from *Yamato* until his dying day. Even the most junior survivors of the hopeless action in the East China Sea are now grandfathers.

Lieutenant Commander Mochitsura Hashimoto had no compunction about lending his skills to the Self-Defense Forces. He ended the war with a stunning success. Given his chance to launch marauding raids against enemy supply lines, he inflicted on the U.S. Navy one of its greatest disasters. On July 28, 18 days before the surrender, he sank the cruiser *Indianapolis* with conventional torpedoes. Only 316 of her 1196 crewmen were saved. Spruance's old flagship had, ironically enough, just delivered the heart of the first atomic bomb to the secret U.S. air base at Tinian in the Marianas. Hashimoto lives today in retirement in a Shinto shrine in Kyoto.

Ensign Mitsuo Watanabe became a teacher, as did Ensign Sakei Katono. Ensign Mitsuru Yoshida became a successful banker, and died in 1979. The coast-watching Lieutenant Goro Matsuoka went into the export business. The English he learned as a prisoner proved invaluable, but he never quite lived down the stigma of captivity. His is the only name in this book that was changed to hide an individual's identity. There were more horrors in store for the young gunner Masanobu Kobayashi. He was in one of the first rescue teams to reach Hiroshima after the atomic attack. During two unspeakable weeks his body absorbed enough radiation to necessitate annual checkups. He became an official police photographer and never learned to drink or smoke.

Ensign Shigeo Yamada did not get back his American citizenship. He did the next best thing by working in the United States for Japan Air Lines. After years in the United States he returned to Tokyo as a Japan Air Lines vice-president in 1979. With his daughters married to Japanese and his youngest son, born in Chicago, living in the United States, he reckoned his family was "a little bit torn." It was the story of his own life.

Few of the leading American characters in this drama lived to a ripe age. The strain of the war years took swift toll of Nimitz, Mitscher, and Spruance, who became America's first ambassador to the independent Philippines—some slight consolation for his failing to get a fifth star at the end of the war. That went to publicity conscious "Bull" Halsey. Rear Admiral Arleigh ("31-Knot") Burke is still alive, at the time of this writing, in comfortable retirement, as is Fred Janney of *Threadfin*, who remained in the postwar navy to become a rear admiral. Michele Mazzocco, the fighter pilot, became an industrial psychologist. That incredible survivor, William E. Delaney, died of leukemia about ten years after the war. Some American veterans of the battle still keep in touch—as do the *Yamato* survivors in Japan. Every year on April 7, the dwindling band of men who fought the fateful battle commune with their dead comrades' souls at the Yasukuni shrine.

APPENDIXES

OPERATIONAL COMMAND STRUCTURE
IMPERIAL JAPANESE NAVY
APRIL, 1945

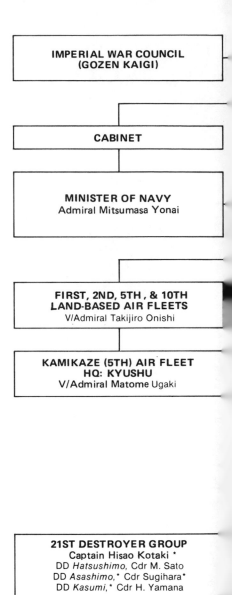

**IMPERIAL WAR COUNCIL
(GOZEN KAIGI)**

CABINET

MINISTER OF NAVY
Admiral Mitsumasa Yonai

**FIRST, 2ND, 5TH, & 10TH
LAND-BASED AIR FLEETS**
V/Admiral Takijiro Onishi

**KAMIKAZE (5TH) AIR FLEET
HQ: KYUSHU**
V/Admiral Matome Ugaki

21ST DESTROYER GROUP
Captain Hisao Kotaki *
DD *Hatsushimo,* Cdr M. Sato
DD *Asashimo,** Cdr Sugihara*
DD *Kasumi,** Cdr H. Yamana

322

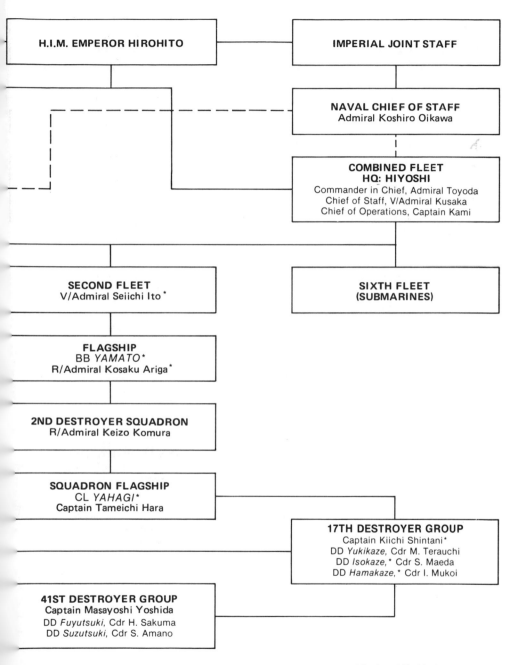

H.I.M. EMPEROR HIROHITO

IMPERIAL JOINT STAFF

NAVAL CHIEF OF STAFF
Admiral Koshiro Oikawa

**COMBINED FLEET
HQ: HIYOSHI**
Commander in Chief, Admiral Toyoda
Chief of Staff, V/Admiral Kusaka
Chief of Operations, Captain Kami

SECOND FLEET
V/Admiral Seiichi Ito*

**SIXTH FLEET
(SUBMARINES)**

FLAGSHIP
BB *YAMATO**
R/Admiral Kosaku Ariga*

2ND DESTROYER SQUADRON
R/Admiral Keizo Komura

SQUADRON FLAGSHIP
CL *YAHAGI**
Captain Tameichi Hara

17TH DESTROYER GROUP
Captain Kiichi Shintani*
DD *Yukikaze*, Cdr M. Terauchi
DD *Isokaze*,* Cdr S. Maeda
DD *Hamakaze*,* Cdr I. Mukoi

41ST DESTROYER GROUP
Captain Masayoshi Yoshida
DD *Fuyutsuki*, Cdr H. Sakuma
DD *Suzutsuki*, Cdr S. Amano

*Sunk or killed in *Yamato* action

ALLIED ORDER OF BATTLE
APRIL, 1945

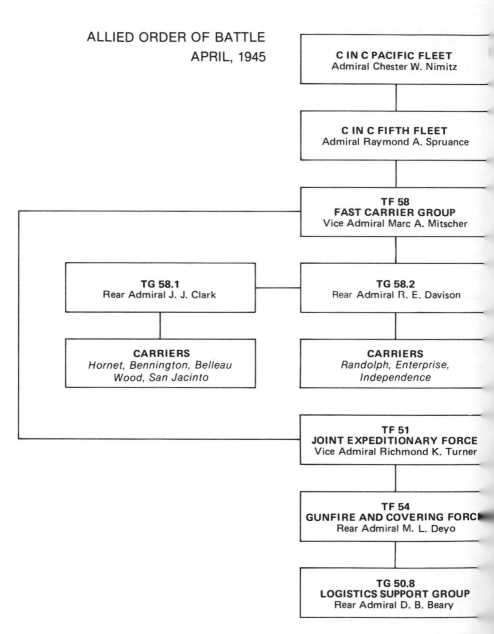

C IN C PACIFIC FLEET
Admiral Chester W. Nimitz

C IN C FIFTH FLEET
Admiral Raymond A. Spruance

TF 58
FAST CARRIER GROUP
Vice Admiral Marc A. Mitscher

TG 58.1
Rear Admiral J. J. Clark

TG 58.2
Rear Admiral R. E. Davison

CARRIERS
Hornet, Bennington, Belleau Wood, San Jacinto

CARRIERS
Randolph, Enterprise, Independence

TF 51
JOINT EXPEDITIONARY FORCE
Vice Admiral Richmond K. Turner

TF 54
GUNFIRE AND COVERING FORCE
Rear Admiral M. L. Deyo

TG 50.8
LOGISTICS SUPPORT GROUP
Rear Admiral D. B. Beary

Note: As of April 7, 1945, composition of Task Groups was constantly changing, mainly because of Kamikaze attacks.

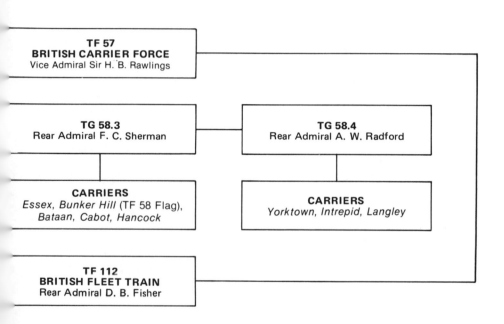

TF 57
BRITISH CARRIER FORCE
Vice Admiral Sir H. B. Rawlings

TG 58.3
Rear Admiral F. C. Sherman

TG 58.4
Rear Admiral A. W. Radford

CARRIERS
Essex, Bunker Hill (TF 58 Flag),
Bataan, Cabot, Hancock

CARRIERS
Yorktown, Intrepid, Langley

TF 112
BRITISH FLEET TRAIN
Rear Admiral D. B. Fisher

IN C Commander-in-Chief
   Task Force
   Task Group

YAMATO, SIDE-ON SECTIONAL VIEW

— HEAVY LINE DENOTES INTERNAL ARMOR
B.R. — BOILER ROOM
ENG. RM. — ENGINE ROOM
HYD. P. RM. — TRIM PUMPS
MAG. — MAGAZINE
ST. — STORAGE
W.T.C. — WATER TIGHT COMPARTMENTS
FLC. — FLOODING COMPARTMENTS
T.T. — TRIM TANKS
O.F.T. — OIL FUEL STORAGE
R. — ROOM
SP. — SPACE

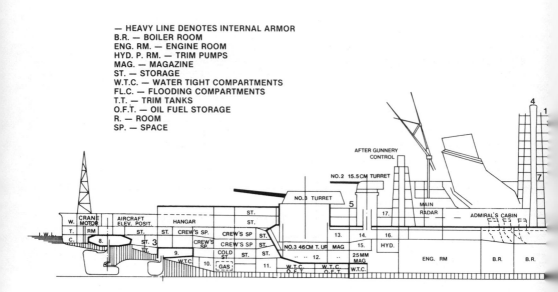

1. SHIP'S CAPTAIN.
2. ADMIRAL'S STAFF.
3. ENSIGN KATONO'S DAMAGE CONTROL.
4. GUNNERY OFFICER.
5. GUNNER KOBAYASHI'S POST.
6. QUARTERMASTER.
7. ADMIRAL'S SEA CABIN.
8. STEERING ENGINE ROOM.
9. AUXILIARY STEERING ROOM.
10. GAS PRESSURE ROOM.
11. OIL PRESSURE ROOM.
12. NO 3 MAIN TURRET MAGAZINE.
13. NO 3 MAIN TURRET SHELL ROOM.
14. NO 2 SECONDARY TURRET SHELL ROOM.
15. NO 2 SECONDARY TURRET MAGAZINE.
16. AUXILIARY MAGAZINE.

17. UPPER RADIO ROOM.
18. MAIN ANTI-AIRCRAFT MAGAZINE.
19. NO 2 MAIN TURRET MAGAZINE.
20. NO 1 AUXILIARY TURRET MAGAZINE.
21. NO 1 MAIN TURRET MAGAZINE.
22. NO 1 MAIN TURRET SHELL ROOM.
23. AUXILIARY TRIM PUMPS.
24. OIL PUMP ROOM.
25. LOWER RADIO ROOM.
26. SONAR ROOM.
27. BILGE PUMP ROOM.
28. FORWARD ANCHOR ENGINE.
29. CHAIN LOCKER.
30. AUXILIARY TRIM PUMPS.
31. FORWARD SONAR ROOM.

M TURRET

NO.2 TURRET   NO.1 TURRET

		CREW'S SP.	CREW'S SP.	CREW'S	SP.	CREW'S SP.	ST.		— WEATHER DECK
		CREW	CREW'S SP	CREW'S SP₁		CREW'S SP	ST.		— UPPER DECK
20.	ST.	CREW	CREW'S SP	CREW'S SP₁		30.	W.T.C.	W.T.C.	— MIDDLE DECK
		ST.	W.T.C	W.T.C	28.	ST.	ST.	W.T.C.	DΩ	— LOWER DECK
19.	22.	23.	25.	W.T.C.	ST.	ST.	27.	ST.	29.	ST.	ST.	W.T.C.	DΩ	— DECK
19.	21.			ST.	ST.	ST.	W.T.C	W.T.C	TRIM T	T.T.	T.T.	31.	— 2ND HOLD DECK PLATFORM
25MM MG.	21.	24.	26.										
W.T.C.	W.T.C.	W.T.C.											

327

YAMATO, BOMBER'S-EYE VIEW OF WEATHER DECK

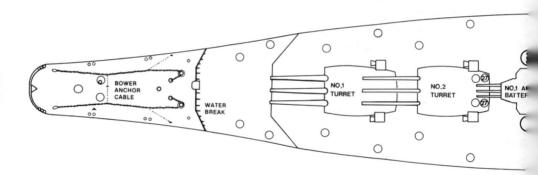

BOWER ANCHOR CABLE

WATER BREAK

NO.1 TURRET

NO.2 TURRET

NO.1 A...
BATTE...

○ = DOUBLE 13 MM M.G.S

⑧ = TRIPLE 25 MM M.G.S

●● = DOUBLE 2.7 CM HA/4A GUNS

328

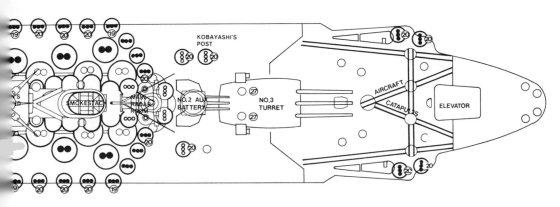

KOBAYASHI'S POST

SMOKESTACK

MAIN RADAR ROOM

NO.2 AUX BATTERY

NO.3 TURRET

AIRCRAFT CATAPULTS

ELEVATOR

Bibliography

Agawa, Hiroyuki. *The Reluctant Admiral.* Tokyo: Kodansha, 1969.

Appleman, Roy Edgar, *et al. Okinawa: The Last Battle.* The Historical Division, Dept. of the Army, United States Government. Tokyo and Rutland, VT.: Charles E. Tuttle Co, 1961.

Ballard, George A. *The Influence of the Sea on the Political History of Japan.* London: Murray, 1921.

Battistini, Laurence H. *Japan and America.* New York: John Day, 1954.

Benedict, Ruth. *The Chrysanthemum and the Sword: Patterns of Japanese Culture.* Boston: Houghton Mifflin, 1946.

Blechman, Barry M., and Robert P. Berman, editors. *Guide to Far Eastern Navies.* Annapolis, MD.: United States Naval Institute, 1978.

Blair, Clay. *Silent Victory: The U.S. Submarine War Against Japan.* Philadelphia: Lippincott, 1975.

Brown, David. *Aircraft Carriers.* New York: Arco, 1978.

———. *Carrier Operations in World War II.* London: Balding & Mansell, 1974.

Browne, Courtney. *Tojo: The Last Banzai.* New York: Holt, Rinehart & Winston, 1967.

Busch, Noel F. *The Emperor's Sword: Japan Vs. Russia in the Battle of Tsushima.* New York: Funk & Wagnalls, 1969.

Bush, Lewis. *Clutch of Circumstance.* Tokyo: Bungei Shunju, 1956.

Butow, Robert Joseph C. *Japan's Decision to Surrender.* Foreword by Edwin O. Reischauer. Palo Alto, CA.: Stanford University Press, 1954. (Stanford University Hoover Institution on War, Revolution and Peace, Publ. No. 24).

Byas, Hugh. *Government by Assassination.* New York: Knopf, 1942.

331

Caidin, Martin. *A Torch to the Enemy*. New York: Ballantine, 1960.

Casey, Louis S. *Naval Aircraft*. London: Hamlyn, 1977.

Chamberlin, William Henry. *Japan Over Asia*. Boston: Little, Brown, 1938.

Churchill, Winston S. *The Second World War*. Vols. III, IV, V, VI. Boston: Houghton Mifflin, 1950, 1951, 1953.

Cohen, Jerome B. *Japan's Economy in War and Reconstruction*. Minneapolis: University of Minnesota Press, 1949.

Coox, Alvin D. *Tojo*. New York: Ballantine, 1975.

Craig, William. *The Fall of Japan*. New York: Dial Press, 1967.

Cross, Wilbur. *Challengers of the Deep*. New York: William Sloane Associates, 1959.

Crowl, Philip A. *Campaign in the Marianas*. Washington, D.C.: Office of the Chief of Military History, Dept. of the Army. (Part of the series, "U.S. Army In World War II; The War in the Pacific").

———, and Edmund G. Love. *Seizure of the Gilberts and Marshalls*. Washington, D.C.: Office of the Chief of Military History, Dept. of the Army. (Part of the series, "U.S. Army In World War II; The War in the Pacific").

Davis, Burke. *Get Yamamoto*. New York: Random House, 1969.

Dull, Paul S. *The Imperial Japanese Navy, 1941–45*. Annapolis, MD.: United States Naval Institute, 1978.

Ellis, Chris. *Famous Ships of World War II*. New York: Arco, 1976.

Fairbank, John K., and Edwin O. Reischauer. *East Asia: The Modern Transformation*. Boston: Houghton Mifflin, 1965.

Falk, Edwin E. *Togo and the Rise of Japanese Sea Power*. New York: Longmans, Green, 1936.

Falk, Stanley L. *Decision at Leyte*. New York: Norton, 1966.

Forrestal, E. P., Vice Admiral. *Admiral Raymond A. Spruance USN: A Study in Command*. Washington, D.C.: United States Government Printing Office, 1966.

Forrestal, James. *The Forrestal Diaries*; edited by Walter Millis with the collaboration of E. S. Duffield. New York: Viking Press, 1951.

Frothingham, Thomas G. *The Naval History of the World War*. Cambridge, MA.: Harvard University Press, 1927.

Fuchido, Mutsuo, and Okumija Masatake. *Midway, The Battle That Doomed Japan*. Annapolis, MD.: United States Naval Institute Proceedings, 1955.

Fukaya, Hajime. *Japan's Wartime Carrier Construction*. Annapolis, MD.: United States Naval Institute Proceedings, 1955.

———. *Three Japanese Submarine Developments*. Annapolis, MD.: United States Naval Institute Proceedings, 1952.

Gibney, Frank. *Five Gentlemen of Japan: The Portrait of a Nation's Character*. New York: Farrar, Straus & Young, 1953.

Grenfell, Russell, Captain. *Main Fleet to Singapore*. London: Faber & Faber, 1951.

Hagoromo Society. *Born to Die*. Tokyo: Ohara Publications, 1973.

Halsey, William F., Admiral, and J. Bryan, III. *Admiral Halsey's Story*. New York: Whittlesey House, 1947.

Hando, Kazutoshi. *Nihon No Ichiban Nagai Hi*. Tokyo: Kodansha, 1965.

Hara, Tameichi, with Fred Saito and Roger Pineau. *Japanese Destroyer Captain*. New York: Ballantine, 1961.

Hashimoto, Mochitsura. *Sunk: The Story of the Japanese Submarine Fleet, 1942-1945*. (Tr. by E. H. M. Colegrave). London: Cassell and Company Ltd. 1954.

Hattori, Takushiro. *The Complete History of the Greater East Asia War*. Tokyo: Hara Shobo, 1965.

Holmes, W. J. *Undersea Victory*. Garden City, N.Y.: Doubleday, 1966.

Hosokawa, Morisada. *Information Never Reached the Emperor*. Tokyo: Dokasha Isobe Shobo, 1953.

Hough, Richard. *The Fleet That Had to Die*. New York: Viking Press, 1958.

Howard, Warren S. *Japanese Destroyers in World War II*. Annapolis, MD.: United States Naval Institute Proceedings, 1952.

Hoyt, Edwin P. *Blue Skies and Blood*. New York: Pinnacle Books, 1975.

———. *Nimitz and His Admirals*. New York: Weybright & Talley, 1970.

Ind, Allison. *Allied Intelligence Bureau*. New York: David McKay, 1958.

Inoguchi, Rikihei, and Tadashi Nakajima, with Roger Pineau. *The Divine Wind: Japan's Kamikaze Force in World War II*. Annapolis, MD.: United States Naval Institute Proceedings, 1958.

Ireland, Bernard. *The Rise and Fall of the Aircraft Carrier*. London: Marshall Cavendish, 1979.

Iriye, Akira. *Across the Pacific*. New York: Harcourt, Brace & World, 1967.

Ito, Masanori. *The End of the Imperial Japanese Navy*. (Tr. by Andreau Y. Kuroda and Roger Pineau). New York: Norton, 1962.

Ito, Masashi. *The Emperor's Last Soldiers*. New York: Coward, McCann, 1967.

James, David H. *The Rise and Fall of the Japanese Empire*. New York: Macmillian, 1951.

Jane's Fighting Ships, 1944-45. Ed. by Francis McMurtrie. New York: Arco, 1979

Jentschura, Hasgeorg, with Dieter Jung, and Peter Mickel. *Die Japan-ischen Kriegsschiffe, 1869-1945*. Munich: J. F. Lehmanns Verlag, 1970.

Johnston, Stanley. *Queen of the Flat-Tops.* New York: Dutton, 1942.

Kahn, David. *The Code-Breakers.* New York: Macmillan, 1967.

Karig, Walter. *Battle Report.* New York: Rinehart, 1948.

Kato, Masuo. *The Lost War: A Japanese Reporter's Inside Story.* New York: Knopf, 1946.

Kido, Koichi. *Diary of Koichi Kido.* Tokyo: Tokyo University Press, 1966.

King, Ernest J., and Walter Muir Whitehall. *Fleet Admiral King.* New York: Norton, 1952.

Kodama, Yoshio. *I Was Defeated.* Tokyo: Radiopress, 1959.

Koyanagi, Tomiji. *The Kurita Fleet.* Tokyo: Ushio Shobo, 1956.

Kusaka, Ryunosuke. *The Combined Fleet: Memoirs of Former Chief-of-Staff Kusaka.* Tokyo: Mainichi Shimbun-Ki, 1952.

Leahy, William D. *I Was There.* New York: Whittlesey House, 1950.

Leckie, Robert. *Challenge for the Pacific.* Garden City, N.Y.: Doubleday, 1965.

Le May, Curtis E., with MacKinlay Kantor. *Mission with LeMay: My Story.* Garden City, N.Y.: Doubleday, 1965.

Lockwood, Charles A., and Hans C. Adamson. *Battles of the Philippine Sea.* New York: Crowell, 1967.

———. *Hell at 50 Fathoms.* Philadelphia: Chilton Books, 1962.

Long, John E. *Japan's Undersea Carriers.* Annapolis, MD.: United States Naval Institute Proceedings, 1950.

Lord, Walter. *Day of Infamy.* New York: Holt, Rinehart & Winston, 1961.

———. *Midway! Incredible Victory.* New York: Harper & Row, 1967.

MacArthur, Douglas. *Reminiscenses.* New York: McGraw-Hill, 1964.

Manchester, William R. *American Caesar: Douglas MacArthur, 1880–1964.* Boston: Little, Brown, 1978.

Matsumato, Kitoro, and Chihaya Masataka. *Design and Construction of Yamato and Musashi.* Annapolis, MD.: United States Naval Institute Proceedings, 1953.

Mainichi Shimbun Sha (Mainichi Newspapers). *The Hirohito Era.* Tokyo: 1975.

Mayer, Sidney L. *The Japanese War Machine.* Secaucus, N.J.: Bison Books, 1976.

Merrill, James M. *A Sailor's Admiral: A Biography of William F. Halsey.* New York: Crowell, 1976.

Moore, Lynn L. *Shinano: The Jinx Carrier.* Annapolis, MD.: United States Naval Institute Proceedings, 1953.

Morison, Samuel Eliot. *History of United States Naval Operations in World War II.* Vols. III, IV, V, VI, VII, VIII, XII, XVI. Boston: Little, Brown, 1947, 1962.

Morris, Ivan. *The Nobility of Failure: Tragic Heroes in the History of Japan.* New York: Holt, Reinhart & Winston, 1975.

Nagatuska, Ryuji. *J'etais un Kamikaze: Les Chevaliers du Vent Divin.* Paris: Stock, 1972.

Nakasone, Seizen. *Tragedy of Okinawa.* Tokyo: Kacho Shobo, 1951.

Nakayama, Sadayoski. *Japan's Phenomenal Shipbuilders.* Annapolis, MD.: United States Naval Institute Proceedings, 1966.

Nitobe, Inazo. *Bushido.* Tokyo and Rutland, VT.: Charles E. Tuttle Co, 1969.

Nomura, Jiro. *Sea of Lamentation.* Tokyo: Yomiuri Shimbun–sha, 1967.

Okumuya, Masatake, and Jiro Horikoshi, with Martin Caidin. *Zero.* New York: Dutton, 1956.

Orita, Zenji, with Joseph D. Harrington. *I–Boat Captain.* Chatsworth, CA.: Major Books, 1976.

Potter, Elmer B., and Chester W. Nimitz. *The Great Sea War.* Englewood-Cliffs, N.J.: Prentice–Hall, 1960.

Potter, John Deane. *Admiral of the Pacific: The Life of Yamamoto.* New York: Viking Press, 1965.

Ranft, Bryan. *Technical Change and British Naval Policy, 1860–1939.* London: Hodder & Stoughton, 1977.

Reischauer, Edwin O. *Japan Past and Present.* New York: Knopf, 1964.

Reynolds, Clark G. *The Fast Carriers.* New York: McGraw–Hill, 1968.

Roscoe, Theodore. *United States Naval Operations in World War II.* Annapolis, MD.: United States Naval Institute Proceedings, 1948.

Roskill, StephenW. *Naval Policy Between the Wars.* London: Collins, 1968.

———. *The War at Sea.* London: Her Majesty's Stationery Office, 1954–61.

Sakai, Saburo, with Martin Caidin, and Fred Saito. *Samurai!* New York: Dutton, 1957.

Seward, Jack. *Hara-Kiri, Japanese Ritual Suicide.* Tokyo and Rutland, VT.: Charles E. Tuttle Co, 1969.

Sherman Frederick C. *Combat Command.* New York: Dutton, 1950.

Sherrod, Robert L. *History of Marine Corps Aviation in World War II.* Washington, D.C.,: Combat Forces Press, 1952.

———. *Tarawa: The Story of a Battle.* Fredericksburg, TX: Admiral Nimitz Foundation, 1973. (Originally published by Duell, Sloan & Pearce, 1945).

Shigemitsu, Mamoru. *Japan and Her Destiny: My Story for Peace.* New York: Dutton, 1958.

Shimomura, Kainin. *Notes on the Termination of the War.* Tokyo: Kamakura Bunko, 1948.

Shiroyama, Saburo. *War Criminals.* Tokyo: Kodansha, 1974.

Singer, Kurt. *Mirror, Sword and Jewel: A Study of Japanese Characteristics.* New York: G. Braziller, 1973.

Smith, Stanley E. *The United States Navy in World War II.* New York: Morrow, 1966.

Stafford, Edward P. *The Big E.* New York: Random House, 1962.

———. *The Far and the Deep.* New York: Putnam, 1967.

Swanborough, Gordon, and Peter M. Bowers. *United States Navy Aircraft Since 1911.* New York: Putnam, 1968.

Takagi, Sokichi. *History of Naval Battles in the Pacific.* Tokyo: Iwanami Shinsho, 1949.

Taleja, Thaddeus. *Climax at Midway.* New York: Norton, 1960.

Tanemura, Sako. *Secret Diary of Imperial Headquarters.* Tokyo: Diamond Sha, 1952.

Taylor, Theodore. *The Magnificent Mitscher.* New York: Norton, 1960.

Terasaki, Ryuji. *Navy Spirit: Life of Commander Jisaburo Ozawa.* Tokyo: Tokum Shoten, 1967.

Thomas, David. *Battle of the Java Sea.* London: Andre Deutsch, 1968.

———. *Japan's War at Sea.* London: Andre Deutsch, 1978.

Togo, Shigenori. *The Cause of Japan.* (Tr. and ed. by Togo Fumihiko and Ben Bruce Blakeney). New York: Simon & Schuster, 1956.

Toland, John. *The Rising Sun: The Decline and Fall of the Japanese Empire, 1936–1945.* New York: Random House, 1970.

Torisu, Kennosuke, and Chihaya Masataka. *Japanese Submarine Tactics.* Annapolis, MD.: United States Naval Institute Proceedings, 1961.

United States Strategic Bombing Survey, Morale Division. *The Effects of Strategic Bombing on Japanese Morale.* Washington, D.C.: United States Government Printing Office, 1947.

United States Strategic Bombing Survey, Naval Analysis Division. *Interrogation of Japanese Officials.* Vols. 1 and 2. Washington, D.C.: United States Government Printing Office, 1946.

Watts, A. J. *Japanese Warships of World War II.* London: Ian Allan, 1966.

———, and B. G. Gordon. *The Imperial Japanese Navy.* London: Macdonald, 1971.

Weal, Elke C. *Combat Aircraft of World War Two.* New York: Arms and Armour Press, 1977.

Winton, John. *War in the Pacific.* London: Sidgwick & Jackson, 1978.

Yokoi, Toshiyuki. *Thoughts on Japan's Naval Defeat.* Annapolis, MD.: United State Naval Institute Proceedings, 1960.

Yokota, Yutoka. *Suicide Submarine!* New York: Ballantine, 1962.

Yoshida, Mitsura. *The End of Yamato.* Annapolis, MD.: United States Naval Institute Proceedings, 1952.

Index